Cash Management: Products and Strategies

Frank J. Fabozzi, Ph.D., CFA
Editor

Published by Frank J. Fabozzi Associates

© 2000 By Frank J. Fabozzi Associates
New Hope, Pennsylvania

ISBN: 1-883249-86-4

Printed in the United States of America

Table of Contents

Contributing Authors

Brian R. Carosielli   Fitch

Frank J. Fabozzi   Yale University

Matthew D. Gelfand   Calvert Asset Management Company, Inc.

Malcolm L. Jones   SunAmerica

Hugh R. Lamle   Chase & MDSass Partners and
M. D. Sass Investors Services, Inc.

Steven V. Mann   University of South Carolina

Frank J. Marckioni   Merrill Lynch Investment Managers

Douglas A. Rivkin   Moody's Investors Service

Richard E. Scott   AMR Investments

Gabrielle M. Danek Winnert   Credit Suisse First Boston

Chapter 1

The Fundamentals of Cash Management Investment Policy

Matthew D. Gelfand
Senior Vice President
Calvert Asset Management Company, Inc.

Cash management is a prime example of the purpose of investing in general: to husband and grow assets in order to cover liabilities. Cash, as opposed to more rewarding but riskier assets such as stocks or bonds, is preferable for meeting large, short-term liabilities that are well defined and predictable. Holding cash is also the only sensible investment choice for meeting uncertain (contingent) liabilities that arise in an emergency.

The range of cash management alternatives is sufficiently wide and complicated to warrant careful planning when deciding on which specific cash vehicles to hold. Thus, the general principles of modern portfolio management can and *should* be applied to professional cash management. This chapter covers the following aspects of developing a cash management investment policy:

- classification of institutional investors
- constraints and circumstances
- investment objectives and risk profile
- cash management policies with *enough* risk
- elements of risk management

CLASSIFICATION OF INSTITUTIONAL INVESTORS

The purpose of cash management is to meet liabilities, which may appear in various forms and circumstances. This section provides a taxonomy of many of these circumstances, organized around types of institutions.

Defined-Benefit Pension Plans

The prototypical institutional investors are defined-benefit (DB) pension plans. DBs have explicit liabilities: their future streams of benefit payments to retirees

1

and their dependents. Indeed, such plans are required by law or their own governing documents to measure, report on, and provide assets in explicit relation to their measured liabilities. The very purpose of pension management is to ensure provision for benefit payments. An element of pension planning is having sufficient liquidity to meet (near-term) benefit payments.

For accumulating plans, current contributions are more than ample. For decumulating plans, some combination of dividend and interest payments, bond maturities, and liquidating long-term assets is necessary. In both accumulating and decumulating plans there are timing differences between contributions or incoming investment cash flows, on the one hand, and benefit payments on the other. These timing differences require cash management to play an explicit role in the plans, even if cash is not a part of investment policy. Moreover, plans that engage in active management of longer-term assets generally have residual cash permanently resident. Managing such cash pools is necessary to maximize returns while maintaining liquidity to cover active managers' trade settlements.

Foundations and Endowments

Foundations and endowments may view their liabilities implicitly as the cash outflows required by operating budgets. Foundations in many cases have penalizing incentives under federal tax rules to pay out 5% of their average assets during the year to eleemosynary beneficiaries (or 100% of the shortfall as taxes to the government). They also have internal administrative expenses.

Colleges and universities have no required spending rates, but, of course, do have demanding operating budgets. Both types of institutions have increasingly recognized the merits of setting and implementing investment policy in conjunction with decisions about operating and grants budgets. Such a policy will coordinate their liabilities more closely with the potential growth of investment assets and the cash flows these assets generate. Unfortunately, the liabilities of foundations and endowments are less certain in size and timing than is the case with pension plans.

As with pensions, investment cash flows of foundations and endowments generally fail to synchronize with operational spending and grant payments, while active portfolio management creates uninvested cash pools due to managers' trading activities. Again, even if cash is not part of a broader investment policy, these institutions must hold some cash and maximize their returns on this cash subject to liquidity constraints.

Financial Institutions

Banks, insurance companies, and other financial institutions have explicit asset/liability management objectives and organizational infrastructures to monitor and administer to those objectives. Cash management is integral to these organizations and ensures that asset and liability risk exposures are coordinated.

For banks, liabilities are customer deposits that may be withdrawn at random, but with some pattern that is subject to forecasting. For insurance companies, liabilities are policyholder claims that surface at random (such as disasters, accidents, or deaths), again with some pattern that can be anticipated. For financial institutions, the nature and structure of cash holdings should be more confined within particular ranges given their role in the asset/liability management program.

Defined-Contribution Plans

Two sorts of cash management problems arise for defined-contribution (DC) plans that manage assets using internally structured investment options, as opposed to providing a broad menu or "supermarket" of mutual funds to participants. As is the case with DB pension plans, foundations, and endowments, natural frictions result from active management of long-term assets. The other cash management problem for internally managed DC plans is akin to that of banks facing withdrawals.

Generally, internally structured DC plans include among their various investment options a cash or stable-value option.[1] Participants often use this option as a savings vehicle to accumulate relatively short-term assets for, say, college tuition or down payments on homes. The option also is a vehicle for highly risk-averse participants to accumulate long-term savings. Actively trading participants can shift between cash and more risky investment options. Thus, stable-value options within DC plans need to function like banks in the sense that they should enable participants to make withdrawals that are unpredictable in size and timing.

Any one participant might have short-term savings or market-timing goals in mind. But pools of participants commingling their short-term funds can "insure" each other's liquidity needs. The insurance function emerges because, at any one time, only a small fraction of the participants in any pool will actually withdraw funds. Moreover, if the DC plan is relatively young, new participant contributions could provide sufficient liquidity at most times to cover normal withdrawals. Thus, the pooling of short-term assets may result in a core of cash that resides more or less permanently in the stable-value fund. Again, it is incumbent on the fiduciaries of such funds to maximize returns subject to their liquidity needs and the stated objectives of their funds.

Corporate Cash Management

Corporations are perhaps the most volatile or unpredictable theater for cash management. Corporations need to maintain pools of cash for various reasons. Some examples: covering contractual obligations and contingencies (operating cash or working capital); strategic purposes such as capital investments or acquisitions; or for speculating, say, issuing bonds at attractively low interest rates although no specific purpose for their proceeds is pending.

---

[1] DC plans are required by Department of Labor regulation 404(c) to offer a minimum of four options with distinct risk/return characteristics. These options usually are at one extreme the stable value option and at the other extreme an all equities option.

Corporations are also encouraged to hold cash, within reasonable limits, to bolster their balance sheets and attract other forms of investment capital. Stock and bond investors use various ratios that depend on short-term asset holdings as one set of measures of a company's financial health and management capabilities. Cash balances can fluctuate wildly and so most of a corporation's cash needs to remain quite liquid, invested in very short-term assets such as commercial paper, money market funds, or repos. However, some amount of cash tends to reside on corporate books more or less permanently. Developing and administering well reasoned cash-management programs can help corporations to invest such cash more efficiently (read: aggressively) and hence to generate yet more cash and profits, with benefits to the firm's bottom line and balance sheet.

CONSTRAINTS AND CIRCUMSTANCES

Each investor faces particular circumstances that influence investment policy, including legal and regulatory constraints, accounting and tax rules, liquidity conditions, and trust mandates. These particulars determine what investors are permitted to do and how much risk they are able to bear when seeking greater investment returns.

Regulatory and Accounting Constraints

Four important constraints of a regulatory nature apply to cash investors:

- Fiduciary prudential standards constrain pensions, trusts, foundations, and — in somewhat different form — corporations from entering into overly risky investments.
- Banks, insurance companies, and other financial institutions are constrained by capital requirements. Similar funding requirements apply to pension plans, constraining these organizations from taking on undue risks. Capital requirements may impose direct constraints since, for banks and insurance companies, the level of capital required as a percentage of assets varies as a function of how risky regulators deem their assets to be. Even where capital requirements are implicit, they can affect risk tolerance given the task of maintaining an acceptable surplus of assets over liabilities, as for pension plans.
- Money market mutual fund regulations (Rule 2a-7) severely constrain the types, maturities, and diversification of securities that portfolio managers may hold.[2]
- Accounting rules, in conjunction with broader financial or reporting objectives, may confine cash managers to investing in short-term instruments

---

[2] A discussion of Rule 2a-7 is beyond the scope of this chapter. The text of the rule appears in 17 Code of Federal Regulations 270, 2a-7 under the Investment Company Act of 1940.

(less than one year to maturity) or instruments with top quality ratings, even if an organization's risk tolerance and liquidity needs could tolerate somewhat more risky investments.

Tax Considerations

Income taxes and other levies can have the greatest influence on investment decisions at the margin. Taxes have a direct effect on the level of returns *pari passu* with the level of taxes. And tax rates and rules, like the weather, are changeable. Variations over time in the relationship between yields on taxable and tax-exempt fixed-income securities are also a function of tax rates, often inducing taxable investors to switch between taxable and municipal instruments of comparable maturity and quality. Even foundations, which are in the main tax-exempt, face minor levels of excise taxes on income and realized gains; certain types of foundations face a 100% penalty payable to the IRS on shortfalls in annual grants relative to 5% of their average assets in a given year.[3] Such penalties or taxes clearly affect the amount of grants foundations will underwrite. They also affect investment choices aimed at maintaining a target level and stability of assets, and liquidity sufficient to fund grants in a given year.

Liquidity Needs and Potential Cash Flows

The needs of investors to pay bills determine the acceptable limits of maturity, or market risk, and default, or credit risk. For purposes of investment policy planning, liquidity can be considered net of incoming cash flows. Pension plans for young workforces that are accumulating for future benefits can avoid cash investments almost entirely, since new corporate contributions will be more than enough for current benefit payments. (Even here, if the timing of contributions differs even slightly from the timing of benefit payments, some cash balances must be maintained to manage the mismatch.) Corporations with major capital-spending programs need to husband liquid assets to ensure coverage of their significant contractual commitments. Investment policy thus should depend on the organization's particular financial circumstances including net operating cash flows, which vary greatly over time.

Internal Governance Structures and Trust Documents

Another feature of the investment policy landscape is the formal structure for overseeing investments, which can affect an organization's investment objectives and tolerance for risk. Trust documents or corporate by-laws may place restrictions on the types of activities in which companies, foundations, or pension plans may engage, including the types of instruments that are eligible for investment.

---

[3] The formula for this grant requirement for operating foundations is more complicated than a simple 5% rule, making allowances for investment returns that fall short of 5% and providing a 1-year catch-up, but under most circumstances, the 5% rule applies. The simpler characterization suffices for purposes of this discussion.

Sometimes these governing rules have been inherited from past circumstances that no longer apply; yet it is too costly — procedurally or politically — to change the internal rules. Not an entirely rational situation, but investment programs must nonetheless grapple with inherited constraints.

Governance structures may either accommodate or constrain risk-taking. Investment oversight committees or personnel who are knowledgeable and involved may be able to tolerate greater risks or invest in more complicated instruments. They will be more cognizant of when risks increase and whether shorter-term investment changes have been implemented to avoid those risks. Oversight groups that are less knowledgeable or that have other priorities may prefer to keep their investment programs simple or to contain risk strictly.

INVESTMENT OBJECTIVES AND RISK PROFILE

Even if the parties involved in setting investment policies were fully aware of the circumstances discussed in the previous section, it would be a difficult task to translate this knowledge into well-defined policies. Some quantitative analysis and decision-making is necessary to define the operational parameters of investment policy.

Elements of Investment Policies

Investment policies should contain (at least) the following elements:

- Investment objectives stated qualitatively and as real (inflation-adjusted) return targets.
- Statements of risk tolerance qualitatively and as maximum tolerable losses or probabilities of losses of particular dollar amounts or percentages of assets.
- Time horizons.
- Specific circumstances that may determine investment decisions, for example, whether an investment sponsor is taxable (and at what rates).

These elements cannot be set independently but, rather, must be mutually consistent. For example, a 10% real return target within almost any time horizon, no less a short-term time horizon, would be inconsistent with a low risk tolerance. A zero tolerance for losses in a cash portfolio, in any time horizon, would be consistent only with investing in very high-quality, fixed-income instruments with maturities comparable to that horizon.

These elements of investment policy must be related as a function of the risk and reward opportunities available to investors. Of all imaginable portfolios, the particular portfolios that provide the greatest available return for a given amount of risk or the lowest achievable risk for a given expected return are called "efficient portfolios."[4,5] Not all combinations of return and risk are achievable (e.g., a riskless 10% real return), nor are all achievable combinations of return and risk efficient (e.g., a low real return of, say, 1%-2% with high risk). The quantitative task of investment policy-setting is to identify that particular efficient portfolio (risk/return combination), within the set of achievable portfolios, that is consistent with an organization's return objectives, tolerance for risk, time horizon, and organizational idiosyncrasies.

Risk and Return

Exhibit 1 illustrates schematically how to characterize the set of efficient portfolios or the "efficient frontier" of risk and reward. The horizontal axis measures risk (or, say, expected standard deviation of returns per year) while the vertical axis measures expected annual returns. Thus, higher points in the graph have better returns, while points further to the right have greater risk, which is worse for investors. Thus, investors would like to move to portfolios further up and to the left in the graph. Unfortunately, the efficient frontier defines the best achievable portfolios — the highest available returns for a given level of risk or the lowest feasible risk associated with a given return. Investors cannot cross the frontier into the upper left corner of the exhibit.

Exhibit 1: Investment Portfolio Basic Characteristics

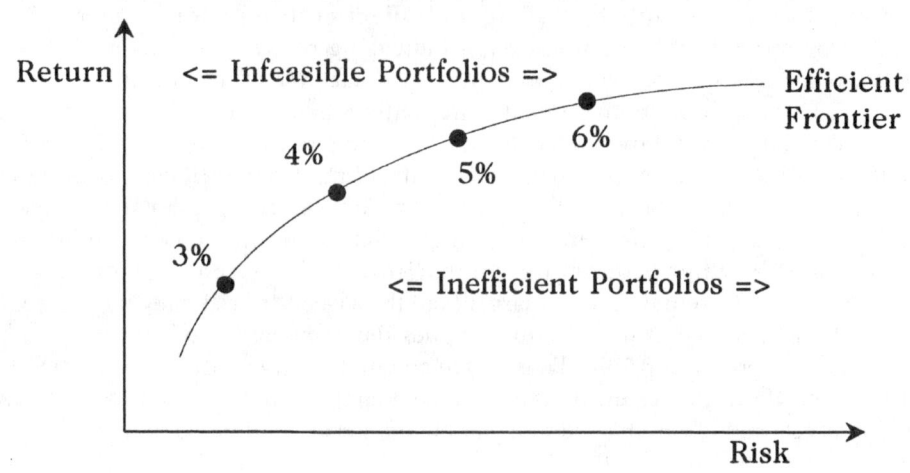

---

[4] Risk in "modern portfolio theory" can be defined by statistics that represent (expected) variability or "volatility" of returns across units of time. The most typical measure is (expected) standard deviation of returns per year. Expected volatility is often estimated by measures of historical volatility.

[5] This chapter provides a strong taste of the issues involved in investment policy setting without detailing how to estimate which particular portfolios are efficient or, in terms of modern portfolio theory, how to "optimize portfolios." This subject receives more complete treatment in all investment management textbooks.

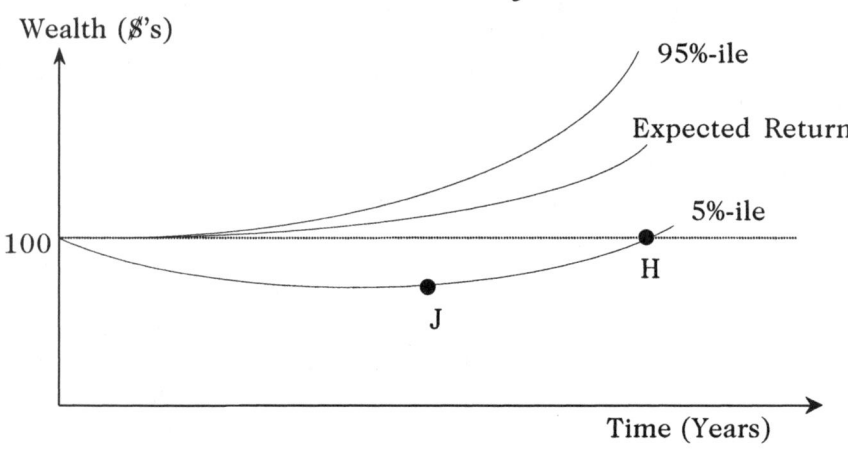

Exhibit 2: Terminal Wealth Percentiles for an Investment Portfolio

Greater returns are available only by accepting greater risk or moving along the frontier to the upper right. But the availability of portfolios on the frontier also implies that investors need not accept inferior results in the lower right of the graph where low-return/high-risk portfolios reside. Investors in this region can improve their results by trading inefficient portfolios for efficient ones (assuming modest or no trading costs), increasing returns, decreasing risk, or some combination of the two, at least until they reach the efficient frontier.

This approach to investment policysetting divides the task between portfolio managers and policymakers. Portfolio managers can estimate the specific contents of each efficient portfolio without deciding which efficient portfolio is best. Policysetters can decide which efficient return-and-risk combination is optimal for their organization without having to determine which specific investments, and in what proportions, constitute the desired portfolio. The policysetters' selection of a return target (and the associated risk they must accept on the frontier of efficient portfolios) implies the composition of the underlying benchmark or policy portfolio. Thus, given an intelligently constructed frontier of efficient portfolios, investment policy can be quantified simply in terms of stated return targets and the associated risk parameters for given time horizons.

The Importance of Time Horizon

Exhibit 2 illustrates a typical pattern of investment results as measured by the prospective values of a portfolio after various periods of time ("terminal wealth") when invested under a given efficient risk/return policy. This exhibit indicates that any investment program has a range of potential outcomes, since future returns cannot be known with certainty. Rather, returns will fall within some range with a particular probability that is dependent on the expected (or policy target) return and the expected volatility of returns implied by choosing an efficient policy. For example, with 90% probability, terminal wealth at any point in time will lie between the upper bound of the 95th percentile terminal wealth and the lower bound of the fifth percentile terminal wealth (labeled respectively in the graph). Of course, with 5% chance, returns could lead to wealth that is better than the 95th percentile outcome or, with 5% chance, to terminal wealth that is worse than the fifth percentile outcome.

The important point Exhibit 2 illustrates is that with some non-negligible probability, investors have a chance of losing assets within any interval of time.[6] Normally, after some additional time, such losses could be recouped, at which point wealth would return to its starting value. Suppose an institution had a long enough time horizon, say, the number of time periods represented by point H in the graph, and they were willing to accept a 5% chance of sustaining any loss of assets before that point in time. In that case, the investment policy implied by a target return equal to the expected return in Exhibit 2 would be appropriate. However, if this organization's time horizon were shorter, say, at point J in the graph, this investment policy would be inconsistent with a 5% probability of losses. A more conservative investment policy would be necessary to avoid potential losses at point J. Typically, longer time horizons permit adopting more aggressive investment stances.

Specific Circumstances

Exhibit 3 illustrates the terminal wealth of an investment program over time when the particular circumstance of the sponsor is to spend assets at a rate equal to expected real returns. As before, this sponsor could experience a range of results. If returns were to be as expected over time, terminal wealth would be unchanged from its initial value; on average, annual investment returns would just equal annual spending. If returns were to be better than expected, say at the 95th percentile, then spending would be less than additions to the portfolio from investments and the portfolio could grow over time. If, on the other hand, returns were to be worse than expected, returns would fail to cover planned spending, and the portfolio would shrink over time, as indicated by the declining curve labeled "5%-ile". Thus, whether an investment policy is appropriate depends in part on the spending policy of the institution and other circumstances that affect net cash flows such as paying taxes or fluctuating operations.

CASH MANAGEMENT POLICIES WITH ENOUGH RISK

Of course, investment policymakers have other tasks besides setting policy. They also have fiduciary responsibilities (which they may delegate) for implementing

---

[6] With some very minor probability, investors could lose their entire investment. The "zero-th percentile" curve, not shown in Exhibit 2, falls to zero at the horizontal axis at some point and never turns back up.

investment programs, monitoring results, and altering programs when results are disappointing or new investment opportunities arise. In addition, merely stating investment return targets and risk-tolerance parameters may ignore circumstances that should be considered in policysetting. Thus, investment policies must contain details beyond summary statements about expected returns and risk. This section considers two such details: performance benchmarks and permissible investments.

Performance Benchmarks and Maturity Risk

Statements about return objectives and tolerable risk levels imply other facts about investment policy. Similarly, these statements suggest which benchmarks may serve as bases for performance comparisons. A spectrum of fixed-income maturities could serve as benchmarks for cash management programs.

Duration

The maturity or duration of a benchmark, and hence of an investor's actual portfolio under normal circumstances, should parallel the maturity or duration of the investor's liabilities — to have some assurance of meeting these obligations.[7] If assets had too much duration relative to liabilities, losses could result were interest rates to rise, since then assets would decline in value by more than liabilities. Savings and loan institutions learned this difficult lesson in the late 1980s and early 1990s.

Exhibit 3: Terminal Wealth Percentiles for an Investment Portfolio with Annual Spending Rate = Expected Return

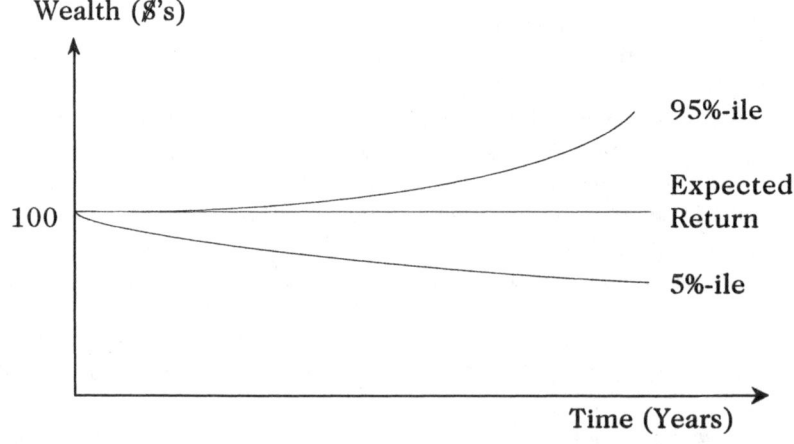

---

[7] Duration measures the interest rate risk of a fixed income security or portfolio and is the approximate percentage change in price or market value for a 100 basis point change in yield.

Exhibit 4: Treasury Yields During an Interest Rate Cycle: July 31, 1986 - April 30, 2000 (%)

Treasury Bill/Note	Start: July 1986	End: April 2000	Change	Low	High	Range
3-Month	5.91	5.83	(0.08)	2.74	9.18	6.44
6-Month	6.00	6.11	0.11	2.91	9.50	6.59
1-Year	6.09	6.17	0.08	3.05	9.59	6.54
2-Year	6.48	6.68	0.20	3.79	9.67	5.88
3-Year	6.70	6.62	(0.08)	4.17	9.59	5.42
5-Year	6.96	6.54	(0.42)	4.21	9.47	5.26

Exhibit 5: Total Returns on Treasury Bills and Notes July 31, 1986 - April 30, 2000 (%)

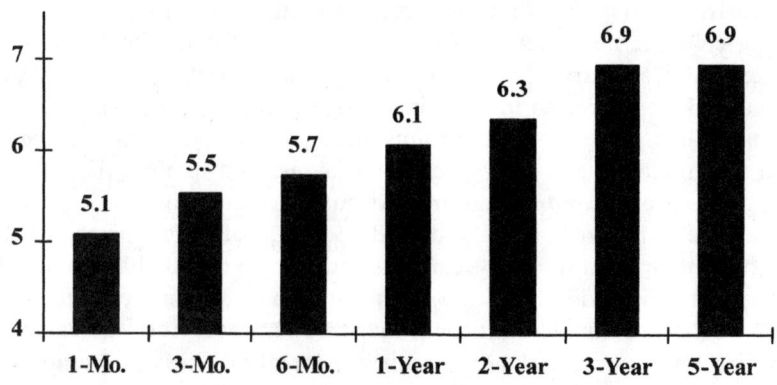

Opportunity

Similarly, (opportunity) losses can result when assets have too little duration relative to liabilities. Many individual investors discover this pitfall when investing too conservatively for retirement. Institutional investors are vulnerable to this error in the form of reinvestment risk for financial institutions, dwindling assets for foundations, and funding risks for pension plans. Accepting as much risk as is tolerable, but no more than that, in order to maximize returns helps to avoid these problems.

Exhibit 4 shows interest rates on various Treasury instruments during an interest rate cycle from July 1986 through April 2000. Within this cycle, yields began and ended at roughly the same levels for all maturities, but with some variability along the way as indicated by high and low yields for each of these instruments. Only 5-year Treasury notes experienced a noticeable yield decline of about 40 basis points.[8]

Exhibit 5 illustrates the absolute returns on these Treasury maturities during the 1986-2000 cycle. Not surprisingly, the instruments with the longest

[8] Although this yield decline combined with the duration of the 5-year note (which measures about 4) gave this note an absolute return advantage compared to the other instruments, the advantage was minor relative to total returns (a bit more than 10 basis points per year of added return).

maturities — and greatest risk — enjoyed the highest absolute returns. The 5-year note, for example, earned 6.9% per year during this period versus 5.1% for 1-month Treasury bills. Because investors demand compensation *ex ante* for bearing greater risk, yields on longer-term instruments are typically higher than on shorter-term instruments. Stated another way, the yield curve is upward sloping. Longer-maturity instruments are riskier because, were interest rates to rise, their value would decline more, leaving investors with fewer assets when they might need to liquidate them.

The question is whether compensation for this added risk is worthwhile, which depends on investors' risk tolerances and time horizons. Exhibit 6 shows excess returns relative to risk for the Treasury maturities under consideration. (Since Exhibit 6 considers excess returns relative to 1-month bills, the measure for this instrument is, by definition, zero.) An intuitive way to view this number is as the "price" in terms of returns for bearing a unit of risk. The 3-month bill, for example, earned an extra 107 basis points of return for every 100 basis points of additional risk compared to the 1-month bill, where risk is measured as standard deviations. Thus, under normal circumstances, an investor with a 3-month time horizon and moderate risk tolerance should invest in 3-month bills, even though 6-month bills provide more than proportionate rewards for bearing added risk. Someone with a 1-year horizon and moderate risk tolerance, on the other hand, could extend their portfolio to 1-year bills and enjoy a 60-100 basis point absolute advantage (as indicated in Exhibit 5) over 1-month or 3-month bills. This investor is amply rewarded for the additional market risk, receiving 90 basis points of excess return per unit of risk albeit a bit less than the 107 basis points of excess return per risk unit on 3-month bills.

Exhibit 6: Return Per Unit of Risk* on Treasury Bills and Notes July 31, 1986 - April 30, 2000 (basis points)

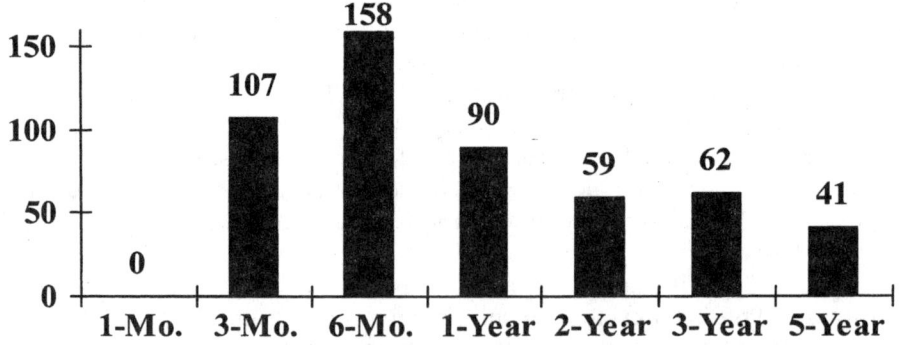

* 100 times excess annual return over 1-month Treasury bill return divided by annual standard deviation of return

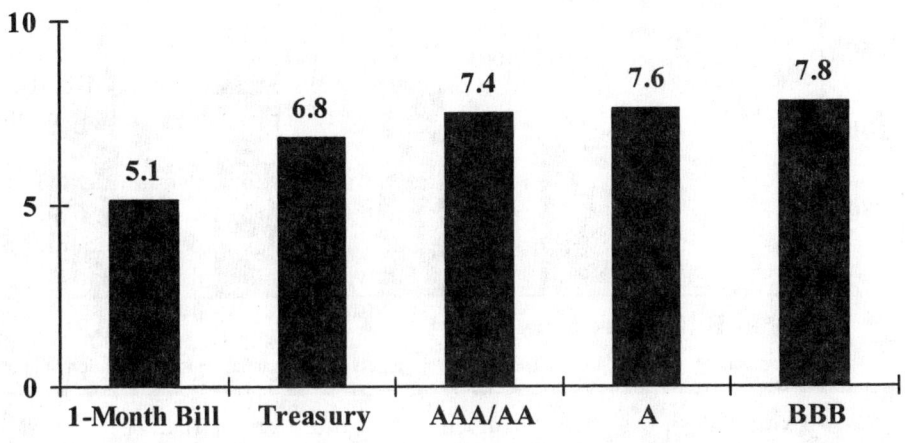

Exhibit 7: Total Returns on 1- to 3-Year Benchmarks,
July 31, 1986 - April 30, 2000 (%)

A more difficult choice for an investor with, say, a 1-year horizon would be comparing 6-month to 1-year bills. The former enjoys a significantly greater relative risk compensation but lower absolute returns on average. Investors with moderate risk tolerance will seek the greater absolute rewards of 1-year bills. However, for more risk-averse investors (e.g., with 1-year horizons but some uncertainty about needing liquid assets before the year is over), choosing 6-month bills to avoid principal risk might be preferable. While avoiding principal risk, such investors would face reinvestment risk — the potential for reinvesting at lower interest rates — when rolling over 6-month bills at maturity. This opportunity cost could result whenever investing in assets having less risk than liabilities. Thus, appropriate maturity benchmarks depend largely on one's time horizon, but may be adjusted to shorter maturities for more risk-averse investors or to longer maturities for more risk-tolerant investors.

Performance Benchmarks and Credit Risk

Another dimension of risk important to choosing benchmarks is credit risk, the potential for losing assets due to borrower defaults. Again, time horizon and risk tolerance affect policy and hence the credit quality of performance benchmarks. Exhibit 7 shows average returns on 1- to 3-year instruments for the same 1986-2000 interest rate cycle as in Exhibits 5 and 6, holding maturity constant to extract from the effects of interest rate risk while considering instruments of various credit qualities. (One-month Treasury bills appear for reference.) As expected, riskier instruments enjoyed greater returns on average over this period, with BBB 1- to 3-year corporate bonds providing 7.8% average returns, 100 basis points better than Treasuries.

Exhibit 8: Return Per Unit of Risk on 1- to 3-Year Benchmarks, July 31, 1986 - April 30, 2000 (basis points)*

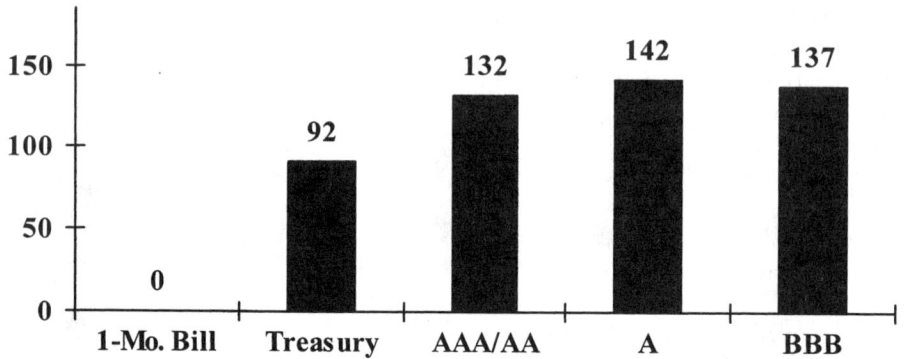

* 100 × excess annual return over 1-month Treasury bill return divided by annual standard deviation of return.

Exhibit 8 shows that instruments with more credit risk also generally enjoyed greater rewards relative to risk or volatility of returns, although the excess return per unit of risk of BBB 1- to 3-year bonds was a bit below that of single-A bonds at about 140 basis points. These exhibits demonstrate that investors tend to overcharge borrowers for credit risk or, said differently, yield spreads tend to be excessive. In other words, yield spreads of lower-rated securities relative to (zero credit-risk) Treasury instruments more than compensate for losses realized due to defaults or credit downgrades.[9]

The issue, however, is that default or downgrade risk could be realized on any given bond at any time. Thus, investment sponsors having shorter time horizons should seek greater diversification and higher credit qualities. Diversification permits holding portfolios with lower average credit quality than would otherwise be prudent since greater yields on lower grade but performing bonds in such portfolios make up today for losses on the relatively few bonds that actually default. Similarly, investors with longer time horizons can afford to accept greater credit risk since yield spreads on performing bonds can, eventually, compensate for relatively infrequent defaults.

---

[9] Various theories attempt to explain why apparently excessive spreads tend to persist. One is that the true default risk of corporate bonds has yet to be observed *ex post*, so that apparently "excess" spreads, in fact, are not in excess at all *ex ante*. Thus, we have so far enjoyed relatively lucky results from the spectrum of potential outcomes against which lenders (investors) have been protecting themselves by charging risk premiums. Another theory is that markets for corporate bonds remain inefficient because information needed to bid away excess spreads is costly if not impossible to collect, creating self-fulfilling outcomes. Incomplete information creates opportunities for uncreditworthy borrowers to issue bonds to imperfectly informed lenders or leads to secondary trading at more random prices than better informed markets would exhibit. These phenomena lead investors to demand higher yield premiums than would otherwise be feasible as compensation for these risk inducing inefficiencies. In turn, excess spreads mitigate the very inefficiencies for which the spreads are meant to compensate and so, again, only appear to be excessive. The risks would resurface were spreads to narrow.

ELEMENTS OF RISK MANAGEMENT

Establishing investment policies and selecting performance benchmarks consistent with such policies are fundamental decisions. In addition, investment sponsors need to decide whether they will engage in active portfolio management as a means of adding to benchmark returns. Active management permits holding positions that differ structurally from benchmarks either by holding securities represented in the benchmark in alternative weightings, or by holding classes of securities not represented in the benchmark. Other chapters in this book discuss techniques for adding value through active management. For sponsors who favor active management, specifying which active positions and non-benchmark securities are eligible for investment is an important element of policy. These sponsors need to codify which active management risks are acceptable and take practical steps to monitor and contain them. This section outlines some of the investment eligibility and risk-management issues with which sponsors must grapple.[10]

Selecting Eligible Investments

Investment guidelines should state limits on the maximum (and perhaps minimum) maturity for any single security in a portfolio as well as on average for the portfolio as a whole. Similarly, guidelines should specify the lowest (and perhaps highest) credit qualities that individual holdings may bear as well as the target, high and low quality on average for the portfolio as a whole.

Although it is beyond this chapter's purpose to analyze other types of risks, outlining some of these other risks will be helpful as a guide for further review. Bonds with embedded call or put options introduce different patterns of pricing behavior relative to interest rate movements than simpler coupon or "bullet" bonds. Collateralized mortgage obligations (CMOs or so-called mortgage derivatives) introduce such option risk, as well as analytical complexities that provide opportunities for adding value, but also for misunderstanding. Investment guidelines should indicate which option risks and which types of instruments are eligible as investments. More exotic investment tools such as leverage, derivatives or short sales may permit managers to manage risk in underlying securities portfolios more efficiently, but also to adopt more active and hence riskier investment positions. In their investment guidelines, sponsors need to specify whether these exotics are permissible and, if so, for which purposes and to what extent.

Monitoring and Controlling Risk

Any investment program, passive or active, must monitor results relative to pre-established performance benchmarks with regard to total returns, risk (volatility

---

[10] The following discussion considers qualitative and administrative aspects of investment risk management. See Hugh Lamle, "Identifying, Measuring, and Controlling Risk in Cash and Extended Cash," in this book for a technical and quantitative view of this subject.

of returns) and benchmark risk (stability of portfolio returns relative to benchmark returns). Active management programs must devote more resources to monitoring and controlling risks because of the added analytical and management complexities involved. To the extent that active investment positions versus benchmark are permissible, they must also be observable and quantifiable. Otherwise, active positions cannot be monitored systematically, controlled and corrected when awry. Trading activities also must be controllable. Even if ineligible trades cannot be prevented, investment fiduciaries should have a means of identifying such positions so mistakes can be corrected quickly and unauthorized trading activities can be more closely monitored or shut down. Especially in cash management programs, active investment positions should be liquid so they can be reversed quickly at minimal trading cost when portfolio managers no longer see added value in them. Finally, manager risk must be contained. Active management positions have the advantage of potentially adding value, but also can detract from performance. Performance could suffer because an active investment style goes out of favor or because an active management firm malfunctions because the company goes out of business or key personnel are no longer available due to career decisions or personal health. Investment policy or procedures must contemplate both types of manager risk.

Each of the above administrative issues has a solution, although no solution is complete or foolproof. Perhaps of paramount importance is education of plan sponsor board and committee members and staff. Well informed oversight can lead to better, more intelligent choices of investment tools and techniques. Education also permits grappling with added analytical complexities in active management programs, which have potential for adding to performance. While not a cure for mismanagement or malfeasance, due diligence in hiring staff and investment product vendors is both preventative and required by fiduciary standards. Portfolio diversification is the easiest medicine to take for stabilizing investment returns, as in the case of managing credit risks discussed earlier. Similarly, manager diversification is important for preventing or mitigating the adverse consequences of managers' style, business and casualty risks. In order to complete the loop of setting investment policy, implementing investment programs, and monitoring results, it is essential to establish adequate accounting, data collection, and reporting systems.

Finally, the world of investing is fast paced, with many actions occurring daily: securities transactions, administrative actions, and policy choices. No one person monitors all the individual decisions made each day, no less remembers these decisions over time. Yet, the reasons for arriving at given portfolio positions today may be important for deciding about how to alter investment decisions going forward. Thus, documenting actions and decisions is important. Documenting the rationale for transactions can be as simple as recording comments in an accounting database; documenting policy decisions may require more elaborate descriptions of underlying thought processes. In whatever form, this documentation is important for institutional memory. In addition, individuals' desire for progress and personal growth leads to natural turnover in the personnel responsible for investment programs. Establishing continuity in staffing and committee memberships is important to maintaining institutional memory and sound investment policy.

Chapter 2

Crafting the Appropriate Investment Policy for an Organization's Unique Needs

Frank J. Marckioni, CFA
Director of U.S. Fixed Income
Merrill Lynch Investment Managers

What is the most important part of the investment process for a successful corporate cash program? This is not a trick question. In fact, there can be a variety of legitimate answers. Some examples:

• Picking the best bonds for the portfolio.
• Interest rate forecasting.
• Being able to supply the cash needed to fund the business plan.

While these are all important aspects, we contend that the most critical part of the process is at the very beginning stages when members of a firm sit down to craft the investment policy for corporate cash: Every later decision that will be made is based on this document. Time must be taken to craft an investment policy that provides a reliable, accurate road map. Otherwise, the corporation will end up driving the wrong way down a one-way street. And nobody wants that! In large measure, writing an effective investment policy is a two-part process:

• Identifying the conceptual objectives of the organization.
• Assimilating these concepts into definable portfolio constraints.

IDENTIFICATION OF OBJECTIVES AND CONSTRAINTS

The first step, in many ways, is a conceptual exercise intended to identify a firm's attitude toward prospective eventualities in its portfolio. The investment policy will be, for all intents and purposes, an extension of the overall business plan. Put another way, it is hard to imagine a competent company forecasting the business plan without regard to cash needs. They directly impact the way their balance-sheet asset needs to be managed. Since every firm has a unique business plan and vision for the future, every company will also have a unique approach to managing its cash portfolio. The elements of this distinctiveness need to be identified before we can craft specific portfolio guidelines.

While some treasury managers are compelled to treat every dollar in their coffers equally, others tend to carve up the balance into subportfolios with different needs, objectives, and constraints. For the most part, the identification of objectives in this chapter addresses a corporate cash portfolio that is not being used to fund day-to-day activities such as payroll, rent, or suppliers' invoices. To meet such daily needs, the portfolio is generally best served by a money market fund or bank checking account. We will concentrate in this chapter on the cash portfolio that has at least some level of flexibility for investing activities. To start the investment policy process, two primary objectives need to be identified: return expectations and risk tolerance.

Return Expectations

Return expectations can be either a relative or an absolute measure. Some treasurers tell us, "I want to earn more than I can in my money market fund" or "I want to get more out of my cash than what my internal manager can deliver." These return expectations are relative to other alternatives. On the other hand, the return objective is absolute when treasurers say, "We need to get a rate of 6% on this portfolio because we need the income to fund a project." In either case, the return expectation will significantly impact how the investment policy is written.

Risk Tolerance

In the world of corporate cash, risk tolerance differs from return expectations in that risk is almost always approached from an absolute basis. It is common for a chief financial officer to comment, "I want to get a competitive rate of return on my cash, but I can't afford to have a loss on the portfolio on a quarterly basis since I have to report to shareholders." Alternatively, treasury personnel might say, "If I earn an extra 10 basis points on the portfolio I might get a pat on the back, but if I lose money I'll be fired." This is the epitome of absolute risk tolerance — with very clear downside risk!

It is rare to hear a corporate cash manager approach risk from the same perspective as a pension fund manager. Pension professionals are concerned with such factors as standard deviation of returns and tracking error. Treasury personnel are much more interested in making sure their cash is there when they need it. This difference in perspective will deeply influence the parameters of the investment policy.

CONSTRAINTS

Identifying the primary return and risk objectives is only a first step in building the conceptual framework for the policy. Other critical elements need to be identified so that all relevant considerations are addressed in the ultimate investment guidelines. These considerations are generally referred to as constraints. The primary constraints are liquidity needs; tax considerations; time horizon; and legal, accounting, and regulatory concerns.

Liquidity Needs

The general level of cash the company will need to keep very liquid to meet commitments will be as unique as the firm's business plan, and may account for specific expenditures. As one example of a liquidity constraint, the plan may call for building out of a fiber-optic network that has specific progress payments. Or it might take into account potential but yet-to-be identified opportunities: "We could be making an acquisition at any time." Liquidity needs must be clearly articulated so that appropriate policy measures can be taken.

Caution must be exercised when projecting liquidity needs. Unless the cash flows that will be required are absolutely certain (such as progress payments on a construction project), it may be a good idea to project only into the short term three to six months for purposes of identifying this constraint. There are far too many uncertainties in business to let long-term cash projections influence investment decisions in a corporate cash portfolio.

Tax Considerations

Since companies have to pay taxes on their earnings, the tax aspect becomes relevant for corporate cash investors. Most important is the effective tax rate the firm is paying on its pre-tax earnings. Keep in mind that anything earned by corporate cash investing will be incremental to the core earnings activity, meaning that the full marginal tax rate will apply. The breakeven levels between taxable and tax-advantaged securities in recent years have been at points where only companies at the highest marginal corporate rate will have their cash investing strategy impacted by federal taxes.

Time Horizon

For the corporate cash manager, the time horizon is closely related to liquidity needs. If the treasurer knows with certainty that all of his or her cash will be used tomorrow for the purchase of a factory, the time horizon of one day will provide clear input to the liquidity constraint of the portfolio. But as we all know, few decisions are so clear-cut, so time horizon becomes far more nebulous. When we are helping companies craft their policy, we frequently are told, "The time horizon for this portfolio is indefinite." The problem with that statement is that there are effectively no securities in the market that have an indefinite maturity.

For purposes of structuring an effective investment strategy, the discussion of time horizon needs to focus more on assigning probabilities to the occurrence of significant events. We usually get tangible answers when we ask: "What are the chances that you will need to liquidate 25% of the portfolio within a 90-

day timeframe?" Objective data of this type will dictate the ultimate exposure to be allowed in the portfolio.

Legal, Accounting, and Regulatory Constraints

Most corporate cash investors account for their portfolio as "available for sale" under FAS 115; as such, the accounting designation of the portfolio is fairly straightforward. But, in many cases, other legal and regulatory concerns must be addressed relative to a company's investment policy. For example, public utilities and insurance companies have numerous concerns involving state regulators, while some commercial bank and trust company clients must deal with both federal and state regulations. These concerns make a good day for the lawyers but a bad day for portfolio managers!

Unique Circumstances

Every company we have worked with has some interesting or unique provision that just has to be addressed: "One of our board members doesn't think anyone has calculated the impact of an earthquake on the Japanese banking sector" or "Our CFO had to liquidate a CMO at below par 15 years ago, so ..." These examples suggest the broad array of company-specific items that have been factored into investment policies. Other more conventional issues can include internal accounting capabilities, size and experience of treasury staff, and whether the company is public and has to report earnings. Unique circumstances of this stripe cannot be ignored when preparing to write the corporate cash portfolio.

ASSIMILATING THE CONCEPTS

Once these elements have been thought through conceptually, the company needs to craft a policy that places clear and definable boundaries on its portfolio managers. For purposes of this chapter, we will confine our discussion to investment issues, pausing here only to recognize that there are other important elements of the policy such as authorized signatories or procedures for making amendments. To illustrate all of the items in this investment policy, we will often be referring to the sample that concludes this chapter, constructed for a large corporate client that has a fairly robust policy in terms of eligible securities and exposure to the yield curve. We chose it because it incorporates all of the important concepts that need to be discussed relative to actual portfolio guidelines.

OBJECTIVES

All policies need to spell out in explicit detail the objectives for the portfolio and the priority of those objectives. The most common objectives for a corporate cash portfolio, in order of importance are capital preservation, liquidity, and return. Why do the objectives need to be stated explicitly when the remainder of the policy places specific investment constraints on the portfolio manager? The portfolio manager's mission should be to make decisions that comply with not only the technical aspects of the policy but also with the *spirit* of the policy.

Even the most comprehensive investment policies will be open to interpretation and subjectivity regarding what may be included in the portfolio. What needs to be explicit, however — and an integral part of every investment decision — is the overall objective of the policy. Suppose, for example, that a corporate cash policy clearly mandates capital preservation and liquidity as the primary objectives. If a portfolio manager is in any doubt regarding an investment decision, then he or she should always err on the side of conservatism as this is in the *spirit* of the policy.

Maximum Exposure

Maximum exposure to maturity/duration of the portfolio and individual securities is perhaps the greatest determinant of portfolio return and volatility potential, especially in the context of high-grade, fixed-income mandates. For portfolios that allow only high-quality instruments, exposure to the yield curve can account for as much as 90% of total returns. To illustrate this point, Exhibit 1 compares the returns of some widely published fixed-income indices.

We use the 3-month bill index as the starting point because it represents the "riskless" passive investment in fixed income. From there, we look at relative exposure of being on the 1- to 3-year part of the yield curve and then the 1- to 5-year part of the yield curve. Going from the 3-month bill to the 1- to 3-year Treasury index, there was a pickup of 130 basis points of annual return.

Incrementally, investing a comparable index comprising 100% investment-grade corporate bonds provided us with 70 basis points of annualized total return. Consider this: We were able to achieve 6.62% of annual returns exclusively from the yield curve in the 1- to 3-year sector, and able to get only an additional 70 basis points from the corporate market. In essence, of the 7.32% of the return received from the corporate index, 6.62% can be attributed to the curve alone. This means that about 90% of the return was achieved solely from exposure to the yield curve. Exhibit 1 also reveals that each of these indices had almost identical volatility. The profile of the 1- to 5-year area shows a very similar situation, adding credence to the notion that the exposure of a high-grade portfolio to the yield curve is by far its single most important determinant of total returns over time.

Exhibit 1: Returns of Fixed-Income Indices
June 30, 1989 — June 30, 1999

	Annual Returns (%)	Volatility* (%)
3-month U.S. Treasury Bill	5.22	0.40
1- to 3-year U.S. Treasury	6.62	1.69
1- to 3-year investment-grade corporate bond	7.32	1.69
1- to 5-year U.S. Treasury	6.98	2.33
1- to 5-year investment-grade corporate bond	7.61	2.32

* Annualized standard deviation of monthly total returns
Source: Merrill Lynch Indices

For most corporate cash portfolios, we would strongly recommend setting limits on both individual securities and on the portfolio as a whole. Too often, we have seen policies that neglect to include one or the other because assumptions are made. For example, we have worked with numerous clients that have a policy containing specific maturity restrictions for each permissible sector but no constraint on the overall portfolio's average maturity. To compound matters, for U.S. Treasury investments the maturity restriction is typically more generous than for other asset classes.

It is very common to see a policy that allows Treasurys to be invested with a maturity maximum of three years, while all other sectors are limited to investing in maturities of less than 12 months. When we discuss this type of policy with the treasurer, he or she makes it crystal-clear that the portfolio has a very strict capital-preservation objective: "Don't lose my cash!" As already mentioned, this policy would not include a portfolio-wide maturity constraint. Effectively, the portfolio could be fully invested in Treasury securities that have three years to maturity. The company in such a case is focused on the notion that Treasury securities will not expose the portfolio to credit risk, which is true. But often overlooked is the tremendous amount of market risk that nonetheless needs to be considered.

Extending this example, if we examine the return profile for the last 10 years of an index that is constantly invested in 3-year Treasury notes, we find that this portfolio actually lost money on a monthly basis 26 times (out of a possible 120 months) or about 22% of the time. Additionally, a portfolio of 3-year Treasurys experienced quarterly losses 17% of the time, or seven times in the last 10 years out of a possible 40 quarters. When we point this out to prospective clients, they generally react first with disbelief, then with swift and decisive action. Our recommendation for this type of intent/outcome dislocation is simply to impose an average maturity constraint on the portfolio: In this example, an appropriate limitation may have been six to nine months.

As may be seen in our sample policy, we do not discuss maturity whatsoever. Instead, we focus on duration, a mathematical exercise that measures the sensitivity of a bond's price to changes in interest rates. There is voluminous published material on the notion, theory, and practice of duration but, for the purposes of this chapter, we will focus entirely on the impact of using duration as the appropriate measure for an investment policy.

In our example, we tend to recommend the use of *effective* duration, which takes into consideration the fact that not all fixed-income securities pay principal and interest in predictable fashion. The two most common uses for effective duration are for floating-rate securities and amortizing assets such as asset-backed securities and all kinds of mortgage-backed securities.[1]

---

[1] See Chapters 11 amd 12 for a discussion of the various types of mortgage-backed and asset-backed securities products.

Floating-rate securities generally pay income to the investor that changes over time based on some common market rate such as the London interbank offered rate (LIBOR) or the 3-month Treasury bill. A very common floating-rate note would have a coupon payment that changes every 90 days based on some increment above or below the then prevailing 3-month LIBOR. Since the coupon will change with market rates, the bond's price will be much less volatile. In fact, without any change in the bond's credit quality, its price should be very close to par when the interest rate resets since it will be paying income based on current market rates. Therefore, this floating-rate note will effectively have true interest rate risk only until the next time its coupon resets to current market rates.[2] For this reason, effective duration is calculated as the duration of the bond until its next reset date, which in most cases is far shorter (hence, less risky) than its actual duration (or maturity, for that matter). Since we are concerned only with the bond's sensitivity to interest rates in this section of the policy, it is most accurate to use effective duration whenever appropriate.

For asset-backed and mortgage-backed securities, effective duration becomes relevant because there is almost always some uncertainty regarding the way the principal amortizes and/or the interest is paid. When this is the case, the market has adopted conventions to calculate what is known as the average life of these securities. Average life refers to the notion that using consensus speeds for the principal and/or interest payments, the expected maturity of the bond can be calculated.

For example, a typical auto loan asset-backed deal has a legal stated maturity of five years, since the underlying loans in the deal are all 5-year auto loans. But, as we know, many if not all of the loans will be paid off before five years due to trade-ins, refinancings, defaults, or simply because the borrower decides to pay off the loan early. While the legal final maturity of the bond is five years, technically, we know that on average we will get the vast majority of our principal back in less than five years. How soon will that be? That depends on a variety of factors such as interest rates, economic cycles, or geography. From our perspective, though, it is most important that the average life of the bond can be calculated by incorporating all of these factors. Since we can calculate the projected maturity of a bond with uncertain cash flows, we can then calculate its duration based on these projections. Such instruments are typically traded based on their average lives, so using effective duration is a far more valuable way to calculate their sensitivity to interest rates.

As shown in our sample policy, the portfolio can invest in individual securities with an effective duration of up to five years, while the portfolio can have a weighted average effective duration up to two years.

Is this a little or a lot of exposure to the yield curve? This question can be answered only by investigating the return profile of this type of portfolio and comparing it with the objectives of the company. We will make such a comparison in detail during our discussion of benchmarks.

---

[2] For other factors that affect the interest risk of a floating-rate note, see Chapter 10.

Eligible Investments

The section of the policy on eligible investments specifies the kind of bonds that are allowed in the portfolio. Many policies, as is the case with our example, detail not only what is allowed in the portfolio but also the types of instruments that are specifically prohibited. Highlighting these prohibited investments is a good idea for companies that want to make it perfectly clear that they do not want certain types of instruments in the portfolio. Since much of the language in our industry can be subjective, it pays to include specific prohibitions.

As our sample policy indicates, most of the common sectors of the fixed-income market are eligible investments. For the sake of brevity we will not review each sector in detail, but will highlight only some of the more interesting selections.

Asset-Backed Securities

Nearly all of the portfolios that we manage allow us to invest in asset-backed securities. And for good reason. In recent years, asset-backed securities have become increasingly important for all types of fixed-income portfolios. As of first-quarter 1999, the outstanding level of asset-backed securities in the market was $641 billion, up from $205 billion just five years earlier. This means that asset-backed securities have gained a fairly wide level of investor sponsorship. It follows that including ABS into a portfolio introduces a valuable tool for diversification and return potential. Our policy stipulates that only those asset-backed securities with a triple-A rating are permitted in the portfolio. This is a common constraint in the world of corporate cash investing. In most cases, we agree that this is a reasonable limitation, ensuring that only the highest-quality and most liquid asset-backed securities will be included in the portfolio.

MBS and CMOs

Mortgage-backed securities include mortgage passthroughs and collateralized mortgage obligations (CMOs).[3] The performance of mortgage-backed securities depends on the underlying collateral of residential mortgages. For purposes of corporate cash investing, however, we usually differentiate between passthroughs and CMOs to be absolutely clear about what is permitted in the portfolio. Many corporate cash investors have an inherent fear when it comes to any kind of mortgage-backed security.

Some of this fear is based on actual market events. In 1994, for one memorable example, much of the mortgage-backed market experienced intense structural risk due to the dramatic backup in interest rates. This was especially true for esoteric CMOs, referred to as mortgage derivatives.

But mortgage-backed securities used prudently can be a beneficial source of diversification and return potential in a corporate cash portfolio. Since these products rely on the payment stream of the underlying pool of mortgage loans, they are generally associated with relative uncertainty regarding the repay-

---

[3] CMOs are explained in Chapter 11.

ment of principal. As is well known, the mortgagor (the homeowner) has the right to repay any or all of the principal at any time, and, for many reasons, this occurs regularly. Perhaps refinancing is seen as an attractive alternative; or the homeowner moves, defaults on the mortgage, or simply pays back the principal on an accelerated basis.

Despite the fact that the market has collected almost 20 years of repayment data on bonds of this type, there is still a fair amount of uncertainty swirling around the cash flows of mortgage-backed securities. Because of this, mortgage product generally has attractive yields, especially considering that nearly all of these instruments are triple-A rated. It would be impractical to review all the theory and practice that has evolved to value and monitor mortgage-backed securities in the context of this chapter. We will focus solely on their direct application to corporate cash portfolios.

When incorporating this asset class into corporate cash portfolios, it is most important to include only those securities that meet the objectives of the policy, most notably that the mortgage-related issues will meet the mandated capital-preservation and liquidity standard. Portfolio managers should focus only on passthroughs and CMO for which cash flows will not be significantly impacted by reasonable changes in interest rates. Many very useful and fairly standard models are used in the market to predict this relationship.

For instance, a "vanilla" short-dated planned amortization class (PAC) bond can have an average life of 18 months.[4] The payment stream is structured so that this will not change if interest rates move ±200 basis points. These kinds of bonds can be particularly attractive to corporate cash portfolios because, even though this is a particularly stable CMO, it would be typically priced more attractively than corresponding single-A-rated corporate bonds that carry some level of credit risk. As will be discussed later in this chapter, there are ways to incorporate language into the policy that helps mitigate structural risk on all securities with uncertain cash flows.

Concentration Limits

Setting limits on how much of the portfolio can be invested in the securities of a single issuer can make certain that the portfolio is adequately diversified. The old notion about not putting all your eggs in one basket is tried and true advice that applies to the world of corporate cash investing where capital preservation and liquidity are the primary objectives.

As shown in our sample policy, there are three key elements to this section. First, U.S. Treasury and federal agency securities are singled out for special treatment. Both of these important sectors have no limits on the amount that can be held in the portfolio. This open-door policy is directly related to the creditworthiness of these entities. For many reasons, even in a portfolio that allows investments in most sectors, a portfolio manager may want to hold most or all of the

---

[4] PAC bonds are described in Chapter 11.

portfolio in government-related issues. It could be a defensive reaction to a market meltdown, as occurred in fall 1998, or simply a decision to hold a significant portion of the portfolio in highly liquid securities, to "keep the powder dry" for opportunities that have yet to materialize. In any case, flexibility is critically important to a portfolio manager in a corporate cash account. The U.S. Treasury is the most creditworthy issuer in the world, and the implied government support behind the federal sponsored enterprises makes them effectively only slightly more risky from a credit perspective than Treasurys. We strongly recommend allowing this type of latitude.

Aside from government-related issuers, our sample policy has a maximum of 5% of the portfolio for any single issuer. This is a very typical constraint for portfolios of this type, and is used in many fixed-income mutual funds. If the portfolio manager decided to invest the entire portfolio in nongovernment-related securities, there would be at least 20 positions in the portfolio; this amount is reasonable for an investment-grade, fixed-income mandate.

The single-issuer constraint, however, is not necessarily so straightforward. For a 5% limit to work, the portfolio needs to be of sufficient size so that each individual position is large enough to find in the market (or, at least, find at reasonable prices). In the institutional market, any position of less than $1 million is typically thought of as an odd lot. Odd lots represent some intriguing dilemmas for investors. First, they are more difficult to find in large supplies, which could disadvantage the portfolio. Second, they usually do not have the same ready liquidity as institutional lots and, therefore, have a wider bid/ask spread. If you needed to sell an odd lot, you might not get a very attractive price. So size may be a factor in what concentration limit is most appropriate.

For a portfolio of less than $20 million, a concentration limit of less than 5% should be the rule of thumb. Does this constraint expose the portfolio to more risk? Yes, sort of. Technically speaking, by having more eggs in one basket the portfolio is less diversified and, hence, more risky. But tradeoffs are available: The increase in risk can be counteracted by raising the credit-quality bar of bonds that are allowed in the portfolio. (The credit-quality issue is addressed in detail later in this chapter.)

The final specific constraint highlighted in this section of the policy relates to repurchase transactions. Our sample policy allows a 25% maximum concentration for the counterparties to repo investments. Why so much latitude? The answer lies in the structure of these securities. Typically, the appropriate repurchase agreements that are allowed in corporate cash policies (and in our sample policy, specifically) are fully collateralized with at least 102% of the transaction's value with either U.S. Treasury or federal agency securities. This level of collateral with such high-quality instruments mitigates much of the risk associated with these instruments. Hence, we feel comfortable recommending an extended concentration limit for repurchase agreements. If anything were to impair the counterparty's ability to pay back the principal of the repo, we would simply take possession of the collateral on our client's behalf.

QUALITY

The policy must provide explicit detail regarding the minimum acceptable credit quality that is allowed in the portfolio; most corporate cash policies focus on the credit quality of bonds individually. The policy in our example allows the portfolio to contain a full range of investment-grade securities (bonds with a triple-B rating or better). For corporate cash portfolios this is a fairly aggressive posture, as triple-B securities represent more risk than many cash investors feel they are willing to assume.

Comparing the inherent risk of triple-B-rated bonds with their corresponding yield advantage reveals that it may, in fact, make sense to consider this type of credit profile for the policy. According to Standard & Poor's, triple-B-rated bonds had a 5-year cumulative default rate of 1.75% from 1981 through 1998. Counter this with the fact that in the 1- to 3-year area of the curve, for 1994-1999, triple-B-rated corporate bonds have averaged an 82 basis point yield advantage over comparable U.S. Treasurys (which don't carry any credit risk).

Suppose your company had held the triple-B corporate portfolio for five years and experienced average default rates; we will make the very conservative assumption that 1.75% of the portfolio would be valueless. (This is actually a very conservative assumption since not all defaulted bonds go to zero value, but let's make that assumption to provide a worst-case scenario.) Over that same 5-year period you would have accumulated 4.10% of incremental yield (82 basis points × five years) to the credit-risk-free Treasury alternative, leaving you with a net 2.35% advantage by holding the all-triple-B portfolio.

This analysis, of course, accounts only for default risk that exists for these securities. Other risks are involved in investing in triple-B-rated bonds; even without defaults, the price of these instruments can depreciate due to many market variables. If the portfolio requires a very high degree of liquidity, there are clearly risks associated with investing in securities with this credit-rating profile.

Let's suppose that you are still unsettled on the inclusion of triple-B rated securities in the portfolio. In that case, we highly recommend the application of a single-A credit standard for individual issues. To get meaningful exposure to asset classes such as corporate bonds and bank notes, it is almost imperative in today's market to allow the portfolio to invest in single-A-rated securities. Large corporate America has taken on the attitude in recent years that a single-A rating provides the best possible combination of balance-sheet flexibility and investor sponsorship. For this reason, the issuance of corporate bonds has become far more centered around a single-A profile. For example, as shown in Exhibit 2 30% of all corporate bond issuance in 1992 was at least double-A rated. This had changed dramatically by 1997, at which time only 14% of corporate bond issuance was rated double-A or better. Exhibit 3 provides a representative sample of corporate issuers with investment-grade ratings.

Exhibit 2: Corporate Bond Issuance by Ratings Category

Rating	1992	1997
AAA	$20 billion	$3 billion
AA	$33 billion	$18 billion
A	$70 billion	$65 billion
BBB	$50 billion	$63 billion

Exhibit 3: Representative Sample of Issuers

Double A	Single A	Triple B
Associated Corp. of North America (Ford)	Caterpillar	Burlington Northern
	Daimler Chrysler	Conagra Inc.
Airtouch	Ford Motor	Cox Communications
AT&T	General Motors	Cummins Engine
Citigroup	Goldman Sachs	Federated Dept. Stores
Coca Cola	IBM	Norfolk Southern
Eli Lilly	Lucent	Raytheon
Gillette	MCI Worldcom	Ryder
J.P. Morgan	PepsiCo	Safeway
Merrill Lynch	Walt Disney	Sprint
Morgan Stanley Dean Witter	Xerox	
Norwest Corp		
Procter & Gamble		
Wachovia Bank		

For money market product, the portfolio stipulates the Tier Two credit quality standard. This term is commonly used in evaluating the applicability of securities for money market mutual funds. Tier Two refers to instruments that would carry a rating of either P-2 (Moody's), A-2 (S&P), or F-2 (Fitch). The corresponding long-term debt ratings of these issuers would generally be around a low single-A profile. For companies seeking a more liquid or conservative profile, it is common to use a Tier One minimum. Many of the policies we see rely solely on Moody's and Standard & Poor's, and impose an A-1/P-1 credit constraint for money market product.

Nationally recognized statistical rating organizations (NRSROs) are the large, well-known firms that assign credit ratings to a vast array of fixed-income securities. Moody's Investor Services, Standard & Poor's, Fitch IBCA and Duff and Phelps, and A.M. Best are among the largest and most widely used providers of this service.

The other key element of the quality section of the guidelines deals with stipulations for structured issuances, mostly asset-backed and mortgage-backed securities. As mentioned earlier, these bonds can be valuable tools in a corporate cash portfolio, but we need to make assurances that only the safest and most liquid issues in these asset classes will be used. Our sample investment policy constrains the portfolio to those securities that will have an average life drift of not more than one year based on a ± 100 basis point move in interest rates. As described earlier, we tend to focus on average life for these kinds of securities to help us determine their appropriateness for the portfolio. For structured securities, as interest rates move in either direction the amortization of their principal is projected to change based on the prepayment models that are used to value these bonds. Since the principal payments are anticipated to change, the average life of the security will also change. Generally, bonds with more change in projected average life will have more price volatility and less liquidity. For purposes of our policy, we try to limit the potential for this average life "drift." We want to be sure we are including those bonds that will have the most stable price changes as interest rates move in either direction. This gives us comfort to participate meaningfully in these sectors of the market while mitigating downside risk.

Currency Exposure

While it is implied that most corporate cash portfolios are going to be invested in domestic securities, it is clearly worthwhile to stipulate this in the policy. For the many firms that need a multicurrency approach to cash management, this would need to be clearly articulated in the guidelines.

Specification of the Benchmark

Benchmark specification takes on a multitask responsibility for corporate cash portfolios. The first task is to evaluate the major risk and return parameters of the policy in an attempt to quantify whether they meet the conceptual objectives of the organization. The initial and by far the most important step in this process is to isolate the portfolio's exposure to the yield curve permitted in the policy.

As mentioned earlier, exposure to the yield curve is the single greatest determinant of potential return and volatility in a high-grade, fixed-income portfolio. To evaluate risk and return we will focus on the policy parameters that stipulate allowable duration ranges for both individual securities and the portfolio as a whole. In our sample policy, the portfolio is allowed to invest in individual securities with an effective duration of up to 5, but the weighted average duration of the portfolio as a whole may not exceed 2.

The issue at hand is to find a suitable proxy that encapsulates that level of yield curve exposure. To do this, we will rely on the purveyors of published fixed-income indices to see if we can construct a customized benchmark to replicate this exposure. For the individual security limit of five years, we found that the Merrill Lynch 1- to 5-year U.S. Treasury index is a fairly accurate representation. This market-weighted index is intended to proxy the entire menu of all Treasurys that mature between one and five years. While this a valid approximation for the portfolio's ability to invest in individual securities, this index has an effective duration of approximately 2.25. This is longer than our policy allows, so we have to balance this longer index with appropriate shorter index that not only will adjust the customized benchmark duration but will also reflect the fact that the portfolio's primary objectives are capital preservation and liquidity. Appropriately, then we have chosen the Merrill Lynch 3-month Treasury bill index to fulfill this role.

To replicate the overall effective duration allowed in the policy we chose weightings of 75% for the 1- to 5-year index and 25% for the 3-month bill index. This customized benchmark has an effective duration of approximately 1.5. This "risk neutral target" portfolio duration reflects the fact that the portfolio is allowed to have an effective duration up to 2. Of course the benchmark needs to be less than the maximum exposure allowed in this regard because the portfolio manager needs to have the latitude of being longer than the benchmark when his or her viewpoint is bullish on rates (that is, rates are going to go down).

Now that we are satisfied that the benchmark we have initially chosen is an accurate representation of the yield curve exposure allowed in the policy, we can now test it both historically and prospectively to see if the return profile meets the client's needs. The historical return profile is summarized in Exhibit 4.

As can be seen in the exhibit, the benchmark has achieved an annual total return of 6.54% for the period 1990-2000, but these returns declined steadily over that time period in an era of generally falling interest rates. For a reference point, the 3-month Treasury bill achieved a return of 5.22% over the same period. But since our investment objectives in this case are more focused on capital preservation, the volatility measures are probably more meaningful. For the period 1990-2000, this customized benchmark had a standard deviation of returns of 1.79%, meaning that on average the portfolio had annual returns of 6.54% ± 1.79% two-thirds of the time. While this measure of volatility is somewhat interesting, it doesn't address the true risk parameter of most corporate treasurers. That's why we also calculated the occurrences of loss in the portfolio over different time periods. Exhibit 4 clearly illustrates that on a monthly basis, there will periods when the portfolio experiences a loss, but on a quarterly basis the probability becomes much, much lower.

Exhibit 4: Historical Return Profile as of March 31, 2000

Effective Duration	1.62
Current yield to maturity	6.32%

Years	Annual Returns (%)	Volatility of Returns* (%)
1	3.68	0.98
3	5.76	1.49
5	6.03	1.56
10	6.54	1.79
15	7.36	
20	8.91	

Incidence of Loss	Monthly	Quarterly	Annually
10 years	19 times	2 times	None
20 years	37 times	3 times	None

*Annualized standard deviation of monthly total returns

Exhibit 5: Historic Risk/Return Analysis
March 31, 1990 - March 31, 2000

	Total Return Annualized (%)	Total Return Volatility* (%)
3-month Treasury bill	5.22	0.40
6-month Treasury bill	5.44	0.49
1-year Treasury	5.85	0.87
2-year Treasury	6.36	1.86
3-year Treasury	7.00	2.70
5-year Treasury	6.99	4.25
10-year Treasury	7.36	6.65
30-year Treasury	8.80	9.71

* Volatility is computed as the annual standard deviation of monthly total returns
Source: Merrill Lynch and Salomon Brothers Treasury Indices total return calculations

What is most important about this exercise is that only the company will know what represents its true tolerance for risk based upon its plans for the cash. While we consult our clients and present the analytic data to support our beliefs relative to the risk and return potential of any given strategy, it is up to the company's treasury managers to determine the acceptability of any given approach. Risk and return are terms that are both relative and subjective. In Exhibit 4, our client is willing to assume occasional occurrence of loss on a monthly basis to achieve long-term return objectives. However, the client does not want much exposure to the possibility of a quarterly loss given its status as a public company that is compelled to report results quarterly. We work with many companies whose profile precludes them from the possibility of a monthly loss, while others are willing to accept significant volatility on the quarterly returns.

Keep in mind that the above exercise only identifies the general profile of potential returns, and only measures the impact of yield curve exposure on the portfolio. During our standard practice of helping clients wrestle with the guideline issue, we generally like to present the impact of curve exposure in a broad context. Frequently, we will use the exhibits discussed below to reveal the relative return and risk profile of being constantly invested in various parts of the yield curve. This is an excellent starting point when considering how the portfolio should be structured.

Exhibit 5 reveals, in a general sense, the profile of returns an investor received for the 10-year period 1990-2000 from being invested in various parts of the yield curve. It is apparent that for investors who a have a pure capital-preservation objective, the portfolio should probably be structured to have maximum curve exposure of less than one year. For others, a more thorough analysis of the exposure needs to be undertaken to determine the optimal mix between seeking incremental relative returns versus the amount of periodic volatility they are willing to assume.

Exhibit 6: Historical Incidence of Loss*
March 31, 1990 - March 31, 2000

	Monthly (120 months)	Quarterly (40 quarters)	Annually (10 years)
3-month T-bill	0	0	0
6-month T-bill	0	0	0
1-year T-bill	5	0	0
2-year T-note	19	4	0
3-year T-note	26	13	1
10-year T-bond	43	15	2
30-year T-bond	46	15	3

* Loss defined as negative total return
    Source: Merrill Lynch and Salomon Brothers Treasury Indices total return calculations

Exhibit 6 details the historical incidence of loss (negative total return) for the same period.

The importance of benchmarking in this context is to determine that the investment guidelines are suitable for what the company would like to achieve with its cash portfolio. This should be an iterative process that culminates in a guideline statement and a concurrent benchmark that represent the most viable strategy given the current objectives and constraints.

By performing this task, we are taking the first steps toward risk management before we have invested a single dollar of the company's assets. Once this is accomplished, the benchmark becomes the "risk neutral" position of the portfolio, or what would be theoretically the target exposure. This means that if the portfolio manager is completely neutral to where the market is going, he or she should basically buy the exposure implied by the benchmark. This is obviously rarely the case; so when the portfolio manager has an opinion on the market, he or she would have mismatch positions relative to the benchmark.

Therefore, on an ongoing basis, the benchmark clearly becomes an appropriate performance measurement tool to evaluate the effectiveness of the manager. We would encourage all corporate cash investors to monitor continually their portfolio manager's performance relative to the benchmark. And this is the case whether or not the performance is meaningfully below or above the benchmark returns. If the performance is below the benchmark, this is an obvious area of concern. If the performance is significantly above the benchmark, then similar concerns should arise — as the portfolio manager had to take some pretty big bets to achieve this return. These kinds of bets may not be in the best interest of the company or may not be in the spirit of the policy.

One of the obvious questions that typically evolves from this discussion is our reliance on Treasury indices when, in fact, the portfolio can invest in so many other sectors. First, as we already mentioned, yield curve exposure is such a large part of the equation that we want to focus our attention on this aspect of the portfolio. In addition, however, the short end of the curve — where it tends to exist in corporate cash investing — seems to have never really gotten the "respect" of the major index providers. Hence, there are no really market reflective indices for fixed income portfolios that have average lives less than two years. For these reasons, we generally construct our benchmark portfolios using Treasury-only indices.

SUMMARY

The practice of carefully crafting an investment policy for corporate cash investing is a critical aspect of optimizing this important balance-sheet asset. By taking appropriate steps, this can be accomplished in a way that will reflect the unique needs of the organization, and strike the balance between not leaving any potential return on the table and having access to cash when opportunities present themselves. While this may require some corporate soul-searching to uncover the true tolerances of executive management, it can be well worth the effort. It is most likely true that the company in question is in the business of something other than managing cash, so it is critical to apply the company's cash the primary line(s) of business in order to maximize shareholder value. At the same time, however, any incremental return that the company can get from its cash portfolio flows directly to the bottom line, so the absolute level of earnings can be significant.

APPENDIX

PROPOSED CORPORATE CASH INVESTMENT POLICY

Objectives

- Preserves principal.
- Meets liquidity needs.
- Delivers a suitable return in relationship to these guidelines, market conditions, and the benchmark set forth in this policy.

Duration Restrictions

The following guidelines will apply to the portfolio as a whole:

- The average effective duration of the portfolio is not to exceed 2.
- The maximum effective duration of any individual security is not to exceed 5 unless otherwise noted elsewhere in this policy.

Eligible Investments

- Obligations issued by the U.S. Treasury or guaranteed by the U.S. government.
- Obligations issued or guaranteed by U.S. federal agencies.
- Commercial paper.
- Repurchase and reverse repurchase agreements fully collateralized by U.S. government and/or agency securities with a maximum maturity of seven days. The market value of the collateral securities, when marked to market, must be equal to or greater than 102% of the face value of the agreement.
- Corporate bonds and notes and medium-term notes
- Obligations of commercial banks including but not limited to bankers' acceptances, certificates of deposit, time deposits, and bank notes.
- Asset-backed securities with a minimum triple-A credit rating from at least one nationally recognized statistical rating organization (NRSRO).
- Mortgage-backed securities.
- Collateralized mortgage obligations.
- Money market mutual funds with a minimum $1 billion average asset size for the previous 12 months.

Prohibited Investments

The following investments are strictly forbidden from inclusion in the portfolio:

- Interest only.
- Principal only.
- Inverse floating-rate notes.
- Speculative investments.
- Derivative instruments except floating-rate notes
- Futures, options, forward contracts, and swaps of any kind.

Concentration Limits

Holdings are further subject to the following limitations:

- Obligations of the U.S. government and U.S. federal agencies: No limits.
- Obligations of all other issuers: With any one issuer, not to exceed 5% of the aggregate market value of the portfolio, except,
- Repurchase agreements: With any one counterparty, not to exceed 25% of the aggregate market value of the portfolio

Quality

The minimum short-term debt rating of money market instruments or other instruments with a maturity less than one year is Tier Two. The minimum long-term debt rating for all other instruments is investment grade by at least one nationally recognized statistical rating organization. The maximum average life drift of all structured securities or securities with any embedded option based on a ±100 basis point move in interest rates will be one year, based on consensus prepayment speed forecasts that are published by major analytic services.

Currency

The portfolio will be invested 100% in US$-denominated securities.

Benchmark

Portfolio performance will be measured against a composite benchmark of 25% Merrill Lynch three-month Treasury bill index and 75% Merrill Lynch 1- to 5-year Treasury index.

Chapter 3

Identifying, Measuring, and Controlling Risk

Hugh R. Lamle
President
Chase & MDSass Partners
Director of Fixed Income and Quantitative Investment
M. D. Sass Investors Services, Inc.

Risk is a four-letter word. So is luck. Investors who don't properly assess risk, improperly depend on luck for success.

Appropriately, most of the chapters of this book are devoted to methods of earning superior returns. That, after all, is what managers get paid for and it is the easiest metric for evaluating strategies and their execution. Risk, unfortunately, is usually measured in retrospect and often too late. Risky strategies that succeed are often confused with safe strategies. This is especially true for the risky strategies that produced a relatively consistent pattern of returns during the measurement period. Because interest rate and credit spread cycles can be quite long, even a multi-year measurement period may only include a part of the cycle or expose only certain risks. Therefore, even a full cycle can be a poor guide to the potential volatility and potential underperformance that is inherent in the strategy under consideration.

Owners of capital must be cautious about whom they entrust with its management, whether their own employees or outside managers, because the distribution of returns and risks between the manager and the owner are inherently not symmetrical. Owners of capital take all the risk of an unsuccessful investment but only earn a few to a few dozen basis points of incremental return with a successful strategy. The investment manager's return for adding value is substantially greater. Internal managers' salaries and bonuses can increase in percentage terms by an order of magnitude compared to the increase in return on the portfolio. Outside managers who build a track record of high relative returns can attract more clients, grow their fees, and increase the value of their firms. Although they have more potential return, both internal and external managers have less risk than the owners of capital. Poor, but not negligent, performance may ultimately result in their services being terminated and the disruption of their future cash

The author wishes to thank his colleague Albert A. Slawsky, CFA for his valuable assistance.

flow, but not reduce their personal assets. Only the client has assets at risk. Given the skewed reward to risk relationship, the owner of the capital must be more vigilant in identifying, measuring, and controlling risk because he or she cannot depend on the manager to be equally cautious. This is not to say that many managers consciously and venally decide to buy a free call on their personal success with the risk that they take for their clients; but rather, that the extremely competitive nature of the markets and the asymmetrical returns described above, can erode the link between the client and the manager working as a team for the client's benefit. This erosion can be subtle and even unconscious on the part of the manager. Unless the client has an appropriate risk control process in place it may reward the manager who takes excessive risk and thereby outperforms, by allocating more assets to that manager. Other managers will naturally be motivated to try to catch up by also taking more risk.

The ease of calculating the standard deviation of returns, value at risk (VAR), the Sharpe ratio, and other statistical measures have given many investors an exaggerated confidence in their ability to measure and control risk. However, these quantitative tools do not eliminate the need for a deeper, more penetrating, prospective analysis of the impact that a plausible, although not recently observed, confluence of events may have on the markets. The purpose of this chapter is to provide a glossary of risk factors and a context for risk evaluation so that the perceptive reader can identify which risks are inherent in each of the strategies discussed in this book, attempt to measure those risks prospectively, seek to control them within acceptable limits for the portfolio under consideration, and understand the tradeoffs in potential return that may result from the risk management policies selected. The vast variety and complexity of money market and bond market risks make a comprehensive discussion impossible in the limited space of a single chapter of a broader book on strategies. Readers are therefore cautioned to view this chapter as only an introduction to the elements of risk. Even at this superficial level, however, it will provide a foundation for evaluating which apparently attractive strategies contain risks that should eliminate them from consideration and which strategies should be modified in the light of their risk dimensions. If you, the reader, are merely provoked to probe more deeply into appealing strategies and managers with a checklist formed from this chapter, I will have succeeded in my goal and you will avoid financial loss and professional humiliation.

RISK DEFINED

Risk is the probability of earning a return below some minimum level for a defined period of time. Some losses are so unacceptably large that even if the probability of their occurrence is very low they must be avoided. Incremental returns from money market and low risk bond strategies, though worth pursuing, are sufficiently modest that an investor will not recover from a major loss in a reasonable period of time. Most often, the reaction to a serious loss is to drastically reduce risk exposure and thereby eliminate any further opportunity to earn reasonably available incremental returns.

CATEGORIZING RISK

Risks are intimately related to the various means of adding return. In fact, it is generally impossible to add return without taking some form of incremental risk, so it is helpful to categorize strategies for adding return by their sources of incremental risk. While it is a useful exercise to analyze risks in isolation, in combination the whole may be either greater or less than the sum of the parts. For example, in certain negative market environments complex security structures lead to less liquidity which, in turn, compounds the security's interest rate and/or credit risks.

IDENTIFYING, MEASURING AND CONTROLLING RISKS

Listed below are broad types of risk. They are not mutually exclusive and other authors may group them differently, but this list does include all of the major risks:

- interest rate related
- credit
- structural
- liquidity
- event
- operational

You must accept some risks, but which ones and in what combination? Each of these risks exists at the security level, but some may be mitigated at the portfolio level. For example, it may be perfectly acceptable to hold some less liquid issues in a portfolio if it also contains sufficient liquidity to meet all of its perceived cash flow requirements plus a cushion to protect against mis-specification of these requirements. In this case, these less liquid issues can be held to redemption if necessary and the incremental income earned. Alternatively, when and if the liquidity premium declines in a more favorable market, these issues may appreciate in value sufficiently, relative to other portfolio candidates, to warrant their sale and the reinvestment of the proceeds into other less liquid instruments.

Interest Rate Related Risks

Interest rate sensitivity is the change in a security's or portfolio's cash flow or market value due to changes in the level of interest rates or the shape of the yield curve.

Price sensitivity is the impact on the security's price or portfolio's market value due to the change in interest rates. The generally accepted measure of such sensitivity is known as *duration*, the longer the duration the greater the sensitivity.

Reinvestment risk is the risk of reinvesting portfolio cash flows at rates below the forecast level. This is particularly severe when securities mature, are called for early redemption or have active sinking funds after interest rates decline and both interest and principal must be reinvested for the remaining horizon at lower yields than planned.

Leverage risk multiplies the security's price or portfolio's value change due to the financial leverage embedded in the security or portfolio. The most obvious form of leverage is buying securities with borrowed funds. Other forms of leverage such as the use of derivatives can create payoffs that are analogous to the use of margin but may not be as obvious. The catalogue is too long and varied to list but includes the sale or purchase of puts and calls, more complex options, financial futures, or similarly structured notes. While the reward risk relationships they create may be attractive, the absolute risk may be excessive in the context of cash and extended cash portfolios.

Credit Risks

Credit risk is the risk that an obligor will not make the required payments when they are due. On a given investment there may be multiple obligors which creates exposure to multiple credit risks. For most publicly traded and many privately placed debt obligations, these default risks are evaluated and ranked by nationally recognized statistical rating organizations such as Standard & Poor's Corporation and Moody's Investor Services, Inc. These rating agencies generally do a good job but they have demonstrated that they are far from infallible. Investors are counseled to do their own credit research. This is especially true when the issuer is in a volatile industry or the security's structure is complex.

The primary credit risk is, of course, that of the debtor on an obligation. However, many issues are insured, backed by a credit guarantee, a letter of credit or a put to a party other than the issuer. In the event of a default by the primary obligor, the credit enhancer may be called upon to fulfill the debtor's obligations. When an issue is credit enhanced, an investor must also assess the ability of the insurer or other enhancer to perform. One must evaluate the terms of the guarantee, put or other enhancement as well to make certain that the guarantor's obligation is not contingent on performance by the issuer. If it is, then default by the debtor may limit the obligation of the credit enhancer.

Credit enhancers are one class of counterparty. Others include sellers of puts and remarketing agents who alter the effective maturity of an issue. Here the buyer relies upon the issuer for ultimate payment, but a default by a remarketer or put seller will result in the investor holding a long-term security which is inherently more risky than the short-term investment she thought she was making.

Broker-dealers who buy or sell issues for delayed settlement and custodians who hold an investor's assets are also subject to default. While the consequences of such failure will be different from a failure by an issuer to make payment in a timely fashion, its likelihood should be evaluated with the same degree of care as the creditworthiness of the issuer.

Credit risk can also impact interest rate spreads. Thus, even if default does not occur the perceived increased probability of default can erode market values and credit downgrades can force sales of securities at depressed prices.

Structural Risks

Many securities' cash flows are affected by interest rate, currency, or other market changes. These range from simple forms such as floating-rate and reset money market securities, notes, bonds, preferred stocks, and swaps to more complex forms with caps or floors, interest-only and principal-only issues as well as structured notes pegged to the shape of the yield curve or cross rates between currencies. These embedded options may contain multiple layers of risk. They include the obvious interest rate related price sensitivities, reinvestment risk and extension risk, as well as the increased credit risk of the counterparty who must make the cash payments. These securities can be modeled to determine their price sensitivity to changes in the relevant markets and to what extent they create adverse leverage in negative environments.

The more complex the embedded options are that create this cash flow and price sensitivity, and the more specific the embedded options are to particular markets, relationships, and counterparties, the less liquid the instruments will be, especially when the markets move against them. In periods of market stress, declining prices may cause leveraged holders of such securities to face margin calls and forced liquidations at substantial price declines from the discounted present value of their forecast cash flows. Properly structured portfolios that have excess liquidity can use these periods of extreme volatility to their advantage if they have properly controlled their risk.

Liquidity Risks

Liquidity risk is the potential widening of bid/asked spreads that results from buyers' unwillingness to buy a security or invest in a sector. An event that would normally lead to increased supply and lower prices is compounded as market makers and other buyers anticipate lower prices and withdraw their bids in the expectation that they will be able to buy the securities at lower prices from anxious or forced sellers. This reduced demand will increase the price concession necessary to sell a security. Often the reduced demand is in anticipation of an increased supply of sellers because of a problem in the market for these securities. As the bids dry up and prices decline, other holders fearing even more declines become sellers. In general, the more complex the structure or the lower the credit quality of an issue, the greater the potential for such a supply/demand imbalance.

A form of liquidity risk can also impact commingled portfolios such as money market funds, bank commingled funds, bond funds, and insurance company funding agreements or guaranteed investment contracts. This occurs when some participants seek to redeem their investments and the fund has insufficient cash to make the payments. The fund may then be forced to sell securities that it had planned to hold to maturity or to borrow against these holding at a higher cost than is earned by the portfolio. The normal transaction costs plus increased price concessions or borrowing costs on these sales will affect all of a fund's holders when in fairness the costs should be borne by those redeeming. As investors who do not need their funds immediately fear being penalized by these costs, they may seek to redeem investments that they otherwise would have held. This can lead to a cascade of redemption requests and more negative impacts. Typically, a negative market environment or some negative event precipitates these accelerated redemptions. Poorly structured funds have in the past faced complete "meltdowns."

Event Risk

Event risk is the potential for a sudden and unpredictable change in the environment that increases the probability of an issuer, class of issuers or credit enhancer not being able to meet its or their obligations. These include industrial accidents, product liability and other litigation, poor operating results on the part of an issuer, credit downgrades, and mergers and acquisitions. Forced liquidations by large holders of these types of securities due to portfolio losses or redemptions related to other securities on their portfolios, and macroeconomic events that increase interest rate volatility and affect issues with embedded options are frequently related to event risk. Often, at the individual issuer level, equity analysis can be a better guide to some of these risks than credit ratings.

Currency risk is the risk that the currency that the issue is payable in declines in value relative to the currency of the liability that the investment is intended to fund.

Operational risk is the risk that some operational aspect of managing the portfolio may be disrupted or fails. Y2K is a good recent example of such concerns. Others include controls regarding authorizations of transactions and transfers of funds and the financial capability of the manager and custodian to attract and retain qualified personal and fund research and development to keep up with the state of the art. Custody of securities should be at a segregated account independent of the broker-dealers and outside investment managers to create an independent record of the securities held and their value. This can prevent both fraud and mis-measurement of returns. Portfolio service providers should be scrutinized for their disaster recovery plans so that the various parties involved with the portfolio can continue to fulfill their responsibilities in the event that natural disaster, fire or other potential disruptions of the operation of their primary business site or data storage.

Total Risk Assessment

Risk assessment requires:

- Portfolio transparency and marking securities to market prices on a frequent and independent basis.

- Stress testing securities, portfolios, and service providers under extreme events and scenarios simulating a market crisis.
- Modeling credit risk at both issuer and credit-enhancer level.
- Providing liquidity in excess of forecast needs to provide for errors in forecasting.
- Measuring aggregate portfolio risk across multi-manager portfolios whether managers have the same or perceived complimentary strategies.

INTEGRATING BUSINESS AND INVESTMENT RISKS

Cash and short-term bond portfolios are rarely an investment strategy in isolation from other assets and strategies. Most often they are a reserve of temporarily excess liquidity that eventually will be used for other portfolio or business strategies. However, their changes in asset value, their earnings, and the timing of their returns can have enormous consequences for the owners of the portfolio. Low returns can penalize corporate earnings. High returns can create a hurdle that can make future comparisons unfavorable and impact share prices and stock option values. Lack of liquidity can cause companies and investors to forego otherwise attractive investments or business opportunities. Clearly, cash and extended cash portfolios must be integrated into the overall reward, risk, and time horizon profile of the enterprise that owns the portfolio.

Portfolio Owner Risk

Portfolio owner risk is a complex subject that impacts many companies with investment objectives in addition to earning a high risk-adjusted return.

Public companies may seek a smooth pattern of portfolio earnings so that the portfolio's return does not adversely impact reported earnings and equity analysts' recommendations. For example, earning too much in one quarter may make quarterly comparisons more difficult in future periods. Some investors may accept lower returns in order to classify securities as "held to maturity" and therefore not have to mark them to market. This may cause them to miss favorable trades.

The business strategies of regulated companies such as insurance companies, broker-dealers, banks, S&L's, and credit unions may be impacted by the amount of capital they have. Frequently discounts are applied to the market values of longer term and/or lower rated securities. This can reduce their desirability as portfolio holdings even if their returns are attractive. Changes in regulations therefore can impact the prices of securities as it reduces the potential universe of buyers and at the same time causes some holders to sell.

Benchmark risk is the risk that an improper performance measurement benchmark will bias portfolio managers to take inappropriate risks to beat the benchmark. Clearly, a benchmark that matches the portfolio's policies and guidelines will reduce this risk.

Mismatch of Assets Relative to Liabilities

Investors with known or anticipated needs for funds take risk by owning securities that mature after they need the funds. This mismatch creates a need to sell securities at times when the investment may be depressed in price even if the ultimate price is assured. Securities maturing before a funding need create reinvestment risk.

SUMMARY AND CONCLUSION

Portfolios, of necessity, are constructed with explicit or implicit trade-off between returns sought and risks accepted. Acceptance of implicit risks without subjecting them to the same scrutiny as those that are explicit subjects portfolios to potential return shortfalls, and even loss, in scenarios that can often be identified, measured, and controlled. Investment managers are generally driven to enhance returns due to the extremely competitive nature of the cash and bond management markets. Clients and senior management of investment-management firms therefore must have thorough and continuous focus on risk management in order to prevent investment strategies from subtly deviating from their intended risk profile. This requires:

- Clear investment policies and guidelines that can be monitored daily and independently
- Performance benchmarks and time horizons that create a mutuality of interest between the owner of capital and the manager of the capital are essential in preventing the inherent asymmetrical return distribution between client and portfolio manager form occurring
- Portfolio transparency and marking to market are essential in detecting portfolio shifts that stray from intended policies
- Clear communication with as much lead time as possible between the client and the portfolio manager regarding shifts in cash flows, tax circumstances, attitudes about risk acceptance, and other factors that can necessitate a portfolio change are important in general and essential when portfolios own more price sensitive and/or less liquid securities.

Managers attempt to add value by selecting and combining securities into portfolios that are intended to maximize the return for a given level of risk.

1. Sector selection — buying sectors at unusually high relative yields in anticipation that the spreads will narrow (their relative interest rates will decline).
2. Security selection — buying issues that provide a relative yield advantage to functionally equivalent quality, duration, and structured issues.

3. Lengthening portfolio durations in a positively sloped yield curve environment.
4. Shortening portfolio durations in a negatively sloped yield curve.
5. Shifting portfolio durations in anticipation of interest rate movements.
6. Leveraging portfolios through borrowing funds at a lower cost than the portfolio yield or by using options or futures and other derivative structures which leverage returns to some future interest rate level or relationship.
7. Buying securities with complex cash flow features (embedded options) such as calls, sinking funds, optional prepayments, coupon resets, caps on variable rates they might pay. Some of these have leveraged effects and can be a substitute for borrowing. At times they can be attempts to get around specific investment policy or guideline prohibitions on borrowing.
8. Credit risk — buying lower rated issues to pickup incremental yield in the expectation that the security will not default and the incremental income will be earned.
9. Liquidity risk — buying issues that are less liquidity and therefore offer a liquidity premium.

Chapter 4

Alternatives in Liquidity Management: DDAs, STIFs, and Sweep Accounts

Richard E. Scott, CCM
Vice President, Institutional Fixed Income
AMR Investments

Being flush with cash is a wonderful problem. The business world thrives on cash, measures cash from every angle, and seemingly, prices cash balances at greater than their nominal value. While a cash rich war chest is better than the alternative — scrambling for liquidity — corporate cash presents its own unique problems and opportunities.

By limiting this discussion to the shortest end of the liquidity timeline, it is presupposed that the treasurer has already built a cash flow model that matches assets and liabilities for the short-, intermediate-, and long-term planning horizons. If a simple pairing of cash sources and uses has not been prepared, the treasurer's first obligation is to construct that cash flow forecast. The liquidity portion of that forecast, and this chapter, addresses those cash flows that will occur within the next two years.

LIQUIDITY MANAGEMENT

Liquidity — positive free-cash balances — comes from a number of sources. Often an organization will experience temporary periods of excess funds. These moments of positive cash flow are usually caused by a seasonality of the revenue cycle (e.g., a retailer whose sales skyrocket during the holidays), the sale of a major asset, or the receipt of long-term financing.

More organizations are now preparing for the unexpected by maintaining liquidity reserves. This is the second most common reason for an organization needing to manage a liquidity position. These cushions of cash are wonderful for weathering a downturn in revenues, and a cash reserve strengthens a balance sheet for certain financial analysis.

A less common reason for needing to manage liquidity is that the returns on cash are a preferred source of income. Hopefully it is a rare occasion that a treasurer decides that a money market fund gives a better return than investing in the primary business. However, this type of decision is common with government entities and not-for-profit organizations.

An organization with a finely tuned cash flow forecast is able to match liquidity investments to cash flow requirements. The treasurers of these organizations are realizing the greatest return out of their cash positions by layering various short-term investment alternatives with progressively longer maturities to precisely match their short-term liability schedule.

DEMAND DEPOSIT ACCOUNTS

Consolidation among the largest banks and affordable access to technology by smaller community banks are changing the cash management relationship between banks and their larger customers. The largest banks are offering unified multi-state and international banking for deposits, disbursements, and information about transactions. Smaller community banks are now offering the core cash management products of online wires, sophisticated ACH systems, controlled disbursement, lockbox processing, and information reporting.

Bottom line for all customers is a wealth of choices. Both net borrowers and net investors can command more services and better pricing from their bank partners. It is important for the customer (the treasurer) to recognize the role of the demand deposit account (DDA) in the overall relationship. For the treasurer, the DDA is the first short-term investment alternative; it is not just a checking account for receipts and disbursements.

In understanding the cash management relationship, a treasurer must also place cash management within the context of the burgeoning access to less expensive debt sources. Secondary, non-traditional and specialty lenders — with few cash management services — are gaining customers, but this necessitates customers engaging multiple bank partners to fulfill all their banking service needs. In addition, borrowers have access to less-expensive direct capital markets (commercial paper, for example). Finally, there is greater competition among traditional lending banks. All banks must aggressively price and package their credit services.

Because of lower credit pricing, the lending bank looks for additional sources of fee income from their borrowers. While the contractual tying of some of these services is forbidden, it is an industry standard practice that a borrower first considers the lead bank for additional services such as depository and other cash management services. It is hard for an unrelated vendor, such as a money manager, to elbow its way into this bank relationship, and the banker knows it. Exhibit 1 portrays the old and new paradigms in banking relationships.

Exhibit 1: Paradigm Shift in Banking Relationships

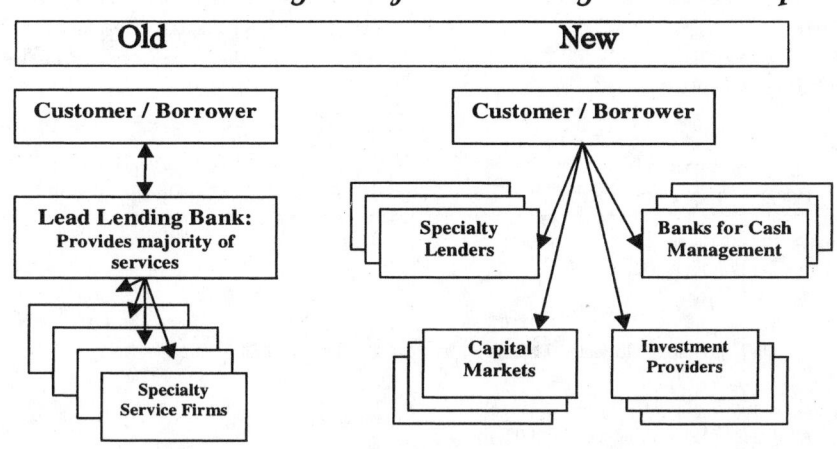

Heavy users of cash management services, such as a large grocery chain's use of currency and check services, provide significant revenue to their banks. On the other hand, the heaviest users of services can also command discounted pricing. In larger markets, the abundance of bank services will also drive down cash management prices.

If credit and cash management services are getting less expensive, where are the profits for the bank? What about bank balances? The rarely discussed benefit to the banks is the account balance left by the customer.

The Role of Bank Balances

Most banks place their corporate customers on account analysis. The analysis sums the bank's service charges, including overdraft charges, and compares those charges to a value placed on the balances left in the customer's DDA.

This calculation is not uniform in the industry, but usually the analysis includes a set-aside for the bank's reserve requirement. Many banks will also factor in any negative balances. Finally, the bank discounts the balances for the uncollected "float" of deposited checks still in the process of clearing. A treasurer should ask his or her bank for a full explanation of the calculation. Exhibit 2 provides an example of a commercial account analysis.

The final figure — sometimes called the "net available balance" — is multiplied by an interest factor. This "earnings credit rate" interest factor is often an arbitrary percentage. Some banks tie the rate to a recent Treasury bill rate, while other banks give no pricing relationship to the market. The net available balance times the earnings credit rate will yield an earnings credit. This credit can be used to offset the account analysis service charges. One pays for the bank's cash management and other services in a "soft dollar" method rather than "hard dollar" invoicing and payment. These balances are also called "compensating balances."

Exhibit 2: Sample Commercial Account Statement

Bank Name			Account Analysis Page 1	
P.O. Box 99999				
Dallas, Texas 75201				
CUSTOMER				
100 MAIN STREET			Period 09-01-99 Thru 09-30-99	
DALLAS, TEXAS 75019			Account Number 123456789	

Balance Information	
Average Daily Ledger Balance	$167,596.73
Average Daily Float	79,758.00
Average Daily Negative Collected Balance	10,000.00
Average Daily Positive Collected Balance	97,838.73
Federal Reserve Requirement (10.0000%)	9,783.87
End of Quarter Ledger Balance	167,794.52

Service Description	Unit Units	Activity Price	Required Charge	Balance
Account Maintenance	1	12.5000	12.50	4,828.00
FDIC Charge / $1,000 (Quarterly charge)		0.4791	80.39	31,049.83
Deposits	16	0.6000	9.60	3,707.90
Currency / Coin Deposited	5,223	0.0009	4.70	1,815.33
Checks Deposited	2,384	0.0600	143.04	55,247.77
Branch Coin Supplied - Indiv Roll	13	0.1000	1.30	502.11
Branch Currency Supplied	11,353	0.0005	5.68	2,193.84
Cashier's Checks	3	2.5000	7.50	2,896.80
OD / Negative Collected Balance Interest	10,000	8.0000%	65.75	25,395.28
Total Analyzed Charges			330.46	127,636.86
Total Charges This Statement			330.46	
Total Required Balance				127,636.86
Additional Required Balance				29,798.13
Earnings Allowance		253.31		
Less: Total Analyzed Charges		330.46		
Analyzed Charge (Transferred from Account xxxxx)	77.15			

The Earnings Allowance Rate is 3.50%. $1.00 of Charge can be offset by $386.24 in Positive Collected Balances. This factor includes a provision for Reserves.

Three factors come into play. First, is the earnings credit rate a competitive short-term yield? Second, is the underlying calculation of the available balances skewed in favor of the bank? Third, were the balances left in the DDA comparable to the amount needed to offset the bank charges?

Answering the competitive rate question is easily done. Compare the earnings credit rate to available overnight investments, such as money market funds and repurchase agreements. The earnings credit rate should be within ¼% to ½% of other market rates.

Answering the question about the calculation methodology is a bit tougher. One can use basic accounting and fairness tests to ascertain that the balance calculated closely reflect the available balances left at the bank. An organization will generally be treated fairly.

Getting through the third question requires looking at the balances and cash management relationship from the bank's point-of-view.

Where does the bank make money on the DDA? First is the float: the uncollected value of your deposits is determined by an availability schedule that the bank publishes. This table details the number of days that the bank will withhold availability on your deposited checks, usually in a bank-by-bank breakdown. It is based on the number of days that it supposedly takes your bank to send your deposited checks to the clearing or paying bank on which they are drawn and collect your money.

The bank makes significant profit on these availability schedules. The bank usually collects the funds much faster than the standard schedule describes and benefits from the use of your funds for the interim. At larger banks, more aggressive availability schedules are available to larger check depositors through negotiation.

The second profit for the bank from the DDA is in the service charges. A large bank's incremental cost of delivering a typical cash management service is 20% to 40% of the published price. Labor-intensive services (currency and check services) have lower margins, and technology-based services (wire transfers, ACH, and information reporting) are nearly pure profit. Again, high-volume users can get a more aggressive price.

The final area of significant bank profit from the DDA is the excess balances. Recall that the calculation of the earnings credit will specify certain balances needed to offset the service charges. Any balances greater than this amount generate bank profits at approximately the federal funds rate. A depositor gets no value from excess balances; they are pure profit for the bank. Above $100,000 in total deposits from a customer, the bank has no FDIC expense, and the account analysis calculation methodology shifts the pain felt from the uninvested reserve requirement to the customer.

What about interest-bearing checking accounts? Public funds (e.g., municipalities) and charitable-cause clients are generally the only organizations with access to interest bearing DDAs. Corporations are prohibited from these accounts by law (Regulation Q), although the banking laws are changing. Usually the interest rate is very low, and any interest earnings must be overcome in the account analysis calculation to avoid "double dipping" for interest earnings and earnings credit.

Many public fund customers require that banks collateralize account balances in excess of FDIC coverage with a pledge of government securities. While managing pledged collateral adds administrative costs (about a ¼%), the bank will often charge for this service. Nevertheless, excess balances still generate income at nearly the federal funds rate for the bank.

What should the treasurer of an organization do? First, manage the bank relationship carefully, particularly if the organization is a net borrower. Next, tirelessly solicit discounts in cash management services, including gaining access to the most aggressive availability schedule if the organization is a heavy check depositor (in volume or value of check items). Finally, the treasurer should keep a careful eye on DDA balances so that he or she never exceeds the required balance to offset services. If the earnings credit rate or calculation methodology is inadequate, the treasurer should minimize DDA balances (toward $0). Even if the treasurer pays for all bank services in hard dollars, he or she is better off with other short-term investments with a much higher investment yield.

If there are balances over the amount required for account analysis or over a minimal amount, where does a treasurer invest the short-term liquidity?

STIF AND SWEEP ACCOUNTS

Once the exclusive domain of the largest banks and their trust departments, short-term investment fund (STIF) and sweep accounts are increasingly available through a variety of bank and non-bank providers. STIF is typically employed in the trust department as a daily investment for any liquidity. A sweep account (which is not an acronym) is typically an investment offering of the commercial side of a bank for "cleaning up" any excess liquidity in a DDA.

It is important to understand the differences and similarities in STIFs and sweeps. The history of the two investments, their providers, their customers, and their legal construction are very different.

Both STIFs and sweeps rely on technology to identify each participating account's investable liquidity. In the trust department, liquidity will result from a variety of transactions or income from the investment portfolio. In a commercial DDA, liquidity will result from the positive cash flow of the debits and credits. For both trust and commercial sides of a bank, the technology systems transfer the available liquidity to a short-term investment instrument. This calculation and transfer (sometimes replenishing a trust account or DDA when cash is needed) occurs on a frequent, usually daily, basis. This is where most of the similarities end.

STIF Account

The STIF account has been used by trust department for decades and goes by a variety of names. Before today's sophisticated trust accounting systems, the calculations and transfers were performed manually.

Most trust accounts are eligible to participate in a STIF. Some trust departments managed the collective liquidity into one investment pool, prorating the income to all the participants. Some trust departments manage individual STIFs for their largest customers, eliminating any investment commingling of trust accounts. Still other trust departments use external management, primarily money market funds, for the liquidity investment. In many cases, a STIF managed by a trust department is a unique legal instrument that is not a registered investment (more on this later).

The revenue in a trust department is derived from fees assessed on the overall trust relationship. The STIF and its supporting technology are part of the overall package of trust services. There is little if any incremental revenue benefit to the trust department that is attributable exclusively to STIF balances, but the performance of the STIF is frequently an important consideration for prospective customers or by the trust's owners and beneficiaries.

Since the typical trust account is focused on asset growth, asset preservation, or asset transfer, the trust department generally deals with a client who is "interest rate sensitive." Often the trust owners or beneficiaries closely monitor the investment performance of the account. In other situations, a fiduciary (such as a trust officer or committee) is held accountable for investment performance.

STIF performance is often comparable to institutional money market funds. An aggressive, customized, or individually managed STIF can actually exceed a money market fund due to its more aggressive credit profile or longer maturity structure. However, this performance comes with greater risk (interest rate risk, credit quality risk, and so on.).

While the yield on a STIF may be attractive and the services of the trust department may be quite robust, usually the trust fees are significant enough to deter a commercial customer from moving its general business from the commercial side of the bank.

Sweep Account

The sweep DDA ("sweep") is a relatively new cash management product, coming into wide use since 1990. Tied to a customer's DDA, the commercial bank's cash management system identifies all balances greater than an agreed upon maintenance or "peg" balance, and then it will transfer the excess funds to a designated investment. Usually the investment is the bank's money market fund, but sometimes the sweep is into a repurchase agreement program. Some banks use an external money market fund if they do not manage a proprietary mutual fund family.

In all cases, the system transfers funds in both directions as required. This functionality is wonderfully convenient for an investing customer, a point that the bank counts on in winning business. But it comes at a very great cost to the customer.

The typical commercial bank customer using a sweep is not focused on investment performance, as would be a typical trust customer. Rather than being interest rate sensitive, they are interest rate aware. In addition, the bank is reluctant to give up the profitability of the customer's excess balances above the account analysis requirement. Therefore, the sweep investment of the bank is a lower yielding money market fund. The lower yield is not the result of inferior performance, but it is the result of a more expensive class of shares.

Mutual funds offer their products to many different customer groups. The groups are stratified into the size of the relationship with the largest investors receiving the least expensive offering of the funds (thus, greatest yield). The same portfolio of investments is offered with more expensive pricing (lower yielding) to successively smaller customers. This structure and pricing, as shown in Exhibit 3, reflects the economies of scale on a per-dollar basis: the largest investors create the least administrative burden per dollar of investment.

Not so with sweep accounts. Although the fund balance may be very large, and even though the administration is totally performed by a computer system, the bank usually designates a more expensive class of fund for its sweep program. The fund will generally yield 0.50% to 1.50% less than a comparable institutional class of money fund or STIF. The same holds true with a sweep program into repurchase agreements: the repo rate is set at 50 to 150 basis points less than the federal funds rate (which closely tracks the money fund rate). These spreads are a big part of the profit for the bank.

In addition to the lower yield, sweep customers are usually charged a cash management service fee for access to the technology. These fees range from $25 to $150 per month.

Bankers initially feared that a money fund alternative to DDA accounts would drain away lucrative balances, a process referred to as "disintermediation." However, customers demanded a product with greater yield (compared to zero or the low interest-bearing checking accounts) and greater liquidity (versus certificates of deposit with limited liquidity). Customers did not want to give up the functionality of the checking accounts. Brokerage firms and foreign banks were increasingly able to offer these services.

Over the past decade, commercial bankers came to understand that the balances customers moved to an investment sweep were replaced or supplemented with funds from outside of the bank. Banks actually experienced winning the relationship battle for the customer by seeing balances move from brokerage and other investment relationships back to the bank.

Exhibit 3: Money Market Funds — Comparison

Class of Shares	Investment Amount	Expense Ratio	Ave.	Net Yield *
· Super Institutional	$25mm & up	10bp to 15bp	12 bp	5.38%
· Institutional	$100k to $25mm	15bp to 25bp	25	5.25%
· Service	$5k to $100k	25bp to 50bp	40	5.10%
· Sweep	tied to technology	50bp to 150bp plus monthly fee	115	4.35%
· Retail	$0 to $5k	75bp to 250bp, plus sales load	150	4.00%

* Assumes a 5.50% Gross Yield on the Portfolio

Commercial banks defensively built sweep products to answer the competitive pressures from the brokerage and mutual fund industry and to provide a DDA-related investment to organizations subject to Reg. Q. But the resulting product gave up very little of the enormous profitability that the banks enjoyed from excess balances. Altogether, the sweep account (with the newly won balances) nearly replaced the profits from excess DDA balances.

BEYOND THE BANK

It should be increasingly clear that a prudent treasurer should look beyond the lead bank for investment management. If balances are adequate to pay for account analysis charges in a commercial account, or if trust account liquidity is adequate to facilitate trustee functions and investment management, then independent investment alternatives should be explored.

How much liquidity justifies an external search? Moreover, if a search is performed, what investment alternatives should be considered?

If there are consistently any balances greater than the desired compensating balance, at least the bank should be asked about STIF, sweep, or time-deposit options. A STIF and sweep are very convenient and offer certain operational risk controls, but these technology products come at the cost of higher bank fees, lower yields, or higher risks in investment portfolios. Certificates of deposit can be denominated to a very small dollar value, but they have very limited liquidity or liquidity with a penalty fee assessed.

If excess balances are between $5,000 and $100,000, many money market funds (including those owned by the bank) will permit an investor into their service class of shares. This yield is 15 basis points to 35 basis points (usually 25 bp) lower than the best yielding institutional class of shares. Already, a treasurer using a service class has improved on the typical sweep product by 25 to 100 basis points!

If liquidity balances range over $100,000 and certainly over $1 million, many funds will make available their institutional class of shares. As discussed, these funds offer daily liquidity and manage their portfolio to maintain a constant $1.00 net asset value. This minimizes the amount of principal risk that an investment could experience.

Over $10 million, but usually at levels of $25 million and up, money managers offer other investment alternatives. These include enhanced cash accounts, separately managed portfolios, and a variety of custom tailored liquidity solutions. Some of these solutions include sophisticated layering of maturities, securities lending, the use of synthetic investment instruments, risk management, currency and interest rate hedging strategies, and equity exposure.

Before glancing at these alternatives, a treasurer should understand the benefits and problems associated with investing beyond the bank.

Registered Investment Products

A registered investment product (and this is not a legal definition but a working definition) has several attributes: (1) it is available to the investing public, (2) it is subject to various mandatory reporting, operational and administrative requirements, (3) it is subject to various oversight authorities, and audits, and (4) it is usually marketed by individuals and firms that are subject to professional training, licensing, and supervision. Registered investment products are securities that are bought and sold by investors who meet certain dollar-value requirements, operational requirements, suitability requirements, and legal requirements. Securities laws require that many investment products register as a protection to the investing public.

On the other hand, nonregistered investments have much broader latitude in all of these areas. Treasurers are under a tremendous burden for analysis and due diligence any time a nonregistered investment product, service, or program is contemplated.

Money Market Funds

The most useful registered investment for liquidity is the money market fund. Yet, these funds come in a variety of risk profiles. The money market fund universe generally breaks down into a 2x3 matrix: rated (meaning AAA or equal) versus unrated; prime versus government versus tax-exempt. This matrix is shown in Exhibit 4.

A money market fund that has been AAA-rated provides an investor with a comfort of additional oversight and conservative investment practices. Typically, a AAA-rated fund has a weighted average maturity of less than 60 days. It owns securities that are highly rated, such as government securities or very strong corporate instruments (e.g., A1/P1 commercial paper). A variety of national rating organizations have developed a short-term rating program. While a fund or short-term instrument can certainly be rated less than AAA, it is rarely used as a strong selling feature of the product. For example, a AA-rated money fund surrenders a distinct marketing advantage to all AAA-rated funds.

An unrated money market fund must conform at least to the minimum requirements, such as having a 90-day or less weighted average maturity and having no individual investment holding with a maturity greater than 13 months. There are other minimum requirements.

Exhibit 4: Money Market Matrix

Portfolio Composition	Rated Funds	Unrated Funds
Prime Money Market Fund	Must maintain high quality corporate securities and portfolio WAM* < 60 days	Not as restrictive. May contain wide variety of investments, but always the WAM < 90 days
Government MMF	Nearly all are "AAA"	WAM > 60 days, maybe certain "riskier" investments
Tax Exempt MMF	Must maintain high quality municipal securities and portfolio WAM < 60 days	Not as restrictive. May contain lower quality municipal investments, but always the WAM < 90 days

* WAM: Weighted Average Maturity

As noted, money market funds fall into three general portfolio characteristics: prime, government, and tax-exempt. A prime portfolio will contain the broadest investment mixture of securities. These include corporate obligations and, perhaps, certain foreign instruments. Therefore, it is impossible to generalize a definition for prime funds. A treasurer should read the investment guidelines and the rest of the prospectus closely, before purchasing, to determine the investments that a particular fund will consider.

The second broad category is government funds. Again, these funds come in a variety of flavors. Some will invest strictly in Treasury securities, while others will include a variety of government agencies. Some will include repurchase agreements as authorized investments, while the most conservative funds do not include repos. The consistent theme in this government category is the lack of any corporate obligations. Generally speaking, government funds have lower risk profiles than prime funds.

The third bucket contains the tax-exempt funds. Primarily, these funds are composed of securities that are exempt from U.S. income tax, principally because they buy municipal investments. Other tax-exempt funds target exemption from a specific state's income tax, such as a California tax-exempt fund. The quality (safety) of these funds rests with the quality of the underlying municipal investments. Municipalities have credit quality ranging from AAA to deeply troubled. By closely reading the prospectus, a treasurer can determine the risk profile of a fund under consideration.

Any prime, government, or tax-exempt fund can be rated or unrated. It is common to find a government fund rated AAA. An increasing number of prime funds are becoming AAA-rated. Why? Supply and demand: treasurers want more yield and less risk.

When considering any investment, a treasurer must address a philosophical risk question. Does the corporation want to take an aggressive approach to its liquidity management? Or, does the corporation want to confine its risk-taking to its core business but not in cash management? The answers to these questions will lead a treasurer to consider aggressive, unrated funds, or to tend toward AAA rated, conservative funds.

From a practical point of view, it is impossible to prescribe a one-size-fits-all solution. Historically, many corporate treasurers have selected prime funds with a recent bias toward AAA rated funds (hence the increasing number of choices). Many fiduciaries and government treasurers prefer government funds. Every taxable organization must "do the math" to determine whether a tax-exempt fund provides a higher after-tax return than a taxable money fund.

Near-Cash Alternatives

Short-Term Bond Funds

Short-term bond funds are registered investments that are not money market funds. They do not seek to maintain a constant $1.00 net asset value, but they do seek to manage their interest rate risk. Sometimes referred to as "enhanced cash funds," these mutual funds typically are very successful in stabilizing their net asset values, and the rate of return is slightly higher than the money funds. The weighted average maturity of these funds ranges from 90 days to two years (there is not a standard or rule). The treasurer must first determine if any share-price fluctuation is acceptable (if not, stick with money funds), and then the treasurer must select a portfolio composition that is consistent with the organization's investment guidelines. Short-term bond funds vary greatly in their portfolios, much more than the money market funds. Minimum investment begins at about $5,000 for the expensive class of shares, and access to the institutional class of shares begins around $1,000,000. Depending on the portfolio, these funds can outperform money market funds by 20 to 100 basis points or more.

Enhanced Cash/Enhanced Yield Accounts and Trusts
Enhanced cash/enhanced yield accounts and trusts are not registered mutual funds. While this difference reduces the mandatory reporting and oversight, it also significantly reduces the operating cost, thus increasing the yield paid to the investor. These accounts and trusts are established by a cooperative contract, trust agreement, or partnership document. They target accounts that seek unique investment attributes (instruments or maturities), higher yield, or a particular accounting treatment, but the customer may be investing too little amount for a separately managed portfolio. Minimum investments typically begin at $100,000 and some programs start at $1 million. Depending on the portfolio, these accounts and trusts can outperform money market funds by 10 to 150 basis points.

Separately Managed Accounts
A separately managed account presents the investor with a tremendous range of alternatives. These accounts can be built to fit any investment requirement. There are two approaches to a separately managed account: internal staffing and external contract. Managing an organization's investment department takes a lot of work.

Separate portfolio management can be quite expensive for accounts under $10 million, but the management expense is quickly defrayed as the account size reaches $50 million to $250 million. Investment accounts consistently over $100 million in liquidity should strongly consider separate portfolio management. Depending on the portfolio, these accounts can outperform money market funds by 10 to 300 basis points.

Layering Maturities
Layering maturities is a strategy rather than an investment alternative. A treasurer with an accurate cash flow forecast can select progressively longer maturity investments to match the longer liabilities. This strategy, assuming an appropriate risk evaluation, can minimize the organization's exposure to principal loss while maximizing the income opportunities. Stated simply, matching assets to liabilities

is the biggest bang for the buck. A layering strategy can add 10 to 200 basis points in yield to the overall liquidity position compared to a total investment in a money market fund.

Securities Lending
If an organization owns significant investment securities (over $10 million) that are in high demand (certain Treasuries, agencies, and equities), a securities lending arrangement can generate 5 to 25 basis points in incremental income. The construction of the agreement is very important because it must address the issues of approved lending counterparties, acceptable collateral, permitted reinvestment, and fee sharing with the lending agent. Securities lending can also be employed if the organization has contracted for separate portfolio management. It is not an option if all investments are in money market funds, mutual funds, commingled accounts, or bank obligations.

Synthetic Investment Instruments and Risk Management
Synthetic investment instruments and risk management are another highly technical specialization. Some firms have significant exposure to currency risk for its liquidity, interest rate risk for its portfolio or commodity risk (fuel costs, agricultural products, etc.). If this is the case, then an organization should explore various alternative investments for liquidity that are designed to minimize these risks.

Equitizing Cash
Finally, if an investment portfolio and an organization's investment policy calls for a specific exposure to equity or other markets without an allocation to cash, the presence of any liquidity can dilute the desired portfolio allocation. However, a portion of the cash position can be used to purchase a variety of readily available index options that will mimic an investment in the equity market. For example, a 10% cash balance in a pension plan can be partially invested (about 10 cents on the dollar) into an S&P 500 index to negate the perceived uninvested cash. After the investment, the organization is left with a 9% cash position whose income is incremental, not a variance, and an equity market exposure equal to the original 10% cash balance. Other indices are available that track many of the more popular markets. Specialists within an organization or employed by a financial services firm can develop this strategy.

SUMMARY

A treasurer must consider a variety of investment options if the organization is holding liquidity. The banks have several liquidity alternatives that offer convenience, and unique, soft-dollar characteristics, but these investments tend to be expensive, thus reducing yield. With little additional effort (in daily activities, reporting, and monitoring), an organization can squeeze out a great amount of additional income from the organization's cash balances.

Bottomline secrets to superior management of an organization's cash war chest: build a great cash flow forecast, write a risk-appropriate investment policy, stick to that policy, build a solid system of controls, explore all available alternatives, closely match (layer) short-term investment assets to liabilities, and be willing to expend a little extra effort. We have explored several alternatives that can generate hundreds of basis points in incremental return. An extra 1% net yield on an organization's $10 million liquidity translates to $100,000 in found money.

Chapter 5

Basic and Nontraditional Repo Investment Strategies

Gabrielle M. Danek Winnert
Director
Credit Suisse First Boston

Repurchase agreements, otherwise known as repos, are money-market transactions in which one party sells securities to another while agreeing to repurchase those same securities at a specific price on a specific forward date. These transactions are similar to secured loans, with the lender of money receiving securities as collateral to protect it against borrower default. Repos are viewed by some market participants as purchases and sales and by others as secured loans. The market refers to the parties lending money as "buyers," while parties lending securities are known as "sellers." The terms "securities" and "collateral" are generally interchangeable.

- One firm's repo is another firm's reverse repo.
- Dealer borrowing money is transacting a repo.
- Dealer borrowing securities is transacting a reverse repo.
- Street convention is for both parties to view trades from the dealer's perspective.

What are the benefits of a repo?

- fully secured investment alternative for investors in the maturity range of five years or less
- efficient cash management tool
- can be executed with a full range of maturities: overnight, open, term, and flex
- variety of repo collateral types are offered: Treasury, agency, strips, mortgages, commercial paper (CP), certificates of deposit (CDs), corporates
- number of delivery options for repo: delivery-versus-payment (DVP), tri-party, and hold-in-custody

WHAT TYPE OF LIQUIDITY IS OFFERED IN THE REPO MARKET?

Liquidity in the repo market has traditionally been driven by the need for a broad range of investors — mutual funds, corporations, insurance companies, municipalities — to invest overnight cash liquidity. Repo was developed as a collateralized alternative to overnight bank deposits, allowing investors to diversify counterparty risk away from the banking community during a series of banking crises in the 1980s. The product has evolved to rival government, bank, and corporate credits across the money-market yield curve (one day to one year), generating enhanced yields over governments and lower credit risk versus corporate and bank debt. Repo is collateralized by a variety of underlying securities, each with unique yield and liquidity characteristics. Government securities are the most liquid and produce the lowest relative yield, while high-yield corporate bonds trade at the other end of the spectrum.

THE MECHANICS OF A REPO: MARGIN AND PRICING

Repo is the sale of securities on a temporary basis, involving the seller's agreement to repurchase the same or equivalent securities at a later date combined with the buyer's corresponding obligation to sell them back. In a transitional transaction, the repurchase price will include an interest component. Interest is paid based on the actual number of days in the trade, using a 360-day basis (referred to as a money-market yield). Most repo transactions in the U.S. market are executed for cash (same-day) settlement, unless both parties agree otherwise. Increasingly, general collateral markets are trading on a forward basis, settling anywhere from one day to one year forward.

In the U.S. repo market, the party lending money receives "margin," the excess collateral provided to the cash lender to act as a buffer in the event that the borrower defaults on its repurchase obligation. Margin also protects the cash lender against an adverse change in the price of securities between the time of default and the subsequent liquidation of collateral. Under the terms of the repo agreement, the right to liquidate upon default depends upon the type of securities collateralizing the repo. When providing margin, securities pledged as collateral are priced at market value minus a "haircut." The size of the haircut varies depending on the maturity, price volatility, liquidity, and current market price of the securities, the term of the repo, and the credit standing of the cash borrower. Securities are always priced at current market prices, including accrued interest, because this best reflects the liquidation value of the repo's underlying securities.

Example: Repo as a Short-Term Investment

Suppose dealer X has $10 million face amount of an off-the-run, 5-year U.S. Treasury note trading at par, and needs to finance the position overnight. Furthermore, suppose that the treasurer of XYZ Corporation has $9,900,990 to invest for one day. In this instance, the parties can enter into a repurchase agreement, where dealer X agrees to deliver $10 million face amount of the Treasury notes to XYZ Corporation and receive $9,900,990 in funds. Here, dealer X is giving the cash lender a 1% margin, based on the market price of the securities (example assumes zero accrued coupon interest). The repo proceeds would be:

$ amount of repo
= (market price + accrued coupon interest) × face value/margin percentage
= (1.00 + 0) × $10 million/1.01 = $9,900,990.

The $10 million in U.S. Treasuries is returned the next morning by XYZ Corporation to dealer X, which simultaneously wires funds to the cash lender for $9,900,990 plus interest for one day's use of funds. Assuming a 5.00% overnight repo rate, XYZ Corporation would receive interest in the following amount:

interest paid to XYZ Corporation = $9,900,990 × 0.050 × $\frac{1}{360}$ = $1,375.14.

Repo margin must be maintained to protect the cash lender from loss should the market value of the securities pledged as collateral fall below the dollar value of the repo transaction. This is accomplished by "marking to market" collateral to reflect price movements in the value of underlying securities. If the market value of the securities declines so that the repo margin is not maintained, the borrower must give the cash lender either additional securities or cash to restore margin.

Substitution of Collateral

During the term of a repo, the lender of securities may need those securities for another delivery; therefore, the lender, having reserved the right to substitute collateral at the inception of the trade, will deliver other securities of equal market value in return for the original collateral.

KEY PARTICIPANTS IN THE REPO MARKET

Following are the key participants in the repo market:

1. The Federal Reserve Bank: implements monetary policy and makes short-term adjustments to financial system liquidity.
2. Primary dealers.
3. Third-party brokers.
4. Leveraged investors: hedge funds, security lenders, spread traders, and total-return accounts.
5. Real-money investors: central banks; municipalities; corporations; pension funds; commercial banks; bank trust endowments; investment companies/mutual funds; financial intermediaries, including credit unions, thrifts, and insurance companies.

DELIVERY OPTIONS IN THE REPO MARKET

Delivery refers to the possession and control of securities "delivered" under a repurchase agreement. There are two delivery alternatives for repo collateral: receiving securities in an independent custodial account or receiving securities in a segregation account for the customer within the dealer's account.

Deliverable Repo

Under a *deliverable repo transaction*, the investor will receive possession of the securities, which creates a "perfected lien" — that is, grants a valid ownership on the collateral. The cash investor receives the rights of ownership. There are two forms of delivery, "delivery versus payment" and "tri-party delivery," the latter being the more popular form.

Delivery versus Payment Repo

In a *delivery versus payment* (DVP) repo, the cash lender's collateral is delivered into a clearing account or general custody account at its bank, against a simultaneous transfer of cash to the dealer. Here is what is involved:

- Cash lender takes possession of collateral in a bank account established, maintained, and paid for by the lender.
- Cash lender incurs the cost of all outgoing (and some incoming) cash and security wire charges.
- Cash lender notifies its bank of the transaction and instructs the bank to effectuate the simultaneous transfer of cash and collateral.

Risk of settlement failures exists for the cash lender. The cash lender and the dealer must mutually agree on collateral prices. A DVP repo is more labor-intensive and time-consuming than other delivery alternatives.

Tri-Party Deliverable Repo

In a *tri-party deliverable repo* transaction, a dealer, cash lender, and third-party custodian bank will enter into an agreement in which the custodian bank acts as an intermediary in the repo transaction. Here is what is involved:

- Custodian bank receives money from the lender and securities from the dealer, credits the dealer's cash account, and simultaneously moves collateral to the cash lender's custody account.
- As collateral moves from the dealer's clearing account to the cash lender's custody account within the bank, the cash lender takes possession of the collateral.
- Custodian bank prices the collateral using an outside third-party pricing service.

- The custodian bank in a tri-party arrangement is most likely the dealer's clearing bank.
- Since the collateral moves within the same bank, the dealer only pays any internal transfer fees.
- Outstanding tri-party repo collateral is marked to market daily and is verified by the bank to ensure that proper margining is maintained as collateral values fluctuate.
- Cash lender can ascertain which specific securities are being held in its custody account at the end of the day. Custodian bank also mails hardcopy confirmations or e-mails electronic confirmation for all tri-party transactions.

Cash lender receives slightly higher yields on tri-party versus DVP repos due to the slightly lower cost of settlement and added trade flexibility. A tri-party agreement governs the legal obligations of the dealer, the investor, and the custodian bank.

Segregation Repo

Under a *segregation repo*, the cash lender receives a pledge of acceptable securities which are segregated within the dealer's own clearing account. It is also commonly referred to as *hold-in-custody repo*, *safekeeping repo*, or *mixed-bag repo*. Here is what is involved:

- Lender wires money to the dealer "free," and the dealer segregates acceptable collateral within its vault or within its own account at its clearing bank.
- Securities must be maintained within the dealer's account in a segregated subaccount for the exclusive benefit of repo customers.
- Dealer sends a listing of the collateral, in the form of a trade confirmation.

Since the cost of transferring securities to an outside account is not incurred, segregation repos are less costly for the dealer. The dealer prices securities. Segregation repos usually offer yields equal to those available on tri-party arrangements. They are easier for cash lenders to administer than DVP. A segregation repo is commonly used when customer securities are in physical form, trades are small in size, or the customer does not desire physical delivery via the local depository.

MATURITY OPTIONS

Repos are executed for maturities between one day and five years (occasionally longer under special circumstances), with most having maturities of one year or less. Generally, there are four basic types of repo maturity terms:

1. *Overnight*: The most common maturity terminates the next business day.
2. *Term*: These are repos executed with fixed maturities for periods exceeding one business day. Subject to negotiation, investors in term repos may terminate the trade prior to maturity at market levels.
3. *Open*: These are repos for an indefinite term that may be terminated by either party on demand. Here, the interest rates change daily to reflect current market conditions.
4. *Flex*: In a flex repo, the cash lender agrees to give the dealer money at a specified rate with a stated end date providing that the cash lender may withdraw some of the cash loaned before the expiration based on a prearranged drawdown schedule.

PRINCIPAL AND INTEREST PAYMENTS FOR A REPO

In a deliverable repo transaction, the lender of securities remains entitled to the economic benefits of ownership of the securities unless it defaults on its repurchase obligation. For example, even though the borrower of securities holds title to the collateral during the term of the repo, the seller is entitled to all principal and coupon interest payments. The purchaser is responsible for wiring the seller any monies received while holding collateral. Since the market always employs full-accrual pricing when determining the value of securities under a repurchase agreement, passing the principal and interest payments to the borrower of money will require issues to be marked to the new market value after a principal or income payment, thereby generating a margin call.

REPO RATES

Repo rates depend on whether the collateral is considered "general" or "special." General collateral is that which meets the counterparty's "general" requirements, while special-issue collateral describes the situation in which the counterparty is looking for a specific security. For example, a dealer reversing in general U.S. Treasury collateral will accept any bills, notes, or bonds, while a dealer looking for special-issue collateral will accept only that specific issue, such as the current 10-year note.

A number of additional factors influence repo rates. In the market for overnight repos, these factors include a benchmark money market rate such as LIBOR or the fed funds rate, the general supply of repo money and repo collateral, the quality of collateral, the method of delivery, the size of the transaction, and the creditworthiness of the counterparty. Thus, the cash lender receives a rate which reflects the riskiness of the transaction, current liquidity within the financial system relative to the demand for money, and the settlement cost to the dealer.

Exhibit 1: Spread Between Opening Fed Funds and Treasury General Collateral Levels

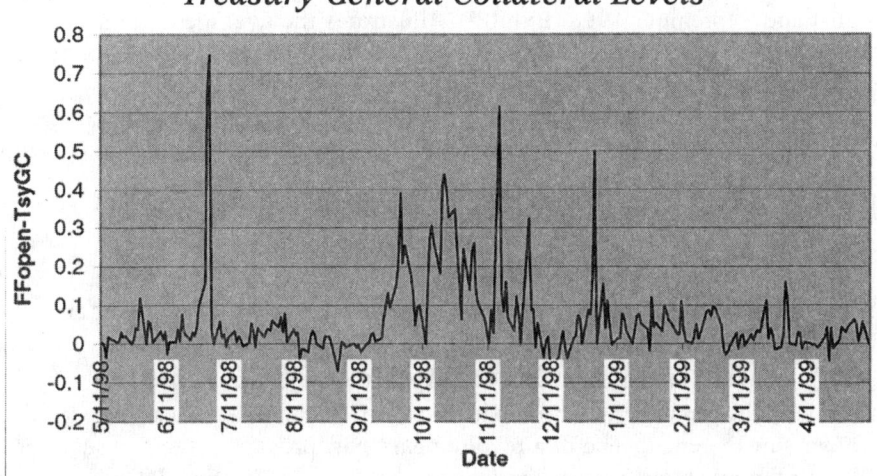

The most visible reflection of the overnight market for money in the United States is the fed funds rate. In general, repo rates will move in concert with the overnight fed funds rate. However, if we look at the data for 1998, as shown in Exhibit 1, the spread between the opening fed funds rate and the overnight Treasury general collateral rate has ranged from –5 basis points (repo trading 5 bps expensive to funds) to +70 bps (repo trading 70 bps cheap to fed funds). It is important to note that repo rates are not established by a formula but, rather, are determined by dynamic market forces and may change daily as market conditions require.

Factors affecting term repo rates include those mentioned earlier along with the shape of the short-term yield curve, the right to substitute collateral, yields on competing money-market instruments, seasonal influences, and interest rate expectations. Special-issue collateral will trade at whatever rate the market dictates at a given point in time. As indicated, the specials market is driven by the supply of, and demand for, a particular security at a given point in time. Dealers seeking a specific issue are most often doing so to cover a short position, or to reoffer securities to another party that is short. The rate at which a dealer can reverse in the issue will depend on the availability of the security on the Street and the demand for the specific issue.

GROWTH OF THE REPO MARKET

The repurchase market continues to sustain its impressive growth. In 1999, the average amount outstanding exceeded $2.47 trillion on a weekly basis, a 24% increase from the $2 trillion level seen in 1997 and more than double the level seen as recently as 1992. The repo market has experienced a dramatic growth in recent years as both the primary and secondary market volume in the U.S. domestic bond markets have also surged to record levels. This is even more impressive if we consider the dramatic decline in global activity after the financial crisis in August and September 1998. Exhibit 2 illustrates the average daily amount outstanding in the repo market (including U.S. Treasury, federal agency debentures, and federal agency mortgage-backed securities).

Exhibit 3 shows the breakdown of outstanding repo activity based on the maturity of the repo. From 1995 to 1998, the volume of repo outstanding in the term markets more than doubled, truly reflecting the growing trend in the repo market away from the overnight markets and into the term markets.

NONTRADITIONAL INVESTMENT STRATEGIES

Interdealer Tri-Party Repo (GCF Repo)

In line with the repo markets becoming more efficient and less costly for dealers, in 1999 we saw the emergence of a revolutionary new product in the Treasury general collateral repo markets, *general collateral financing* (GCF) *repo*. Introduced by the Government Securities Clearing Corporation (GSCC), the industry-owned body that compares and nets U.S. dealers' fixed-income trades, the GCF repo will allow for trade volumes to increase dramatically with a more efficient settlement process. The GSCC is a registered clearing corporation that helps facilitate orderly settlement in the U.S. government securities markets and tracks repo trades settled through its system by product type. A total of $97.9 trillion in repo trades was submitted and cleared by the GSCC in 1998, representing an average daily total of $520.8 billion in U.S. Treasury and federal agency transactions. By October 31, 1999, the GSCC had cleared over $122 trillion of repo trades that could be broken down into $567 billion per day in U.S. Treasury repo and $21 billion per day in agency repo.

Exhibit 2: Average Daily Amount Outstanding in Repo Market ($ Billions)

Year	Reverse Repos	Repos	Total
1981	$ 46.7	$ 65.4	$112.1
1987	275.0	292.0	567.0
1993	594.1	765.6	1359.7
1998	1118.3	1414.0	2532.3

Exhibit 3: Outstanding Repo Activity Based on Maturity of Repo ($ Billions)

Year	Overnight & Open	Term	Total
1995	$717.0	$723.3	$1440.3
1996	826.4	865.4	1691.8
1997	924.4	1117.6	2042.0
1998	1036.1	1496.1	2532.3

GCF repo is a new service designed by the Government Securities Clearing Corporation that will allow the dealer community to trade general collateral repo freely and actively without requiring intraday trade-for-trade settlement on a DVP basis. In the settlement process there will be fewer operational problems with the delivery of odd lots because there will be only one net delivery or receipt at the end of the day. There will be fewer fails, as collateral no longer has to go to multiple dealers — only to the dealer's GSCC account at Chase or the Bank of New York. The risk from a dealer trading for par value instead of for cash value will be eliminated since all trades will be done as a money fill. The clearing charges on the fed wire as well as the margin maintenance activity should both be reduced as the tri-party trades are re-collateralized and re-priced on a daily basis, allowing collateral to be marked to market and margined daily.

Two major benefits to the market will be increased trading liquidity and improved business flow. With the more active trading, the market will eventually start trading to specific dates in order to allow for balance sheet net downs. For example, a dealer will be able to buy a 1-year repo in anticipation of weak economic news and if the dealer is correct, flip the position the following day for a profit with no balance-sheet exposure. With the tighter bid/offer spreads and deeper markets, general collateral (GC) repo will start to look like a cash instrument — that is, a Treasury CD or a Treasury bill.

The market will also provide greater trading opportunities — with the increased liquidity of GC to specific dates, it will be easy to introduce new structured repo products to the market. Traders who in the past have been bogged down with the constraints of collateral stipulations and collateral notification will now be able to spend more time trading. Finally, dealers will be faced with less off-the-run short covering activity because the dealer will never run out of rights of substitution on a trade.

In terms of capital benefits, there will be better balance sheet usage under FAS125 and FIN41 (the accounting rule which addresses repo/resale netting capabilities) due to the increased netting of trades, reduced daylight overdraft charges, and the elimination of the need to deliver collateral to a broker. Instead, the collateral will go directly to the GSCC.

With the emergence of the general collateral financing repo product, the general collateral repo markets can look forward to increased liquidity, tighter bid-offer spreads, and cheaper settlements. GC traders will be able to focus on interest rate and relative value trading and will be freed from the operational burdens of running out of rights of substitution on the term positions they own.

Floating-Rate Repos and Flexible Repos

Repurchase agreements are collateralized obligations that have increased in popularity under the floating-rate structure. The increase in floating-rate repo coincides with the shift in investor interest away from fixed-rate and toward floating short-term instruments.

Exhibit 4: Comparison of Floating-Rate Repo Collateral Spreads

Collateral	Excess Margin	Mid-Market Spread to LIBOR	Day Count	Delivery Method
U.S. Treasuries	101%	−30	Act/360	DVP or tri-party
Treasury Strips	102	−25	Act/360	DVP or tri-party
Agencies	102	−20	Act/360	DVP or tri-party
Agency MBS	102	−15	Act/360	DVP or tri-party
AAA-Rated Private-Label MBS	103	−8	Act/360	DVP or tri-party
AA-Rated Private-Label MBS	103	−2	Act/360	DVP or tri-party

STRUCTURE

Repurchase agreements are collateralized borrowings governed under a standardized Public Securities Association (PSA) master agreement whereby an investor "lends" cash to a dealer and receives securities as collateral. The investor receives interest income at the maturity date of the "loan," calculated on an actual/360 day-count basis. The interest received can be based on a fixed rate or on a floating-rate index. The latter is referred to as *floating-rate repo*. Most fixed-rate repos have maturities that do not exceed six months, while floating-rate repos tend to have maturities greater than six months.

Floating-rate repo appeals to investors and borrowers alike because some of the conventional elements of the floater market can be bundled to create a customized product. Further, it does not rely on an issuer, per se, in that a repo dealer can create a product on the wire to meet an investor's objectives. In effect, the dealer becomes both the issuer and the secondary market maker. This dual role allows the dealer to customize the product, add yield depending on the underlying collateral, and match indices with the investor's needs. Dealers view floaters as a way to satisfy core funding needs through long-term commitments while minimizing interest rate risk to a minimum. Therefore, there is a tendency for repo to trade at a higher yield in the floating-rate relative to the fixed-rate market. Investors willing to commit long-term funding (in excess of one year) to a dealer benefit from these higher yields. Exhibit 4 shows some details of floating-rate repos.

Along with yield, investors benefit from the many index alternatives in the repo market. This variety allows investors to express both a directional view and a relative value view on the market. Further, it allows them to better match their asset/liability profile. The tightest pricing in floating-rate repo tends to come with LIBOR and fed funds, but active markets are also quoted in Treasury bills and prime. Less often quoted indices are the constant-maturity Treasury (CMT) and the Eleventh District Federal Home Loan Bank cost-of-funds index (COFI), since they have low correlation with the funding benchmark rate. For example, a corporation that borrows at prime may want to reinvest short-term cash in a prime-based asset. Repo can then be structured as a prime-based floater.

The trading conventions of the floating-rate repo market are similar to those of the corporate or bank floating-rate-note (FRN) market. The reigning indices are LIBOR, Treasury bills, federal funds, and prime. LIBOR floaters are set off the 1-month, 3-month, or 6-month LIBOR rates, and are reset and paid at monthly, quarterly, or semiannual dates, respectively. The most commonly quoted Treasury bill-based floater is reset weekly and paid quarterly off the weekly auction of the 3-month U.S. Treasury bill.

Federal funds floaters are perhaps the most bearish index available, in that they reset daily and pay monthly. An investor unwilling to commit to the market for even a few days typically opts for the federal funds floater. This index can also be viewed as very conservative in that it takes no market risk. Costs are measured in lost opportunity, not in price markdowns. This index perhaps best captures the concept that dealers are willing to pay higher rates for long-term funding commitments. Otherwise, an investor would be no better off than if he had invested funds daily. Investors who depend on the repo market for overnight liquidity also prefer federal funds-based floaters linked to a long-term commitment in that they are assured of full investment throughout the year and do not have to worry about dealer balance-sheet limitations crowding them out of the repo market over initial accounting dates. With a federal funds floater, the investor avoids having to invest core liquidity daily, since it is done automatically under the terms of the long-term commitment.

FLOATING-RATE REVERSE REPO

Since the dealer is running a matched book in floating-rate repo, we must also take a look at the reverse side of this transaction. In a reverse repo, the customer is "borrowing" funds from and lending their bonds to the dealer. In effect, the customer becomes the issuer by leveraging its existing securities portfolio of government or mortgage securities. Most investors use the reverse repo market to earn additional yield over the yield promised on the underlying security. Investors will "borrow" cash from the dealer and then utilize that cash to purchase securities with a yield higher than the reverse repo rate.

Invariably, a new issuance of corporate, bank, asset-backed, or agency floaters will be accompanied by a heightened interest in the floating-rate reverse repo market as investors look to arbitrage the credit spread between the two markets. It is this matched book activity, whereby the dealer acts as intermediary between investor and borrower, that generates liquidity in the floating-rate repo market.

As an offshoot of the asset-backed market, the floater repo market has developed liquidity in flexible principal paydown schedules. In a *flexible repo*, a cash lender agrees to give a dealer money at a specified rate with a stated end date providing that the cash lender may withdraw some of the cash loaned prior to expiration based on a prearranged drawdown schedule. This type of transaction allows the cash lender the ability to lock in a term rate while still maintaining liquidity. In addition, flex repos allow the borrower of cash in the reverse repo market to pay down the principal borrowing based on a predetermined schedule.

Once again, the borrower receives the option to deviate from that schedule without recourse. Therefore, the borrower can effectively call the reverse repo on all or part of each principal paydown date. That call feature is typically exercised to match the prepayment or extension risk of another asset. However, unless otherwise stated, there is no contractual obligation to adhere to the original paydown schedule if the economic incentive drives the borrower to prepay or extend.

Investor interest has expanded greatly in the floater reverse repo market because it allows investors to reinvest their cash borrowings. A common strategy is to match perfectly the reverse repo index and final maturity to the terms of a corporate floater, taking on the corporate credit risk and locking in a net interest spread. A more aggressive strategy involves borrowing cash on a floating basis and reinvesting it for a similar maturity in a fixed-rate asset. That fixed-rate asset includes fixed-rate repo. Using a combination structure, an owner of government securities could reverse-repo those securities under a floating structure for one year and receive a fixed rate on a reinvestment in other tri-party government collateral. The investor would effectively be executing a swap through the repo market — receiving fixed and paying floating.

STRUCTURED REPO PRODUCTS

Structured repo products are the newest tools in the fixed-income repo market. Over the past few years, the repo market has developed several tailored repo products to suit individual customer's needs. By allowing for custom design and extreme flexibility, structured repo products facilitate the process of finding the optimal solution to a customer's investment goals and funding needs.

Time and time again, customers have repeated that their repo investment goals are investment diversity, yield enhancement, and cheaper funding costs; therefore, some recommendations for achieving these investment goals would be repo swaps or structured term repo products including cancelable term repos, convertible term repos, and repos with embedded options. A repo swap will allow customers to modify the duration of their assets and liabilities by swapping out of longer-term fixed-rate obligations into shorter-duration, floating-rate liabilities or the reverse. A structured term repo, on the other hand, allows a customer to increase the yield or reduce the funding costs of a term repo by selling their repo counterparty valuable optionality.

REPO SWAPS

Repo swaps allow a customer who is locked in a term repo to diversify his returns versus a floating-rate index — most often, LIBOR. By exchanging the cash flows from a longer-term trade for a floating index return, the portfolio manager can effectively adjust the duration of his portfolio. This will allow the portfolio manager to more closely achieve the desired asset/liability mix.

For example, assume a repo customer owns a $200 million position in 2-year-term general collateral repo. The customer is now concerned that rates over the next two years may rise substantially and he will be locked into this lower-yielding term repo. To protect himself, the customer could swap out of this term repo into a floating-rate repo versus LIBOR and lower his exposure to a rise in interest rates. Assuming today is April 1, 2000, and the current fixed-term repo rate he is locked into is 6.50% until February 15, 2002, the customer could enter into a repo swap with dealer X where he would pay the 6.50% and receive a floating rate of 3-month LIBOR minus 30 bps, reset quarterly to dealer X until February 15, 2002.

CANCELABLE TERM REPO

A *cancelable term repo* allows customers to enhance the yield of their repo investments by cashing in on optionality in return for higher investment yields. In a cancelable term repo, a customer grants dealer X the right to cancel the term repo at a specified time if the dealer believes it to be advantageous. In return for this right, dealer X pays the customer an enhanced rate of return on his term repo investment.

For example, assume the current 2-year term repo rate is 6.50%. Dealer X offers $100 million U.S. Treasury repo collateral to a customer for two years, non-cancelable in one year at 6.67%, quarterly pay, Actual/360. The customer will receive 6.67% quarterly from dealer X for the first year. At the end of the first year, dealer X has the right to cancel the term repo agreement. To sum up, the customer has received 17 basis points in yield enhancement versus the 2-year term repo rate to sell the right to cancel the repo after one year to dealer X. If interest rates were to drop substantially, dealer X would cancel the trade and the customer would forgo the opportunity to collect the higher rate for the remaining one year. However, the customer is guaranteed to collect the 6.67% rate for at least one year.

CONVERTIBLE TERM REPO

A *convertible term repo* also allows customers to enhance the yield of a term repo trade by selling optionality. In this type of transaction, the customer sells dealer X the right to convert a trade from a fixed-rate term repo to a floating-rate term repo trade. This allows the customer to lock in an attractive fixed rate for a predetermined time period; thereafter, the customer will receive either a floating rate or continue to receive the fixed rate depending on whether dealer X chooses to exercise the option.

Exhibit 5: Spread Between Treasury General Collateral and 10-Year in Repo 1997

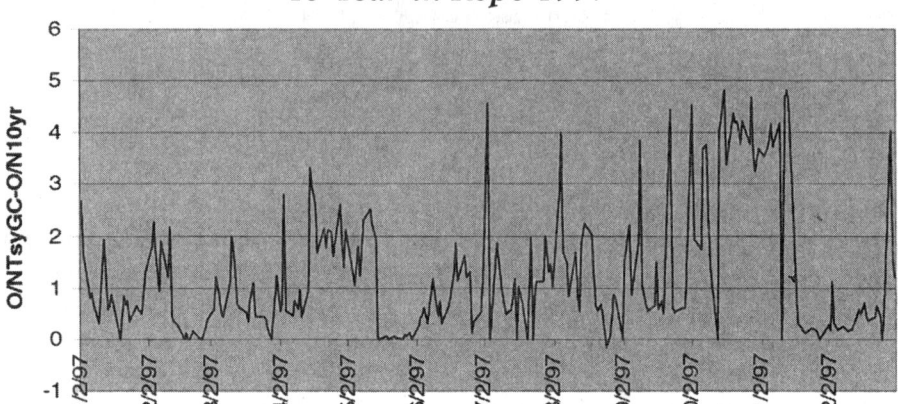

For example, assume the current 2-year term repo rate is 6.50%. Dealer X offers $100 million U.S. Treasury repo collateral to a customer for two years, nonconvertible one year, Bermudan style (i.e., the option may be exercised at specified dates) at 6.69%, quarterly pay: Actual/360. The customer will receive 6.69% quarterly from dealer X for one year. At the completion of the first year, dealer X has the right to either continue to pay 6.69% or pay 3-month LIBOR minus 30 basis points for the remainder of the trade. The Bermudan style aspect of the trade allows dealer X to make the choice whether it wants to pay the fixed rate or the LIBOR floater every three months. Once dealer X chooses to pay the floating rate, it must do so for the remainder of the trade.

REPO WITH EMBEDDED OPTIONS

Repo data for 1997-1998 shown in Exhibits 5, 6, 7, and 8 clearly indicate that the volatility in the specials market has increased dramatically. In 1997, the spread between overnight Treasury general collateral and the 10-year note in the overnight repo market averaged 130 basis points with the low being 0 and the high being 480 bps. In 1998, we saw that same spread average 160 bps; while in 1999, it widened out to a 200 bps average. The change in volatility of the bond is even more dramatic. In 1997, the bonds versus overnight Treasury GC traded at a mean spread of 60 bps, while in 1999 that mean spread jumped out to 150 bps.

What is driving the scarcity that leads to this increased activity in the on-the-run Treasuries? A strong U.S. economy and increased federal tax revenues allowed the U.S. Treasury to pay down $97.9 billion in debt leading to a 10.3% decline in the issuance of Treasury securities in the first half of 1998. The U.S.

Treasury reduced the level of both coupon and bill offerings in the first six months of 1998. Coupon issuance dropped 13.9% in the period, while bill issuance dropped 9% compared with prior-year levels. Coupon issuance totaled $240 billion in the first half of 1998 compared with the $278.9 billion in the comparable 1997 period. In the secondary market, average trading volume increased by 13.4% from $209.4 billion in 1997 to $237.4 billion in 1998. Going forward, we can expect that the strong U.S. economy and the increased federal tax revenues will allow the U.S. Treasury to continue to pay down its debt through both smaller auction sizes and aggressive buyback programs.

Exhibit 6: Spread Between Treasury General Collateral and 10-Year in Repo 1998

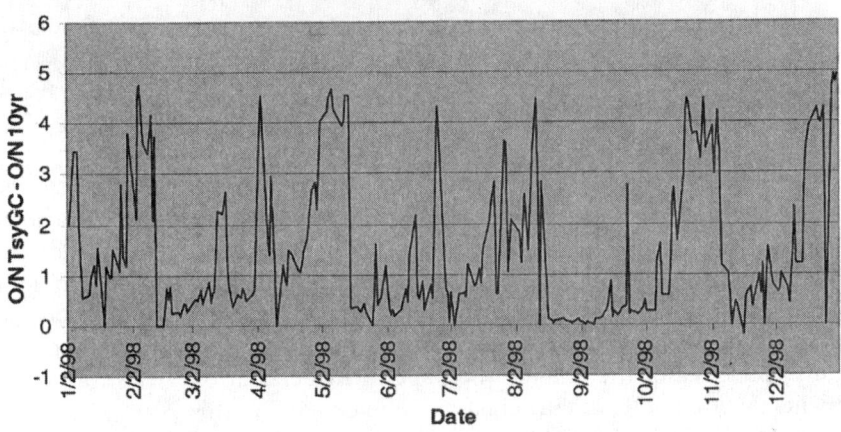

Exhibit 7: Spread Between Treasury General Collateral and 30-Year in Repo 1997

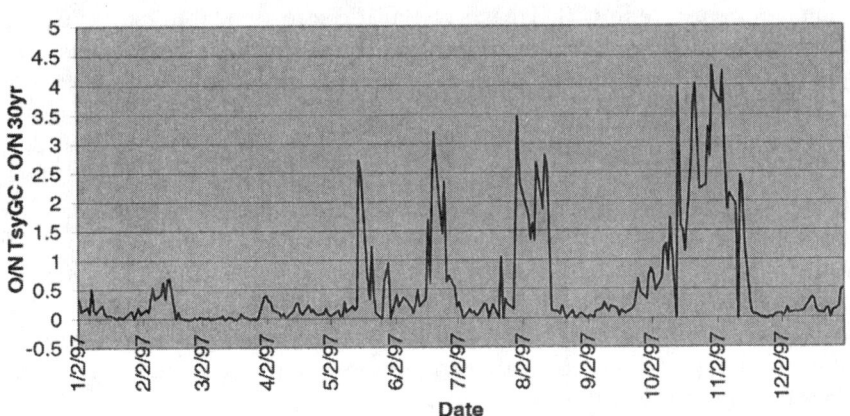

Exhibit 8: Spread Between Treasury General Collateral and 30-Year in Repo 1998

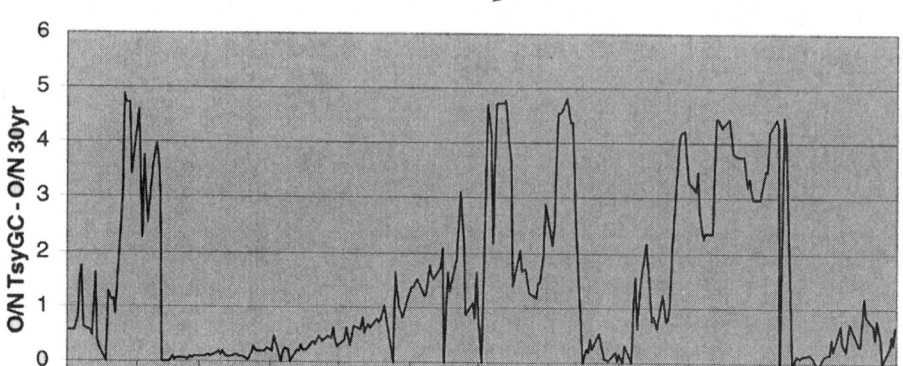

The scarcity and thus the volatility in the Treasury market is also being driven by basis trading, the short hedge used by MBS trading and underwriting, derivatives swaps and options, government trading and arbitrage, corporate trading and issuance, and customer activity. Finally, the mix of leverage versus real-money buying helps dictate where the issues will trade. The more real-money buying, the greater the chance the paper will be kept off the street by those accounts that do not lend, thus creating more demand for the issue.

So, how can investors protect themselves from the adverse affects of the fluctuations in "specialness" costs, yet still benefit from a repo movement in their favor? Repo options allow customers to specify term and level of protection against unfavorable movements in term repo, while still maintaining the upside advantage. Investors in U.S. Treasury securities are subject to daily fluctuations in financing costs in the repo market. Changes in these financing costs can substantially affect the returns for those who transact in Treasury securities when these securities trade "special" in the repo market. Two possible options an investor would have are repo puts and repo calls.

A repo option is the right, but not the obligation, to buy/sell repo at a predetermined (strike) price on or before a predetermined (expiration) date. When buying a repo put, a customer pays a premium to be long the option to lend a given amount of a specific issue at a certain level to a specific date. In contrast, a repo call allows a customer to pay a premium to borrow a given amount of a specific issue at a certain level to a specific date. The repo option can be used by a customer who would like to fund overnight or on term but would like protection in case repo rates move suddenly against him.

To illustrate a repo option, assume a customer is short $100 million of the current 10-year note and is concerned that the issue will trade increasingly special as the auction approaches. Currently, he is using the overnight reverse repo market to cover his position; therefore, to protect against "specialness," he purchases a European repo call struck at 3.50% for the term May 1 to May 15 for 20 bps. For instance, if on May 1 the 10-year to May 15 is trading at 2.50%, the customer will exercise the call option.

Chapter 6

Reverse Repurchase Agreements: Risks and Strategies for Money Market Funds and Cash Pools

Douglas A. Rivkin
Vice President/Senior Credit Officer
Moody's Investors Service

Investors in money market funds that engage in reverse repurchase agreements sometimes have a difficult time understanding the strategies involved in these transactions. Moody's analysts remain concerned that investors may not fully understand the ramifications of reverse repos on their funds' risk profiles. In this chapter we explain the basics of reverse repo transactions, the strategies behind their use, and lists some of Moody's key considerations in assessing these transactions. In the first part of this chapter we review the mechanics of reverse repo transactions, and in the second part we discuss some of the risk factors inherent in them.

Reverse repurchase agreement transactions typically share similar, if not identical, risk characteristics with securities lending transactions. We note, however, that these transactions are not the same. The decision to use one or the other is typically motivated by very different strategies. Nonetheless, reverse repo agreements can change the risk profile of a money market fund in unexpected ways. Moody's believes that investors in money market funds that engage in reverse repurchase agreements should fully understand the nature of the risks inherent in these transactions and their potential impact on a fund's risk profile.

The distinction between reverse repos and securities lending is determined by both the fund's investment strategy and by the party that manages the lending transaction. Securities lending transactions, which are typically managed by a fund's custodian (the lending agent) under contract with the fund, are generally used for the purpose of generating additional fee revenue for the custodian and the fund. Reverse repos on the other hand, have no lending agent. They are managed by the fund's advisor on an individual or counterparty contractual basis and are typically used as an investment strategy for fund yield enhancement. More simply put, securities lending transactions, in being managed by the custodian, are a passive or background fee generation strategies for the fund. Reverse repos, however, in being managed by the fund's advisor, are generally a proactive investment strategy. This distinction carries a number of implications for the fund advisor's investment strategy.

COLLATERALIZED REPOS VERSUS REVERSE REPOS

From a money market fund's point of view, a reverse repurchase agreement is really the opposite side of a collateralized repurchase agreement. The reverse repo is a simultaneous transaction between a fund (lender) and a counterparty (borrower). The fund lends security(ies) to a counterparty in return for cash or collateral (see Exhibit 1), with an agreement to buy back the security(ies) at maturity (essentially unwinding the initial transaction). During the lending period, the fund retains ownership rights to the lent security(ies) and receives any interest or dividends generated during the transaction period. Funds typically engage in two types of reverse repo deals: those collateralized with securities and those collateralized with cash.

Exhibit 1: Transaction Parties
Securities Lending

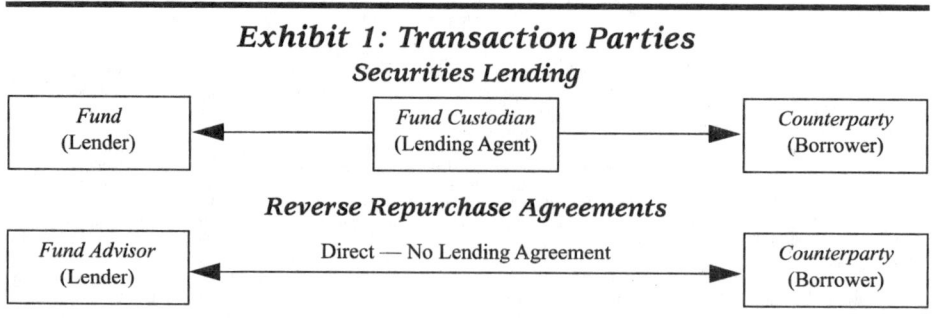

| Fund (Lender) | Fund Custodian (Lending Agent) | Counterparty (Borrower) |

Reverse Repurchase Agreements

| Fund Advisor (Lender) | Direct — No Lending Agreement | Counterparty (Borrower) |

Exhibit 2: Reverse Repurchase Agreement Transaction
Cash Collateral

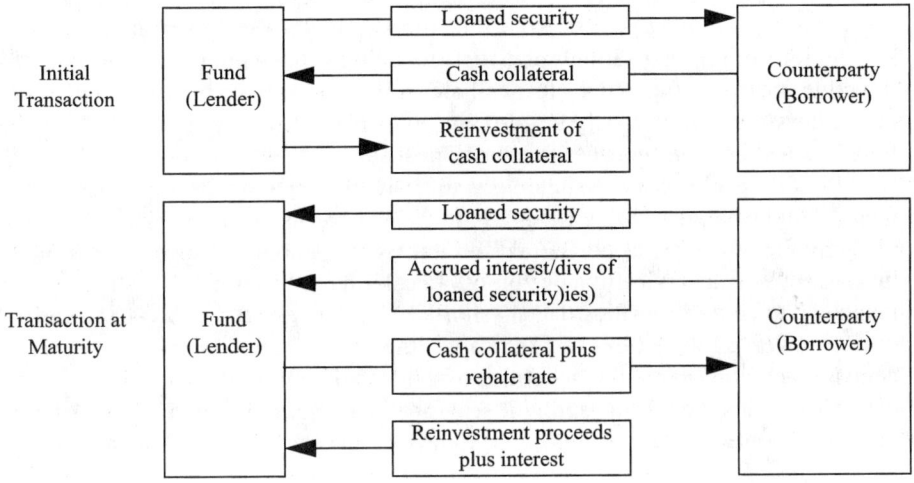

Exhibit 3: Reverse Repurchase Agreement Transaction
Securities Collateral

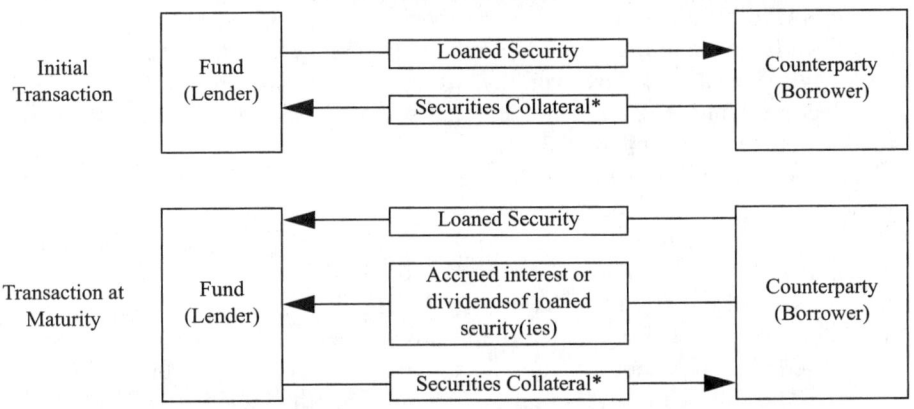

* Loan fee may be included in collateral valuation.

When engaging in a reverse repo agreement collateralized with cash, the fund will attempt to earn a positive spread to be netted from the reinvestment of the cash collateral, less a "rebate rate" paid to the counterparty (for the use of the cash) when the transaction matures (see Exhibit 2). Reverse repo transactions collateralized with securities earn a pre-negotiated fee based on the value of the collateral pledged (see Exhibit 3).

UNDERSTANDING THE COUNTERPARTY/DEALER SIDE

To better comprehend repurchase agreement and reverse repurchase agreement transactions, it helps to understand the counterparty (dealer's) strategy. The broker/dealer community developed the repurchase agreement market as a cost-effective means to finance securities held in inventory.[1] To further leverage profits, dealers may additionally employ an investment strategy in which they make long or short bets on their net inventory positions.

The dealer puts its inventory to work by engaging in repurchase agreements with investors (mutual funds). In this instance, the dealer is taking in cash and pledging the securities as collateral. To increase the amount of specific securities in inventory (or as a service to a customer) a dealer may "reverse" securities back into inventory to cover securities that it "shorted." In many of these cases a dealer may initiate reverse repo offers to funds and other investors. The market supply and demand factors of particular securities will dictate how big of a spread is offered. A dealer who runs a book in repo will seek profits by selling repo agreements at one rate and reverse repo agreements at a slightly higher rate to earn a spread.

BASIC STRATEGIES:
HOW MONEY MARKET FUNDS USE REPOS

Money market funds will engage in reverse repos with a range of motives, as described below, and they will deploy numerous investment strategies to achieve their goals. We caution, however, that all of these reverse repo strategies will have an affect on a fund's risk profile, and that some of these approaches can subject a fund to significant levels of risk.

Moody's believes that it is extremely important for investors to understand their money market funds' strategies and their funds' internal capacity for employing reverse repos, along with the overall appropriateness within a fund's investment objective. Does the strategy make business sense for the fund? Is the risk reward trade-off worth the boost in yield? The answers to these questions may be found by speaking with a fund's advisor. However, one should understand the entire range of strategies and risks up-front to correctly interpret a response.

The following reverse repo strategies should be evaluated in the context of the investment objective risk tolerance of a fund, as well as the regulatory rules governing the fund.

Liquidity Management

A fund that is in need of cash to meet redemptions may sell securities, borrow from its line of credit, or employ a reverse repurchase agreement to raise cash. The

---

[1] The terms repurchase agreement and reverse repurchase agreement are named from the dealers point of view in the transactions. A repurchase agreement is the dealers agreement to "repurchase" loaned (used for collateral) securities from the investor.

reverse repo, when used as a liquidity-providing strategy, may be cheaper than borrowing and can enable the fund to avoid selling portfolio securities and the possibility of a loss. This back-up liquidity strategy can be a smart use of reverse repurchase agreements; however, the fund is still subject to risks inherent in the transaction.

Yield Enhancement

Funds may use reverse repos to increase yield. This is achieved via positive spreads offered by counterparties. Incremental yield can vary greatly depending on the market supply and demand for the particular security that is being "reversed."

Asset Leveraging

Some regulatory bodies allow funds to leverage up to one-third of their net assets. Asset leveraging is often the byproduct of a yield enhancement strategy. We remind readers, however, that asset leveraging translates into additional aggregate exposure. This exposure is derived from both the market risk related to a lent security(ies) and to the reinvestment risk on the cash collateral or pledged securities' collateral.

We further caution that a fund's risk characteristics become magnified when its asset size — or its liabilities — become inflated by reverse repurchase agreements. Thus, extensive leveraging can result in risk levels that exceed the value of the fund itself. Because the reverse repo is a leveraged deal by nature, any leverage will cause measurable portfolio risk to be greater than 100% of a fund's net assets, given the incremental exposure to the reinvested securities.

Maturity Leveraging

Funds may enter transactions in which the cash collateral from the reverse repo is reinvested at a different maturity than that of the lent securities. This may also occur in transactions where the pledged collateral securities have a different maturity than the lent securities (for example, cash collateral from a rolling 1-day reverse repo may be invested in a 30-day security). Such maturity leveraging is often the byproduct of a yield enhancement strategy.

Maturity leveraging, however, will affect the fund's "true" weighted average maturity (WAM), which is a proxy for a fund's interest rate risk. (As the WAM increases, so does risk.) The true WAM accounts for all of the fund's securities (including lent securities) and the securities purchased with the cash collateral or acquired as collateral.

Credit Leveraging

Credit leveraging occurs when cash collateral from the reverse repo is reinvested in lower credit quality securities with potentially higher returns. Credit leveraging can also involve transactions where the lent security is of higher quality than the collateral received — in exchange for (a higher spread or yield). For example, cash collateral from a 1-day reverse repo of a security rated P-1 might be invested in a security rated P-2. Credit leveraging is often the byproduct of a yield enhancement strategy.

Matching Program

Funds may match reverse repo transactions by investing cash collateral in securities with identical — or nearly identical — maturity and similar credit characteristics to those lent. For example, cash collateral from a 7-day reverse may be invested in a 7-day repo with similar credit characteristics to the securities that were lent out in the reverse repo. While this approach still employs asset leveraging and possible yield enhancement, it tends to limit both market risk and credit risk exposure in the fund.

Structured Protection

Puts or setoffs may be used to protect a fund from risks associated with a reverse repo. For example, term reverse repo agreements may allow for each reversed security to be called, on demand, overnight by the fund so the security(ies) can be liquidated if necessary. Among other protection measures are a fund's discretionary right of setoff in case of counterparty default. These strategies, if used correctly, may offer the fund greater protection during extreme market conditions. We note that spreads on these deals may be narrower.

RISKS TO MONEY MARKET FUNDS

The following is a listing of the risk features inherent to reverse repurchase agreement transactions. Moody's includes these risk factors in every review of funds that engage in reverse repo transactions.

Market Risk

A lending fund retains ownership rights to the lent security(ies), and is therefore subject to the accompanying market risk exposure. Additional market risk exposure may occur through the reinvestment of the cash collateral or the collateral pledged in securities.

Counterparty Risk

As with a repurchase agreement transaction, weaker counterparties may expose a fund to the possibility of a failed transaction. In the case of a counterparty default with a cash collateral transaction, the fund will most likely come out whole. If the counterparty default occurs with securities pledged as collateral, the collateral may be subject to a court-imposed stay (this depends on relevant bankruptcy laws).

Credit Risk

In addition to the credit risk of the lent security(ies), a fund will be exposed to the reinvestment credit risk of the cash collateral or the collateral pledged in securities.

Concentration Risk

The additional risk incurred from exposure to a single — or to very few counter-parties.

Leverage Risk

A fund that is leveraged for more than 100% of its assets is exposed to increased market risk, credit risk, counterparty risk, and operational risks.

Operations Risk

The transaction, execution, and delivery of the securities in a reverse repo transaction exposes the fund to higher operations risks than would apply in a transaction with standard money market instruments.

Reporting Risk

Reverse repo transactions are often difficult to spot or fully understand in a fund's portfolio holdings report. Complete transaction detail is necessary to make a proper risk analysis.

Chapter 7

Innovative Investments for Money Market Funds

Brian R. Carosielli
Associate Director
Managed Funds Group
Fitch

Growth in money fund assets, coupled with increased investor demand for higher yields, has challenged prime money fund managers to find investments that enhance portfolio yield without adding significant risk. Consequently, managers have been increasing their exposure to various types of innovative money market instruments. These innovative securities offer higher yields to compensate money fund investors for their structural complexity and, in some cases, lower market liquidity.

As with any new asset type, these innovative money market instruments allow investors that understand the risks, and are able to perform a thorough investment analysis, to capitalize on higher yields before these securities become core investments for most prime money fund portfolios. This chapter covers the following innovative money market instruments:

- Asset-backed commercial paper.
- CDO money market notes.
- Funding agreements.
- Extendible commercial notes.

This chapter will focus on the benefits and concerns surrounding these innovative money market instruments from both an investor and rating agency perspective. This includes descriptions of these securities as well as insight on how Fitch views prime money market funds that purchase innovative money market instruments.

PRIME MONEY MARKET FUNDS

Before discussing the characteristics of these innovative money market instruments, we first need to define the main purchaser of these securities.

Prime money funds are money market mutual funds that invest in a variety of high-quality, short-duration assets. Unlike taxable money funds that purchase only obligations of the United States government and its agencies (known as U.S. Treasury or government funds), prime funds may invest in the public debt of private-sector issuers. For example, prime funds may purchase assets such as commercial paper, medium-term notes, extendible commercial notes, bankers' acceptances, corporate debt, CDO money market notes, certificates of deposit, and funding agreements, as well as obligations of the U.S. government and its agencies/instrumentalities.

Rule 2a-7 Eligibility

Money market funds that distribute shares to investors located in the United States are governed by Rule 2a-7 of the Investment Company Act of 1940 ("the 1940 Act").

Neither the SEC nor the courts have provided guidance as to whether many of the innovative money market instruments discussed in this chapter are eligible securities for money fund investment. Therefore, prime funds should make independent determinations of Rule 2a-7 eligibility, which may include internal counsel review before purchasing these securities. When making these determinations, prime funds must discern if these innovative money market instruments meet the three criteria for an eligible security.

First, based on certain features of such structures, the securities meet the first test of an eligible security, namely that it is a security within the meaning of the 1940 Act.

Second, that the securities are structured to meet the "remaining maturity" criteria for an eligible security by having maturities of less than or equal to 397 days. Also, by purchasing instruments that offer floating-rate coupons, investors generally treat the maturity of the security as the earlier of the period remaining until the next interest rate reset date or days to maturity. This feature allows the fund to ascribe a shorter interest rate exposure element than days to maturity for purposes of calculating the fund's weighted average maturity (WAM) under Rule 2a-7.

Finally, a majority of the prime funds that buy these investments have satisfied the credit quality criteria for an eligible security by only purchasing investments that have one of the two highest short-term rating categories from at least two nationally recognized statistical rating organizations (NRSROs).

ASSET-BACKED COMMERCIAL PAPER

An *asset-backed commercial paper* (ABCP) conduit is defined as a bankruptcy-remote *special purpose entity* (SPE) that issues commercial paper to finance the purchase of trade receivables, term assets, or rated assets from one or more sellers (i.e., transferors of assets). Some of the term assets purchased with the commercial paper proceeds may include credit card receivables, auto loans, installment loans, and equipment leases. Examples of rated assets that are purchased by conduits are asset-backed, mortgage-backed, and corporate securities.

ABCP conduits are typically established by commercial banks or finance companies to create balance sheet relief or to provide low-cost financing to their customers. More recently, conduits have been created to take advantage of arbitrage opportunities in the fixed-income markets. These arbitrage opportunities are usually exploited by issuing commercial paper and then purchasing longer-term, higher-yielding assets with the proceeds.

There are several key characteristics of ABCP conduits that investors need to understand before purchasing these securities. First, ABCP conduits are typically categorized by their level of programwide credit enhancement, which determines whether a conduit is fully or partially supported. In fully supported programs, the repayment of CP relies on a financial guarantee in the form of a credit agreement, surety bond, letter of credit, or third-party guarantee to cover all credit risks. Moreover, investors' risk rests with the financial strength of the guarantor and is not affected by a default on the underlying assets. The rating of a fully supported program is dependent on the ratings of program enhancers and liquidity support providers. In contrast, partially supported ABCP programs rely primarily on the cash flow or market value of a pool of assets for repayment of the CP. Investors in partially supported programs are exposed to losses on the underlying program assets to the extent that such losses exceed pool-specific reserves and programwide credit enhancement

ABCP programs are also categorized as either *single-seller* or *multiseller programs*. Single-seller programs are bankruptcy-remote SPEs that issue ABCP to fund the assets of a single originator or seller. Multiseller conduits combine the assets of several unrelated sellers into one diverse portfolio of assets supporting the CP issuance and are typically sponsored by large commercial banks or finance companies. The multiseller conduit itself is also a bankruptcy-remote SPE that meets certain legal requirements. The asset portfolio is purchased and managed for the issuer by an operating or administrative agent, generally a division or dedicated group within a sponsoring bank or finance company, in accordance with the conduit's operating guidelines. Conduits have well-developed credit and investment policies to manage asset liquidity and regulate the size, quality, and diversity of sellers and obligors participating in the program.

The ABCP market currently consists of more than 200 active programs and approximately $551 billion in outstanding issuances. Furthermore, ABCP makes up approximately 49% of the more than $1.1 trillion dealer-placed commercial paper market. Since the end of 1995, the amount of ABCP outstanding has increased over 445%. This phenomenal growth is due to several factors, including continued expansion of existing programs, increased demand by prime money funds, the entrance of new programs, and the introduction of new asset types to be financed through conduits.

Exhibit 1: Rating Analysis for ABCP

Legal Structure	Fitch reviews legal documentation to ensure that all CP vehicles are structured as bankruptcy-remote special purpose entities and that appropriate legal opinions are rendered.
Credit Protection	All transactions funded in ABCP vehicles are structured to an investment-grade rating that is commensurate with the program's short-term rating. Many programs also have a layer of programwide credit enhancement (i.e. surety bond, cash collateral accounts, or letters of credit) as an additional level of protection.
Liquidity Support	Liquidity support is an integral part of every ABCP program as it ensures timely repayment of ABCP in the event of a market disruption, or an issuer's inability to "roll" the CP (issue new CP to pay maturing CP). Most ABCP programs are structured with 100% liquidity support.
Credit and Investment Policy	A program's credit and investment policy serves as the "owner's manual" for how an ABCP vehicle operates. Fitch reviews each program's policy, which establishes the program's investment guidelines.
Surveillance	Fitch requires that each program provide a monthly portfolio performance summary that allows the analytical staff to monitor each program's compliance with its credit and investment policy. In addition, Fitch conducts annual due diligence reviews of each issuer.

Prime money funds have increased their ABCP exposure over the past several years. According to IBC Financial Data, approximately $183 billion of ABCP was held in prime money funds as of May 31, 2000, which consists, on average, of 18% of total prime fund assets. IBC Financial Data also estimated that the number of prime money funds purchasing ABCP increased to 396 in 1999 from 213 in 1998; in other words, 75% of the approximately 528 existing prime money funds have exposure to ABCP.

ABCP is an attractive asset class for prime money funds because it offers yields comparable to those of London Interbank Offered Rate (LIBOR). Along with offering attractive yields, ABCP also allows funds to diversify into different asset classes, including various types of receivables. ABCP programs are structured very soundly, which allows for full and timely payment of principal and interest at maturity. In addition, the ABCP market is an established and liquid market. Even during the most severe market disruptions, prime money funds should be able to sell their ABCP holdings at fair prices.

Prime fund managers and other short-term investors share similar concerns when evaluating an ABCP investment. Among other things, investors are concerned with timely payment of principal and interest, the credit quality of the underlying assets, and structural protections. During the ABCP rating process, Fitch's analysis addresses these concerns through a full review, as detailed in Exhibit 1.

Rating Agency Perspective

ABCP is a viable investment alternative for prime money fund managers that have a solid understanding of the structure, risks, and regulations associated with this asset class. In addition, fund managers should buy ABCP only if it is consistent with the fund's investment strategy and policy. This must include a thorough analysis of the investment's compliance with Rule 2a-7 as well as the implementation of procedures to monitor various SEC diversification guidelines.

Furthermore, Fitch is encouraged by the heightened investor demand for increased conduit disclosure. Prime money funds are requiring more complete information, so they can have a reasonable basis for investment decisions. In some cases, if a prime money fund does not receive this information from a conduit sponsor, it will invest its money elsewhere.

Fitch is also pleased to see the heightened role of the sponsor in determining a conduit's status (i.e., obligor and guarantor exposure) under Rule 2a-7. By having the conduit sponsor and investor examine the asset diversification of a conduit, within the context of Rule 2a-7 investment guidelines, the chance of violating these guidelines decreases.

By performing a thorough investment analysis, using the ratings of NRSROs, and following the diversification standards established by the SEC, a knowledgeable portfolio manager can invest comfortably in ABCP.

CDO MONEY MARKET NOTES

Collateralized bond obligations (CBOs) and *collateralized loan obligations* (CLOs), collectively known as *collateralized debt obligations* (CDOs), have been some of the most dynamic and burgeoning sectors of the fixed-income markets over the past several years. Outstanding rated CDO issuance increased to more than $99.5 billion in 1999 from approximately $2.5 billion in 1995. This exponential growth has been amplified by innovative cash-flow structures and improved risk-management techniques. Due to these cash-flow engineering advances, CDOs are now structured to appeal to a wider variety of institutional investors, including prime money funds.

Recently, CDO issuers have begun including money market classes (or tranches) in their structures. These tranches are structured to be eligible investments under Rule 2a-7. CDO issuers are targeting money market funds because of the lower all-in financing cost versus issuing term notes. The primary trends that have contributed to the growth in this market segment are more sophistication and development in the structures, advanced cash flow analysis, squeezed margins, increased competition, and the general need for differentiation amongst issuers. CDO money market tranches vary in issuance size and usually take the form of short-term notes, extendible notes, revolving note programs, or asset-backed commercial paper.

This section will focus only on CDO money market tranches that issue notes and will not cover ABCP, which was covered in the previous section.

Overview of CDO Structures

CDOs have been issued in various forms for more than a decade. CBOs are bonds collateralized by a portfolio of other bonds, most often high-yield securities, emerging market debt, bank loans, mortgage-backed securities, asset-backed securities, or any combination of the above. CLOs are backed by portfolios of negotiated and syndicated high-yield or investment-grade loans. In both cases, cash flows from the underlying financial instruments are used to pay off investors in rated securities, with priority given to senior tranches of debt. As a result of this cash-flow prioritization, debt issued by the CDO can be rated higher than the underlying securities.

Furthermore, CDOs are classified as being either cash-flow or market-value. *Market-value CDOs* are collateralized by the mark-to-market values of the underlying securities. *Cash-flow CDOs* are collateralized by the expected principal and interest cash flows of the underlying assets. Most CDO securities are issued pursuant to Rule144A of the Securities Act of 1933, which means they are quasi-public non-SEC-registered securities that can be distributed only to "qualified institutional buyers," "qualified purchasers," and "accredited investors."

Market-value CDOs are designed with liquidation "triggers" that require the structure to unwind (or liquidate), selling the underlying collateral if the trigger event is not remedied within the applicable cure period. Typical trigger events are failure of overcollateralization tests and minimum-net-worth tests. Triggers are established to help limit the losses that a CDO could incur by forcing the structure to sell assets before market conditions worsen (known as "deleveraging").

Cash-flow CDOs have various coverage tests that assure investors that there will be sufficient cash flow to pay principal and interest on the money market notes. Tests for par coverage, interest coverage, weighted average rating, weighted average maturity, and minimum average coupon are routinely performed to verify cash-flow stability. If a cash-flow structure fails a coverage test, cash flows are redirected from the subordinate tranches to the senior tranche (e.g., money market notes) and/or trading activity is restricted until the structure is back in compliance with all coverage tests.

Exhibit 2 demonstrates how subordinated tranches provide credit protection to the senior debt (e.g., money market tranche). The market value or cash flow of the underlying collateral provides credit enhancement to the rated tranches. In the example in Exhibit 2, the value of the collateral would have to decline by more than 50% before the senior tranche would experience any losses.

Overview of CDO Money Market Notes

Fitch has seen rated CDOs issue three types of money market notes — short-term, extendible, and revolving. All three types qualify as Rule 2a-7 eligible securities, as determined by investors, because their maturity dates are 397 days or less. The majority of these notes have coupons that reset off of LIBOR. However, each type has slightly different features. *Extendible notes* (not to be confused with extendible commercial notes) allow a prime fund to extend the maturity of the notes for another period less than or equal to 397 days from the prior maturity date. *Revolving notes* are securities that are part of a program that continually issues notes, in which only one series of notes is outstanding at a time; the characteristics of the notes may change with each series. Short-term notes are notes that have maturity dates of 397 days or less.

Reasons for Investment

CDO money market notes are an attractive asset class for prime money funds because they offer yields that are higher than traditional money market investments. Currently, many CDO money market notes offer yields equivalent to LIBOR plus a spread. Fitch has seen CDO money market notes priced at yields of approximately 5 to 50 basis points over LIBOR. These yield levels depend on the degree of subordination in the structure, strength and reputation of the investment manager, asset type, and current market conditions.

CDO money market notes enable prime money funds to diversify into new asset sectors. By purchasing CDO money market notes, a prime fund receives indirect exposure to a professionally managed, diverse pool of high-yield, bank loan, asset-backed, and mortgage-backed debt. Also, the money market notes have protection against the loss of principal due to overcollateralization. Generally, exposure to losses in the asset pool is reduced by the common practice of limiting the maximum exposure to individual credits to 4%–5% of total assets. Furthermore, most money market notes are customized to meet prime money fund needs and preferences. Prime funds can usually negotiate the maturity and terms of the notes.

As with any new security, prime money funds need to consider the risks associated with CDO money market notes before purchasing these investments. Most of the risks inherent in CDO structures can be classified into three broad categories — credit, liquidity, and manager.

Exhibit 2: Sample CBO/CLO Structure

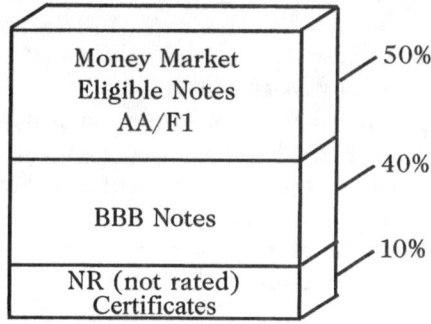

Credit Risk

Since money market notes are normally the senior tranches of CDO structures, they are protected by large amounts of subordinated debt, as shown in Exhibit 2. In other words, if a CDO deal was performing poorly, the money market tranche investors would be made whole before the investors in the subordinated tranches received any payment. Therefore, the risk to the money market tranche investor is that there is inadequate subordination to absorb losses. If there is inadequate subordination, money market note investors may not receive full payment of their principal and interest. Shortfalls in proceeds could be due to significant decreases in the market prices or expected cash flows of the collateral due to credit, market, or liquidity risks.

The risk of inadequate subordination levels in Fitch-rated transactions is addressed by Fitch's practice of conservatively setting subordination levels to protect rated tranches. Investment-grade rated tranches are designed to survive through multiples of worst-case observed historical performance. Moreover, since the inception of CDOs more than 10 years ago, no senior noteholder has incurred any loss of principal or interest. Fitch performs ongoing surveillance by running overcollaterization tests and evaluating details such as the market value for each asset in the portfolio and compliance with portfolio guidelines.

Liquidity Risk

As with all securities, it is up to the fund's management to determine the liquidity of a security. Even though most CDO money market notes are distributed under Rule 144A, some fund managers believe they still have little liquidity because the secondary market for these tranches is not yet active. The lack of secondary market activity is primarily due to the "newness" of certain CDO structures, as well as the relatively small size of some of the money market note programs compared with other short-term fixed-income securities. As is the case with many newer security types, dealers may not make bids on CDO tranches that are not originated or distributed through their company. Potential factors that determine liquidity in the CDO market include the size of the transaction, number and experience of dealers in the transaction, ratings of the transaction, and access to transaction information.

Manager Risk

When analyzing a CDO money market note for investment, in-depth evaluation of the asset manager's strategy, expertise, and experience is of paramount importance. The role of CDO managers is vital because the markets in which they operate are highly specialized. The manager's expertise at finding relative value between investments in similar assets or among vastly different asset types, as well as sector selection must be assessed. Moreover, the ability of the manager to operate within the constraints defined in the structure's operating documents is crucial.

Fitch's recommended approach to management assessment covers the following major areas: performance history; credit analysis and research capability; management's ability to evaluate bond indentures and loan covenants; access to deal flow, risk management, institutional resources and systems; and asset/liability management skills. The manager should also have experience investing in the collateral asset types, having endured at least one market downturn. Lastly, an investor should understand the asset manager's role in a CDO transaction, including equity stakes and expected returns.

Rating Agency Analysis for CDO Structures

Fitch focuses on the following areas when rating a CDO structure: assessment of the asset manager, collateral evaluation, modeling and stress-testing, legal structure, and surveillance.

Assessment of Asset Manager

When evaluating asset managers for market value structures, Fitch looks for proven experience with actively managed and frequently priced portfolios, as well as a demonstrated ability to manage portfolios through market upheavals. In the case of cash flow structures, it is important that the manager have proven experience in managing the target asset mix as well as a demonstrated ability to manage portfolios through credit cycles.

Collateral Evaluation

Fitch examines the liquidity and volatility of the market value CDO's underlying assets when evaluating market value structures. Furthermore, borrowing-based advance rates are utilized to determine the amount of debt that can be secured by a particular type of asset at a given rating level. For cash flow structures, the credit quality and maturity of the cash flow CDO's underlying assets are closely examined. Default and recovery assumptions are assigned to the assets based on weighted average debt ratings and asset type. Furthermore, Fitch requires both market value and cash flow CDOs to maintain a minimum level of issuer and industry diversification.

Modeling and Stress Testing

Fitch runs a model of the proposed market value structure through a series of stress tests that include severe and repeated market value declines. Then, Fitch utilizes the stress tests' results to help determine if the proposed ratings are consistent with the risk to investors. For cash flow structures, the analytic process is heavily focused on actuarial stress tests that rely on multiples of observed historical defaults for the defined asset class(es), as well as the timing and distribution of losses and recoveries relative to the "reinvestment" period and "amortization" period.

Legal Structure

Fitch reviews legal documentation to ensure that both market value and cash flow CDO transactions are structured as bankruptcy-remote special-purpose entities that have a security interest in the underlying collateral and that all appropriate legal opinions are rendered.

Surveillance

Fitch requires each market value CDO to provide weekly and monthly portfolio performance summaries that allow its analytical staff to monitor each program's market value, as well as its compliance with the investment guidelines. In addition, due-diligence reviews of each asset manager are conducted annually, as well as quarterly reviews of the issuer's financial statements.

Cash flow structures are required to provide monthly compliance reporting and quarterly and annual financial statements that allow analytical staff to monitor each program's compliance with its credit and investment policy, as well as to verify that actual collateral defaults are in line with projected defaults. In addition, as with market value structures, due diligence reviews of the asset manager are conducted annually.

Rating Agency Perspective

In addition to undergoing a thorough assessment of the asset manager and the structure's investment policy, a prime fund manager needs to have the resources to analyze and track the underlying assets of a CDO money market note. The analysis for these securities is ongoing because some CDO structures are actively managed and could potentially experience changes in asset composition. As mentioned, the money market note is typically senior to any other debt outstanding, but an investor should be comfortable with the trigger features or coverage tests and the amount of subordinated debt below the tranche. By evaluating these features, investors can assess the structural integrity of the transaction.

Fitch believes that the prime fund manager should invest in CDO money market notes only after it has reviewed the structure thoroughly, has a solid understanding of the risks, is comfortable and familiar with the asset manager, and has established resources to monitor these securities. Furthermore, fund managers should buy CDO money market notes only if it is conducive to the fund's investment strategy and policy. In addition, Fitch considers prime money market fund holdings of CDO money market tranches to be illiquid for purposes of its money fund rating guidelines, unless a review of the particular holding reveals additional information. As such, rated funds should limit their exposure to CDO money market notes and other illiquid assets to less than 10% of total assets.

Upon assigning an AAA or AA rating to a prime fund, Fitch requires that all CDO money market notes be rated 'F1+' or 'F1' or the equivalent by an NRSRO. Analysts at Fitch thoroughly analyze the probability that investors will receive timely payment of all their principal and interest. This includes rigorous stress tests that subject the CDO structure to increased default market value, credit spread, and liquidity risks in varying economic scenarios. Fitch ratings provide investors with a benchmark from which to compare the results of their own analysis.

CDO structures survived the credit spread crisis that occurred in fourth-quarter 1998. By emerging from this drastic spread-widening relatively unscathed, CDO managers have helped bolster market confidence in the CDO market. Heightened market confidence will likely lead to continued CDO issuance and, consequently, the availability of more money fund eligible tranches. Increased issuance will provide prime fund managers who are willing to perform a thorough investment analysis, and utilize NRSRO ratings, with more opportunities to invest in money market notes of CDOs.

FUNDING AGREEMENTS

Funding agreements are contracts issued by insurance companies (the issuers) that provide the policyholder with the right to receive a fixed or variable rate of interest and the full return of principal on the maturity date. The market for funding agreements consists primarily of nonqualified institutional investors, as defined under the Internal Revenue Code, that purchase the contracts directly from insurance companies or brokers.

The National Association of Insurance Commissioners and many state guaranty funds have classified funding agreements as insurance policies; therefore, funding agreements are regulated under state insurance laws. Funding agreements are structured so they do not have to be registered with the SEC under the Securities Act of 1933.

Insurance companies developed funding agreements as a means to maximize their existing guaranteed investment contract (GIC) underwriting expertise and distribution capabilities. In a GIC market that has been characterized by increased competition and declining sales, funding agreements have provided insurance companies with an additional source of revenue.

GICs can be defined as benefit-responsive contracts that are issued to tax-qualified pension plans, which guarantee an interest-crediting rate for a specified period. Funding agreements and GICs have similar characteristics, but funding agreements differ in two fundamental ways: they are sold to nonqualified institutional investors and they include embedded demand features.

A majority of the funding agreements sold are highly customized to meet prime fund preferences. For example, an investor in a variable-rate funding agreement can choose from a myriad of appropriate money market indexes that are used to determine the interest-crediting rate, including: 1-month, 3-month, 6-month, or 12-month LIBOR; federal funds; and the 1-year Constant Maturity Treasury Index (CMT). In addition, funding agreements that are purchased by prime funds typically include embedded demand features, which entitle the policyholder to receive principal in a defined number of days after giving notice to the issuer. Prime funds may choose from 7-, 30-, 90-, 180-, 365-, or 397-day demand features. These funds may also customize their extension agreements, day of interest rate reset, and policies regarding issuer downgrades.

Benefits of Funding Agreements

Funding agreements have become an attractive asset class to many prime funds because of their attractive yields. Traditionally, funding agreements have offered higher yields than similarly rated commercial paper or other variable-rate instruments.

Portfolio managers have also been enticed by the diversification benefits that funding agreements offer. Since many insurance companies do not issue commercial paper, funding agreements allow prime funds to receive credit exposure to the insurance industry (in particular, mutual insurance companies). In addition, funding agreements allow for a high degree of contract customization, which creates the opportunity for portfolio managers to build a security that meets their investment criteria and desired risk profile.

Risks of Funding Agreements

Even though investor demand for funding agreements has increased in recent years, many portfolio managers still oppose their use in prime funds. One of the most common arguments against funding agreements is that they should be considered illiquid securities. Because of the absence of a secondary market, accompanied by minimal contract standardization, many parties believe that funding agreements have no liquidity. No secondary market exists for funding agreements because they are insurance contracts and, therefore, cannot be traded. In addition, some argue that the demand features in funding agreements will actually decrease portfolio liquidity if a large percentage of the outstanding contracts is put back to the insurer over a short period and the insurer has difficulty fulfilling these large contractual obligations.

Another concern is the lack of clarity and continuity in state insurance regulations regarding the claims priority of funding agreements in the event of issuer insolvency. According to some state insurance laws, funding agreements are treated as obligations of the insurance company, giving the contracts senior claims status over all creditors and making them *pari passu* with all policyholders. However, some states have not clarified the claims status of funding agreements, which creates uncertainty as to how these agreements would be treated in the event of an insurance company's liquidation.

Because of the default in 1991 of two large insurance companies, Executive Life Insurance Co. and Mutual Benefit Life Insurance Co., some portfolio managers are concerned about the claims priority of funding agreements. In the case of Mutual Benefit, GIC investors did not suffer any loss of principal, while Executive Life GIC investors experienced minor losses of principal and interest.

More importantly, both groups of investors incurred a long delay in the return of their principal. In both cases, the state insurance regulators treated GICs as *pari passu* with all other policyholders.

To date, there has been only one instance where a funding agreement issuer was unable to meet investor redemptions within the allowable time period specified in the contract, since money market funds first began utilizing these instruments.

In August of 1999, General American Life Insurance Co. was unable to provide timely payment of both principal and interest to investors who redeemed their funding agreement contracts. These funding agreements were "put" back to General American following a downgrade of the insurance company by several NRSROs. Fitch was not among the rating agencies with a rating on General American. The contracts that were put back to General American contained demand features that required the issuer to return the investor's principal and accrued interest within seven days. General American was temporarily unable to meet investor redemptions on its funding agreements due to a large volume of redemptions, and consequently experienced the inability to liquidate assets to cover these liabilities over a short period of time. Approximately three weeks after this incident, General American agreed to be acquired by Metropolitan Life Insurance Co., and shortly thereafter investors received the amounts owed under their funding agreement contracts.

After further analysis, it appears that General American's inability to meet investor redemptions was due primarily to poor asset/liability management and overzealous underwriting, rather than structural problems with the contracts. Some of the assets purchased with the funding agreement proceeds were illiquid, as well as more sensitive to changes in market conditions than the funding agreement liabilities. If more liquid and less price sensitive assets were purchased with the funding agreement proceeds, General American probably would have been able to systematically liquidate the assets in enough time to meet redemptions. In addition, over 30% of General American's general account insurance liabilities were in the form of 7-day funding agreements. By having a large percentage of their total liabilities in the form of short-term funding agreements, General American exposed itself to the risk of having to liquidate a significant amount of assets over a brief period of time. When an investor is forced to liquidate assets in this scenario, they may incur unnecessary execution losses caused by unfavorable market conditions. Fitch believes that the problems associated with General American funding agreements are due to factors related to the issuer, not the product.

As mentioned earlier, funding agreement investors are exposed to the inherent credit and liquidity risks of an insurance company. Therefore, a portfolio manager needs to thoroughly analyze the investment operations and financial strength of the funding agreement issuer. The portfolio manager should consider the asset/liability management techniques, investment policies, lines of business (i.e., funding agreements as a percentage of total liabilities), and liquidity of an insurance company when determining the adequacy of its investment operations. When measuring the financial stability of an insurer, a portfolio manager can utilize the financial strength and claims-paying ability ratings provided by Fitch and other NRSROs.

Rating Agency Perspective

As with any money market investment, funding agreements must meet a strict set of criteria before being eligible for purchase in a Fitch-rated prime fund. Fitch has specific parameters that must be followed when investing in variable-rate securities such as funding agreements.

First, all eligible variable-rate securities should support a stable portfolio net asset value (NAV) by providing a market value that approximates par at the security's interest rate reset date. Moreover, the interest rate index that is chosen must be one that moves in tandem with short-term market rates, i.e., 1-month LIBOR and federal funds. Long-term interest rate indexes, such as the 10-year CMT, and indexes that lag market rates, such as the 11th District Cost of Funds Index, are not appropriate for prime funds. Also, Fitch will not permit investment in variable-rate securities with complex coupon formulas similar to those found in some structured notes.

Since most funding agreements have demand features, it is important to evaluate the quality and liquidity of the feature. Fitch's managed funds group looks to the rating of the issuer when determining the issuer's ability and willingness to honor the demand feature, especially during periods of stress. When assigning a claims-paying ability rating for an insurance company, Fitch factors in the ability and willingness to honor all obligations, including funding agreements with their associated demand features. Second, the credit quality of the issuer, as well as the level of concentration with any single issuer, is also measured. Finally, Fitch defines any funding agreement that does not have a 7-day demand feature as an illiquid security.

Fitch believes funding agreements are viable investment alternatives for prime funds if they are structured properly and entered into with creditworthy issuers. Furthermore, by performing a thorough company/investment analysis and utilizing NRSRO ratings, an investor can make an accurate assessment of the financial strength and claims-paying ability of an issuer.

EXTENDIBLE COMMERCIAL NOTES

Since the inception of commercial paper ratings, CP issuers have been required by rating agencies to have bank short-term liquidity support. Bank short-term liquidity support ensures timely repayment of CP in the event of a market disruption or an issuer's inability to "roll" the CP. It is important to note that bank liquidity facilities typically cannot be drawn on in the event of an issuer default.

Traditionally, commercial banks were the main source of short-term liquidity for CP issuers. Over the past several years, the cost of bank short-term liquidity has increased, while the supply of available liquidity has diminished. The reduction of available liquidity support reflects several factors, including more banks providing liquidity support for their own ABCP conduits, several large Japanese banks exiting the liquidity support market, continuing bank consolidation, and an increasing number of new CP programs. As liquidity support became sparse and more expensive, investment banks identified a need to find alternative sources of liquidity support for their clients. When researching possible sources of liquidity, investment banks realized that one of the most reliable and affordable sources of short-term liquidity support was from money market investors. This spurred the development of extendible commercial notes (ECNs). ECNs are short-term investment products that typically have initial redemption dates from one to 90 days but are extendible to final maturities of 390 days. To date, the majority of ECN issuance has been placed with traditional money market investors, including prime money market funds.

Overview of Extendible Commercial Notes

The ECN market has grown substantially since its inception in August 1998. As of June 19, 2000, there had been approximately $38 billion in issuance, $6 billion of which is outstanding, from over 40 ECN issuers. To date, the majority of outstanding ECN issuance was created to augment a company's existing CP program. ECN issuers are primarily highly rated companies with significant amounts of outstanding CP.

As previously mentioned, ECNs are issued with initial redemption dates of between one and 90 days from the issuance date, as well as extension features that allow for final stated maturities of 390 days. These notes are structured to allow the issuer to repurchase its outstanding ECNs (at par) from investors at the initial redemption date. If the issuer is unable to roll or redeem the ECN at the initial redemption date, they may choose to extend the maturity of the security. Depending on the initial redemption date of the ECN, the maturity can extend 300–389 days. For example, if an ECN had an initial redemption date of 90 days, the ECN's final maturity at the redemption date would be 300 days if the issuer chose to extend the maturity of the notes.

ECNs are issued at a discount (similar to most CP), which means the difference between the value at the initial redemption date and the price paid is the interest earned by the investor. Should the issuer extend the maturity of an ECN, there is an automatic step-up in the ECN's coupon rate. Once this step-up occurs, the ECN will begin to pay a floating-rate of interest every 30 days. The step-up rate is determined by a formula that factors in the issuer's lowest prevailing short-term rating and the current LIBOR. Based on the issuer's rating, the ECN's coupon rate will reset at the 30-day LIBOR plus a spread equal to the larger of a fixed spread or a set percentage of LIBOR (see Exhibit 3). The increased coupon rate provides an economic disincentive for the issuer to not extend the ECN's maturity, thus giving the investor reasonable comfort that the security will be redeemed at the initial redemption date.

Reasons for Investment

As with many innovative money market instruments, investors believe the main advantage of ECNs is that they yield an average of 4 to 7 basis points more than corporate CP from the same issuer. Moreover, because of this yield advantage, prime funds may now be able to justify the purchase of traditionally lower yielding CP issuers that they do not currently own. The purchase of these more popular issuers will increase the diversification of some prime funds' holdings. Furthermore, funds that already buy the CP of the prospective ECN issuer need to perform little additional credit analysis before purchasing the ECN, as the credit risk is similar with both products. Also, some market participants argue that the liquidity support provided by ECNs is more reliable than the traditional liquidity facilities provided by banks. Their reasoning is that, under certain conditions, bank liquidity support may be cancelled or may not be obligated to provide funds, whereas ECNs provide guaranteed liquidity support under all circumstances and conditions beyond the initial redemption date.

Risks

The risks associated with investing in ECNs are very similar to those associated with investing in corporate CP. As with corporate CP, an ECN investor's primary concern is the ability of the issuer to make timely payment of principal and interest. A unique feature associated with ECNs is the potential for the issuer to extend the maturity of the security on the initial redemption date. Although investors receive a very attractive step-up in the coupon rate upon extension, it is likely that this event would occur during a period of turmoil in the financial markets and/or would coincide with rapid credit deterioration of the issuer.

Exhibit 3: ECN Coupon Formulas

Prevailing Assigned Rating*	Percentage of LIBOR	Minimum Fixed Spread	Example: LIBOR = 5.50%	Example: LIBOR = 3.00%
F1+/A-1+/P-1	110%	25	6.05% = (L + 55)	3.30% = (L+30)
F1/A-1/P-1	115%	50	6.32% = (L + 82)	3.50% = (L+50)
F2/A-2/P-2	130%	150	7.15% = (L + 165)	4.50% = (L+150)
F3/A-3/P-3	150%	250	8.25% = (L + 275)	5.50% = (L+250)
< F3/A-3/P-3	175%	400	9.63% = (L + 413)	7.00% = (L+400)

* If split ratings are assigned to the issuer, the reset rate will be set based on the average of the corresponding spreads to LIBOR for each rating. If short-term debt ratings are on Rating Watch Negative for possible downgrade (or any other comparable designation by any other rating agency), then the next lower category will apply for the reset rate.

Source: Goldman Sachs Group, Inc.

Another concern of potential investors is the breadth of the secondary market for ECNs. Currently, there is only one broker/dealer making an active secondary market for a majority of the outstanding ECN issuance. In addition, only a handful of investors currently purchase ECNs. Goldman Sachs Group, Inc. estimates that approximately 270 investors currently buy ECNs, compared to more than 5,000 that purchase CP. Both factors are important concerns in periods of economic turmoil when liquidity may become scarce and/or expensive for newer and less actively traded asset types. In contrast, the breadth of the secondary market for corporate CP is not a concern because multiple dealers and investors participate in the market for most issuers' CP.

Rating Agency Perspective

When determining the applicability of ECNs for investment in prime money funds, Fitch has considered several factors. First, the risk of ECN extension for highly rated issuers is mitigated due to the following factors:

- Increased funding costs to the issuer.
- Alternative sources of liquidity likely to be drawn first.
- Reputation risk to the issuer.

As previously mentioned, if an issuer choose to extend its ECNs, it would be forced to pay coupon rates significantly higher than prevailing CP rates. Also, an ECN issuer would likely tap internal or external sources of liquidity, such as bank lines of credit, additional CP or term issuance, or cash, before allowing its ECNs to extend. These sources of liquidity would be preferable to the issuer instead of the increased costs and reputational damage associated with an ECN extension. Lastly, the issuer would probably have difficulty issuing any subsequent ECNs and may even face increased funding costs for its CP due to investor uncertainty about the company's financial stability and/or practices for managing short-term debt.

As mentioned earlier, some investors are concerned about the breadth of the ECN secondary market. This is because only one broker/dealer currently makes an active market in a majority of the outstanding ECN issuances, and there are only a handful of investors actively purchasing ECNs. Fitch has surveyed the market and is of the opinion that, in times of economic turmoil, broker/dealers currently underwriting/agenting ECNs would provide liquidity on a best efforts basis, as they are established market makers in the CP industry and, thus, would expose themselves to significant reputation risk by not providing liquidity for ECNs that they have underwritten/agented. However, broker/dealers are not legally obligated to provide liquidity for securities they underwrite/agent. Therefore, Fitch recommends that funds view ECNs as illiquid securities until there is an active secondary market for these investments.

Furthermore, investors should be secure with the credit quality and the extension feature of the ECN before considering the security for purchase. In addition, a prime fund should verify that it is not violating its issuer concentration limits by purchasing ECNs. Finally, when determining Rule 2a-7 eligibility, some funds are classifying ECNs as short-term variable-rate securities. This means that these funds use the earlier of the period remaining until the next interest rate reset date or the final stated maturity when determining an ECN's maturity for portfolio WAM calculation purposes. The first interest rate reset date is assumed to be the initial redemption date.

If an extension were to occur, Fitch expects that the fund would re-examine the practice of using the earlier of the period remaining until the next interest rate reset date or the final stated maturity for WAM calculation purposes. Under Rule 2a-7, a fund should follow this practice only if there is a reasonable expectation that the security would reset at a price approximating par. Depending on the factors causing an ECN extension, this expectation may no longer be accurate, and a fund may need to use an ECN's final maturity date when determining portfolio WAM.

ECNs are relatively new and untested investments. Therefore, until ECNs become widely accepted and liquid money market instruments, it would be prudent for a prime fund to purchase ECNs only from top-rated issuers while limiting its aggregate exposure to the product. As such, Fitch recommends that prime funds treat ECNs as illiquid investments and, therefore, limit their portfolio exposure to ECNs and other illiquid assets to less than 10% of total assets. Additionally, a fund's comfort with the asset type, as well as its confidence in the individual ECN issuer, should also be considered.

CONCLUSION

As investor demand for higher money market yields continues and competition among prime funds increases, funds will pursue investments that provide more yield while exposing the fund to minimal risk. At the root of these developments are many issues concerning increased liquidity, credit, and event risks for some of these innovative securities. Prime funds will continually need to analyze the risk and return tradeoffs of each new security type as the market for these instruments develops. As market acceptance and knowledge of these securities increases, the yields of these innovative securities will begin to decrease. Until this occurs, money funds which are able to dedicate the time and resources needed to analyze many of these innovative money market instruments will be able to capitalize on the new, and potentially profitable, opportunities that these instruments offer.

Chapter 8

Funding Agreements

Malcolm L. Jones
Director, Institutional Marketing
SunAmerica

Funding agreements — one of the fastest-growing financial instruments available to today's cash manager — are contracts issued by insurance companies to the nonqualified institutional market.

The contractholder, or policyholder, of a funding agreement receives interest — either fixed or variable rate (by way of a fixed spread to an index) — plus return of principal at contract maturity. Funding agreements may also provide opportunities for investors to exit the contract prior to maturity by way of an embedded par put option (usually with 7, 30, or 90 day's notice).

Funding agreements (FAs) are similar to guaranteed investment contracts (GICs) that insurance companies have been selling to the qualified pension market for many years. Funding agreements have been around since the mid-1980s but have seen explosive growth during the 1990s due primarily to the responsiveness and versatility of the funding agreement structure itself. According to Townsend and Schupp,[1] the sales of funding agreements doubled from 1997 to 1998, reaching $32 billion — a dramatic increase from the (estimated) $2.5 billion in sales in 1995. For 1999, funding agreement sales set another record, though growth slowed substantially.[2] This explosive growth has been driven by added product features: some long-dated funding agreements back note programs, others may include a put option feature or rolling 13-month maturity to meet the demands of the money market mutual fund sector.

Funding agreements can include short-term put structures, municipal funding agreements, and funding agreement-backed note issuance programs (primarily offshore). This chapter provides an overview of the short-term product as used by cash managers. It examines both the sellside and buyside of the market, and ends with a cautious look forward, given somber events of summer 1999.

WHAT ARE FUNDING AGREEMENTS?

To expand on the basic definition opening this chapter, a funding agreement is an insurance contract sold as a private placement and issued without registration

---

[1] The Townsend & Schupp Company, *1998 Funding Agreement Report.*
[2] The Townsend & Schupp Company, *1999 Funding Agreement Survey.*

under the Securities Act of 1933. As a type of insurance policy (explicit in certain states), funding agreements enjoy a senior status in the priority of payments compared with debt (commercial paper, for example) of an insurance company. An exception is the Commonwealth of Massachusetts where funding agreement contractholders are considered general unsecured creditors. In all three major life insurance company insolvencies occurring in the past decade, GICs issued by those companies were treated as policies by their respective regulators. Funding agreements are part of the spread management line of business for insurance companies and do not represent debt on their balance sheets.

Short-term funding agreements are similar to the GIC business that insurance companies have been writing for years, but without the (typical) benefit-responsive risk; they do have additional optionality risk in the form of puts. Funding agreements offer a guaranty of the contract's par value.

Risks and Ratings

Institutional investors that buy funding agreements from an insurance company take on the risk that the insurer can satisfy all policyholder claims when due, since, in most cases, the insurance company's general account supports funding agreement liabilities. As contractual obligations of the insurer, funding agreements themselves were generally not rated. Investors instead looked to the financial strength ratings of the insurer to determine its ability to meet those obligations. Recently agencies have begun to apply their ratings to funding agreements.

Independent credit analysis goes hand in hand with a review of the carrier's financial strength. Institutional investors have primarily required short-term ratings of A-1 (Standard & Poor's) and P1 (Moody's). Long-term ratings of active funding agreement providers range from the mid-A level to AAA/Aaa and further differentiate the financial strength of various funding agreement providers. Fitch also rates some insurance carriers, and all three agencies have begun to rate money market mutual funds.

Active Participants

The most active domestic participants in purchasing funding agreements are 2a-7 money market funds, bank short-term investment funds, and securities lending cash managers (see "The Buyside" section later in this chapter). Cash managers most often purchase variable-rate funding agreements offering a spread to a given index, usually 1-month or 3-month LIBOR (London interbank offered rate). Securities lending accounts often use the Federal Funds rate, and other indices are available. The choice of suitable index is determined by the needs of the purchasing fund.

Since funding agreements are not securities with a liquid secondary market, they are issued at a slight premium to other money market instruments such as commercial paper, even though they enjoy a superior lien status. This "illiquidity premium" varies by market segment and has been narrowing in recent years. While there have been occasional secondary market transactions involving funding agreements, in general, funding agreements have no secondary market.

Contractual Aspects

Each funding agreement is a contract negotiated between buyer and seller. These contracts can be customized to meet an institutional investor's requirements for such aspects as cash flows, fixed- or variable-rate preference, or legal structures. However, this same flexibility is reflective of nonstandardized contract terms that, in turn, present a concern to potential investors, terms that must be analyzed — usually by a fund's legal department. Note that insurance companies file the contract form with their state of domicile and with each state in which they write business.

Structured Liquidity

For funding agreements purchased by cash managers, structured liquidity is built into each contract. In the case of a 2a-7 regulated money market fund, structured liquidity in the form of an unconditional put or rolling maturity enables the fund to own funding agreements. Such agreements can be customized to meet the unique demands of an institutional investor. A key feature of funding agreements is that market value equals book value, viewed as a big plus by institutional investors charged with keeping a stable net asset value. Since no secondary market exists, market value is determined by what the policyholder can reasonably expect to receive given the features (such as reset frequency or put options) of the contract — and that is generally book value. Funding agreements also offer exposure to the insurance industry for institutional investors, since only a minimal amount of insurance company commercial paper is available for purchase. Funding agreements can aid a fund in meeting diversification requirements. Due to the very limited secondary market, all funding agreements, other than those with a 7-day put feature, are placed in the illiquid basket of a money market fund.

Maturity

Funding agreements issued to cash managers have in the past not had a final maturity. Rather, they had an evergreen structure, relying on the embedded put features to determine the eventual termination date of the contract. Recent contracts issued to 2a-7 funds have had rolling 1-year final maturities (a flexible maturity, always less than 397 days, giving the policyholder and the insurance company the right to extend the maturity of the contract) that extend monthly with positive consent from the contract holder. For certain 2a-7 funds, rolling 1-year maturities with no put but with monthly (or even daily) interest rate resets have proven popular. The interest rate reset frequency (coupled with a final maturity structure) enables a fund to take advantage of the maturity-shortening provision of 2a7; the funding agreement with a 30-day reset frequency can be considered a 30-day piece of paper for purposes of calculating weighted average maturity (a measure of interest rate sensitivity). For liquidity purposes, the 13-month final maturity is, of course, the arbiter.

Appealing Aspects

Funding agreements have proven popular with cash managers because they provide risk-adjusted incremental returns to the portfolio. They have been popular with insurance companies because they have been (with a notable exception, see "A Disturbance in the Force" later in this chapter) a profitable, risk-understood/risk-managed segment of their institutional spread business.

THE SELLSIDE

Funding agreements with optionality features (which make them attractive to money market funds and other short-term cash managers) have been a supply-constrained — not demand-constrained — instrument. While upwards of 25 insurance companies have issued funding agreements with these features, the top five issuers represent 50% of the market. There are currently about 10 companies actively issuing funding agreements though in any given week, for a particular structure (e.g., 7-day put feature) or terms, the number of issuers may be zero. Funding agreements with short puts have been marketed to institutional investors as a "core" holding and it is expected that the puts would not be used for trading purposes but are offered to:

- enable the fund to meet its investment requirements
- assist in meeting legitimate cash flow demands of the fund
- provide an exit provision in the event of credit event risk of the issuer (again, see "A Disturbance in the Force")

Superior Overall Credit

As stated earlier, the market for funding agreements is dominated by highly rated insurance companies and funding agreements (as insurance policies) enjoy a superior lien position. In fact, the strength of funding agreements may go beyond their issuers' high credit ratings and the superior lien position of funding agreements. Of all industries covered by S&P, the insurance industry has the third lowest default probability, 3.30% (1981-1999). The default risk for all industries in the same period was 7.99%. Default risk among GIC/funding agreement providers (typically higher rated insurance companies) was less than 0.50% for the same period. Furthermore, the insurance industry has the highest recovery rate (by a huge margin) of any of the industries tracked by S&P. The average defaulted corporate bond recovery rate was 56%; however, for insurance policies for companies coming out of rehabilitation the recovery rate was close to (or above!) 100%.[3]

---

[3] As reported in *Standard & Poor's Credit Week*, January 26, 2000.

Asset/Liability Management

The key to the spread side of an insurance company's business is asset/liability management. While the funding agreement product with its inherent optionality has performed as expected over time (basically, the business has persistency or is "sticky" and stays on the books of the insurance carrier for multiple years), an insurance company must manage the asset side of the equation to handle any and all possible withdrawals. The insurance company must manage both its assets and liabilities to provide sufficient liquidity to meet potential policyholder demands regardless of the external market environment. In other words, for a company issuing 90-day puts in some of its funding agreements, the investment portfolio behind such liabilities must be managed to allow for all of that business being put on any given day. In many cases this requirement places a capacity limit on the amount of short-term funding agreements (those with put options) that an insurance company can offer. Insurance companies believe that the put risk is quantifiable, underwriteable, and manageable.

Management Capabilities

It is important that an insurance company have strong fixed-income management skills and solid asset/liability management capabilities including the ability to model the rapid redemption of all putable funding agreements and to maintain sufficient liquidity to pay when due all liabilities. As Moody's Investors Service said in its April 1998 report on funding agreements, "… the put options sometimes extended to FA holders creates liquidity concerns and event risk."[4]

Perhaps the most difficult part of asset/liability management is the modeling of the duration of liabilities containing put options. Such business typically has had good persistency, and puts are rarely exercised. But investors must not assume that assets can be purchased to match the expected terminal duration of the liability without taking into account the optionality of the liability. This optionality aspect can expose the insurance company to significant asset/liability mismatch in the event of a run on the "bank" (insurance company). The ability to manage this segment of an insurance company's spread business on a profitable and yet risk-responsive basis is perhaps the truest test of a company's asset/liability expertise.

Other Inherent Risks

Beyond the liquidity event risk (a run on the bank) that needs to be managed, other specific risks to be managed by the insurance company include:

- contract notice period (the shorter the put, the less flexibility management has)
- basis risk
- derivative or counterparty risk (interest rate swaps)

---

[4] Moody's Special Comment, "Funding Agreements — A New Frontier of Stable Value," April 1998.

- duration risk (asset-liability mismatch)
- reinvestment risk
- credit risk
- less liquid securities in the portfolio
- concentration of potentially short-term liabilities
- lack of investor diversification

Insurance companies attempt to mitigate these risks by limiting the total amount of liabilities subject to put options, limiting exposure to fund complexes or decision makers, or prohibiting certain put options (for example, 7-day puts). Insurance companies attempt to earn a positive spread on their funding agreement business by taking minimal duration risk, taking some credit and/or interest rate risk, and controlling for the other risks mentioned.

THE BUYSIDE

While the focus of this chapter is on funding agreements purchased by cash managers, FAs are also issued to the municipal GIC market and the funding agreement-backed note market, the latter being the fastest growing segment in 1998-1999. But cash managers rule when it comes to short-term funding agreements, especially money market funds, bank short-term investment funds, and securities lending cash managers.

A study of 1998 funding agreement sales by The Townsend & Schupp Company found that cash management — money market funds, bank short-term investment funds (STIFs), corporate cash, and securities lending) — accounts for over 57% of the funding agreement purchases with money market funds being the single largest buyer segment. The buying pattern remained much the same through 1999. A study of Moody's rated prime money market funds showed that 46% invest in funding agreements with an average holding 4% of assets in funding agreements. Moody's study also showed that money market fund purchases of funding agreements doubled from 1997 to 1998 and continued to grow in 1999. This growing demand from prime money market funds has established funding agreements as a new asset class. Money market funds have the strongest demand for funding agreements with a 7-day put option that would allow the contract to be placed in the liquid basket of the fund. However, this is the segment where, understandably, there was the least supply by the insurance industry. The majority of money market fund purchases have puts longer than seven days or have a rolling 1-year final maturity with no put.

With the expansion of rated money market funds (most rated AAA/Aaa), increased attention from a different side of the rating agencies (different than the side that rates the insurance companies) has occurred. All credit agencies rating money market mutual funds have concluded that funding agreements are eligible investments for such funds. At the same time, all of these agencies have been quick to highlight the risks involved in a fund investing in funding agreements. Not surprisingly, the largest risk cited was the "run on the bank" scenario where an insurance company would have insufficient liquidity to meet all demands when due. In its December 1998 report on funding agreements, Moody's says the following about a put option run:

> While an FA put run has not yet occurred, there is nonetheless the possibility ... [a] credit event such as a short-term rating downgrade of an issuer ... could serve as a trigger for money funds holding that insurer's FAs to engage their put option... In the case of a weakened credit profile for a short-term FA, a fund manager's only choice may be to engage the put option.[5]

A DISTURBANCE IN THE FORCE

Summer 1999 saw not only the release of a new *Star Wars* film but also the occurrence of the first put run in funding agreements. The victim was General American Life, a St. Louis-based insurer and leading participant in the offering of short-term funding agreements. General American's push into funding agreements had been unique. A reinsurance contract with ARM Financial Group Inc. was in force whereby ARM (through its insurance subsidiary, Integrity Life) assumed 50% of the funding agreements written by General American. Importantly, General American was still the "issuer" of the entire funding agreement amount, but was now exposed to not only its own asset-management risks but also the risks of ARM.

Of approximately $6.8 billion in funding agreements issued by General American, over $5 billion was held by money market funds. Almost that entire portion had been issued with 7-day puts. Moody's estimated that General American "had approximately 60% of the entire seven-day short-term funding agreement market."[6] Also, these 7-day put contracts represented a very large percentage of the total assets of General American Life. As a colleague of this author said, "a seven-day put is no substitute for good credit analysis," and, "in the event of a put run, an insurance company's asset/liability management better be darn good." It turns out that General American's asset/liability management consisted of borrowing short and lending long with disastrous results. The stage was set.

Downgrades Waiting in the Wings

ARM's subsidiary, Integrity Life, had financial strength ratios below those of General American. Until July 1999, General American Life had carried AA/AA-/A2

---

[5] Moody's Special Comment, "High Yield, Stable Value Attract Money Market Funds to Funding Agreements," December 1998.

[6] Moody's Special Comment, "General American: A Study in Liquidity Risk," August 1999.

long-term and D-1+, A-1+ and (implied) P1 short-term credit ratings from Duff & Phelps,[7] S&P, and Moody's, respectively. Things began to unravel in July 1999. ARM reported a huge second quarter loss and General American announced that it would recapture the liabilities (and corresponding assets) that it had reinsured to ARM/Integrity Life. Moody's lowered Integrity Life's ratings to Baa3 from Baa1 and also lowered General American's claims-paying ratings to A3 with the possibility of further downgrades. At the A3 level, most money market managers believed the implied short-term rating to be P2. With ratings at that level, General American's funding agreements were on their way to being no longer eligible for 2a7 funds to hold. Rule 2a7 requires two top category ratings from two NRSROs (nationally recognized statistical rating organizations). Even though S&P confirmed its AA−/A-1+ rating, the run had begun. The run became inevitable, and the outcome predictable, when Moody's quickly lowered the carrier's rating to Ba1 on August 9. S&P followed a day later by lowering its long-term rating to BBB− and short-term rating to A-3.

Liquidity Crisis

Suddenly, General American Life was faced with paying over $5 billion in principal plus interest, all over approximately seven days as puts were exercised. While the company was solvent, with assets exceeding liabilities, it had a short-term liquidity crisis. The puts occurred predictably at exactly the wrong time — when ratings were under pressure and the need for liquidity was greatest. An attempt to liquidate a substantial portion of its investment portfolio (already encumbered with embedded losses in a weak bond market) in such a short time frame would have produced even greater losses. This point highlights the issue of how quickly a company can liquidate assets in a stress scenario and at what prices. While such a sale probably could have provided sufficient money to pay the puts when due, it would have put other policyholders at risk. On August 10, General American announced that it was unable to pay when due the total value of puts recently exercised by institutional investors. General American chose to seek relief from the State of Missouri by being placed under administrative supervision and, as a result, Moody's further lowered their rating B1; and Standard & Poor's lowered their rating to BBB−. A substantial majority of the puts exercised were not paid when due. General American was sold to Metropolitan Life on August 25, 1999. At the beginning of October, all puts were paid in full with accrued interest.

What was learned from the General American Life default? First, this was a company-specific event, not a problem that reflected either a fundamental problem with funding agreements or with the insurance industry as a whole. It also is a problem that was resolved with all contractholders receiving all of their principal plus accrued interest, albeit not when originally due. It also demonstrated that access to liquidity is a critical component of the asset-liability man-

---

[7] In 2000, Duff & Phelps was acquired by Fitch.

agement of any insurance carrier issuing funding agreements with short puts. Some funds have reportedly decided they will no longer purchase funding agreements; others are taking a wait-and-see attitude, and all are asking more detailed questions of their other funding agreement carriers.

CONCLUSION

The final comments on funding agreements could have written themselves prior to the General American situation. Namely, funding agreements provide risk-adjusted positive incremental returns for investors. For insurance companies, funding agreements are a profitable and risk-managed portion of their spread business. As this chapter was written in mid-2000, demand for funding agreements was again picking up.

For funding agreements purchased by cash managers, investors are more credit focused and examine short-term funding agreements and their providers with a closer eye. There are fewer insurance companies offering funding agreements and no 7-day puts were being offered directly by insurance companies.

A premium (in the form of lower spreads) was being paid for the highest credits versus lower-rated carriers. The domestic funding agreement market has survived the events of 1999 and funding agreements remain a prudent option for cash managers.

Chapter 9

Assessing Short-Term Funding Agreements in Money Market Funds and Cash Pools

Douglas A. Rivkin
Vice President/Senior Credit Officer
Moody's Investors Service

In 1997 through 1999, U.S. money market funds increased their investments in insurance company-issued short-term *funding agreements* (FAs).[1] Drawn to the market by the FAs' competitive yield spreads, U.S. money market funds look to short-term FAs as an alternative to other money market fund securities. The high number of U.S. prime money market funds that purchase FAs have firmed their position as a major asset class for money market funds. We note, however, that

---

[1] For a discussion of Funding Agreements from Moody's insurance group, see the Moody's Special Comment "Funding Agreements – The New Frontier of Stable Value," April 1998 and "Institutional Investment Products: The Evolution of a Popular Product," April 2000.

---

while the FA market promises yield, stability, and liquidity, the U.S. money market fund industry's holdings in short-term FAs do subject investors to the risks of the insurance company providers. This fact became reality with the default of General American Life Insurance Company (General American) FAs in August of 1999.

On the underwriting side, insurance companies, in an effort to grow their guaranteed investment contract (GIC)/FA businesses (and address a slower pension GIC business), are targeting the $1.6 trillion U.S. money market fund industry in their push to seek new funding sources.

Their efforts seem to be working. At present, the majority of outstanding FA contracts are held by money market funds and other short-term investors. A study in early 2000 of Moody's rated prime money market funds reveals that 36% now invest in FAs, with an average holding of 3% of assets and a highest exposure at 8.1% of assets. New FA sales slowed immediately after the General American default, but have since resumed to a healthy pace in the first half of 2000. In all, the universe of FA contracts now totals roughly $30 billion spread out over 25 U.S. insurers. (Reporting inconsistencies in both the insurance industry and the money market fund industry make it difficult to get actual numbers.)

Some money market funds have been purchasing short-term "investment-only" GICs and FAs from a few insurers for years. Although FAs have been around for many years, they have primarily been customized for municipalities as "muni GICs" and have had limited use in money market funds. Their popularity has exploded only recently, with the insurance companies' stepped-up marketing efforts.

JUST LIKE A GIC

Funding agreements are stable-value, spread-based, products that have become a popular version of the traditional pension GIC. Their investment characteristics are summarized in Exhibit 1. FAs are fixed-rate or floating-rate, privately placed insurance company liabilities, not registered with the Securities and Exchange Commission, guaranteed by the insurer's general account or a separate account. Short-term FAs differ from traditional GICs in a few ways. They are offered to the nonqualified institutional market as opposed to pension GICs, which are primarily offered to the qualified market. Also, they have liquidity put options instead of the "benefit responsive" features of pension GICs.

Historically, GICs and FAs have not been individually rated. To help satisfy investment rating requirements, money market funds are using the FA insurer's long-term financial strength rating, and/or the insurer may seek a short-term financial strength rating to help fulfill fund rating needs. Recently, many insurers have attained short-term financial strength ratings that directly assess FA risks.

Exhibit 1: Short-Term Funding Agreements versus GICs
A Comparison of Investment Characteristics

Investment	Target Institutional Market	Main Features
Short-Term Funding Agreements	Nonqualified short-term investors	Liquidity put option Final maturity extending rolling repurchase
GICs		
Pension	Qualified plan Medium- or long-term investors	Group annuity contract Benefit responsive
Synthetic	Qualified plan Medium- or long-term investors	Benefit responsive Direct security ownership Insurance wrapper
Muni	Nonqualified Short-, medium-, or long-term investors	Stated maturity or put option
Investment Only	Nonqualified Short-, medium-, or long-term investors	Stated maturity or put option

Credit Risk

On a credit risk basis, FA investors are taking on the risk of the insurance company as the full faith and credit supporter of the FA liability, because the FA is a direct obligation of the insurance company. An insurance company's credit and insurance financial strength ratings will indicate the relative credit risk that the money market fund is taking on and the likelihood of any problems at the company. Money market funds generally buy FAs from large high quality insurers with diversified businesses.

The continued viability of an insurance company, is therefore critical to the success of its FA program. This success will be determined by the very nature of the insurance business — specifically, how well the insurance company manages risk.

Short-term FAs, meanwhile, add a new dynamic into an insurer's risk management, making it necessary for insurers to account properly for the credit sensitivities of the money market fund industry. For insurance companies to remain successful in the short-term FA business, they will have to maintain high credit-quality ratings, understand the 2a-7 regulatory market, develop a strong money market fund customer base, offer competitive returns, and manage asset/liability risks appropriately.

The significant growth in FA holdings by the money market fund industry means that the insurers have more liabilities in the highly liquid, short-term money market fund industry. This balance between these industries is still somewhat immature, however the recent General American default made clear that the credit and liquidity sensitivities of money market funds by their predominate choice to liquidate in that case versus hold a weakening credit.

The General American Case in Perspective[2]

The General American case is cited numerous times throughout this chapter since it provides excellent examples for FA risk analysis. It must be noted, however, that the complex liquidity and asset problems that caused General American FAs to default in August of 1999 is generally thought to be extreme as compared to any industry standards. Also, it must be noted that in the end, all General American FA contractors were made whole after Metropolitan Life purchased the distressed company in late 1999.

In short, General American with $6.8 billion of putable FAs, at the time of default in August of 1999, had an estimated 19% of the short-term funding agreement market with $5 billion or an estimated whopping 60% marketshare of the riskier 7-day put contracts. When certain market and credit events caused many FA investors to engage their 7-day puts around the same time, General American was unable to meet those requests and defaulted.

Other life insurers, then and now, have a much more moderate exposure to the short-term FA business. The probability of a similar liquidity crunch with current insurers is small.

WHY MONEY MARKET FUNDS INVEST IN FUNDING AGREEMENTS

FAs are custom designed to meet an institution's investment needs regarding cash flows, terms, fixed or floating rates, and legal structures. Money market funds primarily purchase short-term FAs that mature or can be liquidated, via a put option, in under one year. Short-term FAs are designed to qualify as 2a-7 eligible money market fund investments.

Highly Competitive Yields/Spreads

FAs offer money market funds some of the most competitive yields in the industry. In fact, their yields are often higher than most other securities in a fund's portfolio. Reported spreads have been 2 to 20 basis points above high-quality commercial paper, with similar maturity characteristics (versus the FA put option period).

Money market funds primarily purchase floating-rate FA contracts based on fixed spreads on money market indices including: LIBOR, Fed Funds, U.S. treasuries, the prime rate or commercial paper. Yields will vary based on the credit rating of the insurance company, the FA asset/liability strategy,[3] the contract put option, final maturity, and the current yield curve environment.

---

[2] For a discussion of Funding Agreements from Moody's insurance group, see the Moody's Special Comment "General American: A Case Study In Liquidity Risk," August 1999.

[3] The FA asset/liability strategy refers to the method an insurance company uses in managing an FA liability. These liabilities are carried in an FA "deposit fund" which is an insurer's recordkeeping account for FAs. An FA deposit fund does not imply a legal structure.

Stable Value

FAs protect the fund's capital with a guarantee of the contract's par amount from the insurance company. This stable-value feature is very enticing to constant NAV money market funds because an individual fund's FA contribution value (par investment) remains fixed throughout the life of the contract.

Put Option Provides Liquidity

Short-term FAs have a maturity of 13 months or less, and/or incorporate an unconditional put option with a 7, 30, 90, 180 day, or 1 year notice period in the contract. Most outstanding FAs in money market funds have the put option feature, and the majority of those puts are over 30 days. Recently, and in light of the General American default, most new FA contracts are sold with puts of 90 days or more.

In general, FA programs do have sufficient liquidity to meet moderate put option requests. FA liability portfolios generally have durations in the 1 to 3 range, with a portion of assets in cash and short-term liquid securities. Additionally, insurers often have other liquidity sources to tap if needed.

The timeframe of the FA's put option will determine how money market funds classify the FA investment. Short-term FAs have no secondary liquidity market, so those with a term over seven days are carried in the 10% illiquid bucket of securities allowed by the SEC. FAs of seven days or less are considered to be liquid.

Put Options Rarely Exercised

The competitive yields and stable value of FAs make them very desirable for money market funds to hold in today's market. For those reasons, a money market fund manager will rarely use a funding agreement's put option. Practically speaking, money market funds can hold FAs perpetually. This negates a portfolio manager's need to replace FAs, since they generally will not reach maturity.

Final Maturities

Many of the early short-term FAs were sold with a put option and without a final maturity, essentially producing a perpetual short-term investment. Recent trends and money market fund regulatory requirements have required fund managers to request stated final maturities on all new FAs.

However, many insurers have instituted features that make an FA contract renewable on a monthly basis, effectively producing a forward-rolling, 1-year or 13-month final maturity. With this feature, a money market fund manager will repurchase the FA each month unless he or she decides to not renew the FA contract.

AREAS OF CONCERN FOR FA INVESTORS

Asset/Liability Risk Management

An insurance company backs FAs through an active asset/liability management process. Therefore, an insurer must fully understand the level of risk on both the asset and liability side of its FA deposits. Poor management in this area can pose risks to investors, as outlined in Exhibit 2. A well-managed asset/liability program is critical for the proper risk and liquidity structuring of an FA and GIC program.

Regulatory/Legal Issues

Insurance companies are not federally regulated. Instead, they are regulated by the insurance department of the state in which they are domiciled and by each state in which they write business. Each state determines whether an FA is a policyholder liability, and this is the critical determination for priority of claims relative to outstanding debt and policy obligations.

While some states specifically mention FAs and GICs in their regulatory laws, other states have left the issue unresolved. To address this concern, some insurers in those states that lack clear definition on this issue have requested and received "comfort" letters from legal firms that are familiar with the state's insurance laws. Moody's believes that money market fund investors should be familiar with state insurance laws regarding their FA exposure.

Exercised Puts

Because FAs are desirable to hold, there is a very low incidence of put execution, and consequently insurer FA liability assets may be managed more aggressively. In the short history of the FA market, there has been little variation in put executions baring any credit or market trigger event. In the General American case, nearly all of the outstanding puts were exercised in the wake of concurrent credit and market events that had a material impact on the insurer. It is likely that intermittently, future credit or market conditions will increase put executions. The frequency or severity of such executions is difficult to predict.

Exhibit 2: Funding Agreements
An Insurers Asset/Liability Management Risks

Risk	Scenario	Possible Result
Put Option Commitments	Leverage through duration drift. The duration of the assets held for FA liabilities could be much longer than the outstanding FA put option commitments.	The shorter the outstanding puts, the less room to maneuver assets if put options are exercised.
Low Asset Quality	The insurer holds a high percentage of low-credit-quality securities.	Higher potential for credit loss.
Less Liquid Securities	The insurer holds a high percentage of less liquid securities.	Higher potential for market loss.
Asset Leverage	The insurer is leveraged in liabilities relative to assets.	Mismatch may leverage loss.
Reinsurance	The insurer's FA liabilities are reinsured by a less creditworthy insurance company.	Weaker insurer may default on liabilities.
Concentration in Short-Term Liabilities	An insurer has a large portion of its total liabilities due in a year or less.	Higher sensitivity to investor sentiment change.
Franchise Reputation	Investor sentiment turns negative, causing panic run on an insurer's liabilities.	Damaged reputation deters investors.
FA Liability Structure	An insurer's FA liabilities are not separated from its general account.	Liabilities are not insolvency or regulatory seizure remote.

Possibility of a Liquidity Put Option "Run"

General American has provided the first put option run experience on an insurer's FA business and thus confirms the possibility that one could arise again from a market and or credit event that negatively affects an insurance company's confidence-sensitive and credit-sensitive markets. A credit event such as a short-term rating downgrade of an insurer, by itself or in conjunction with other events, could serve as a trigger for money market funds holding that insurer's FAs to engage their put options, as was the case with General American.

The risk of a put run is defined by the fact that U.S. money market funds are publicly held, highly credit- and liquidity-sensitive cash pools. Fund portfolio managers actively monitor their investments and are required to mark their portfolios to market weekly. Typically, these fund portfolio managers will liquidate securities for which the credit profile has weakened, or let them roll off. In the case of a weakened credit profile for a short-term FA, a fund manager's only choice may be to engage the put option.

A put option run on an insurer's FA liability portfolio could force that insurer to realize losses and seek other liquidity sources to meet FA contractholder requests. The FA market's brief history as a significant asset class in money market funds has not provided any meaningful put engagement experience to predict the roll-off of an insurer's FA liabilities. In the General American case, an orderly roll-off did not occur due to a put option run. In the GIC market, orderly roll-offs of an insurer's liability portfolio have occurred; however, in several other cases GIC providers have suffered losses through liquidations.

Very short puts, those of 7-day and 30-day terms, pose the most risk of a put option run due to the short timeframe in which the insurer has to meet liquidity requests. The majority of outstanding and exercised puts in the General American case were the shortest 7-day type that forced the insurer to default. Recent industry trends away from 7-day and 30 day puts to the 90-day or longer puts have greatly reduced the risk of a put run of very short-term options. These longer puts provide more time to an insurer and therefore may help it manage an orderly roll-off of put requests.

As in the commercial paper market, funding sources (short-term FAs) may dry up quickly after a significant rating downgrade. The commercial paper market's "self policing" nature has historically weathered these downgrades in an orderly fashion, as outstanding paper simply matures on schedule. An orderly roll-off of an insurer's FA liabilities may not be possible, since the engagement of outstanding put option commitments is not highly predictable.

Limited Precedent of Historical GIC/FA Problems

As with GICs, any problems at the insurance company level could place the FA contractholders' principle and interest at risk. While GICs from the large insurance company insolvencies in the early 1990s (Executive Life, Mutual Benefit, and Confederation Life) did receive preferential treatment relative to general creditor status, future outcomes of insolvencies may vary as determined by state or other regulators.

After the problems in the early 1990s, many GIC users sought separate-account GICs or synthetic GICs — products for which the investor would own, directly, longer-dated securities with an attached insurance "wrapper." (The direct ownership of long-term securities would render synthetic GICs ineligible for use in money market funds.). Separate-account GICs, from an investment standpoint, separate the assets of a GIC from the insurance company's general account and may offer some protection should an insurance company run into problems. As with other insurance regulatory issues, this separate-account claim is a gray area to be determined by a state's insurance department or other regulatory body.

The General American case did provide some valuable lessons. The main lessons are the need for adequate liquidity (versus solvency) to meet FA obligations and the vulnerability of reinsuring with a lower quality insurer. While these lessons are clear, their value is limited because at the time of default General American was the most aggressive FA provider by such a wide margin, and therefore its FAs were not comparable to the rest of the FA providers.

Likelihood of Timely Payment Risk

In addition to the risk posed to investment principal and interest, FAs are vulnerable to a more probable risk regarding timely liquidity or maturity payments. This stems from the possibility that a troubled insurance company could be seized by a state's insurance department and enter a phase of rehabilitation or possible liquidation. In this case, months or years could pass before FA contractholders would be able to access their funds. During insolvencies in the early 1990s at Executive Life, Mutual Benefit, and Confederation Life, insurance regulators seized each insurer's assets and placed a moratorium on surrenders.

Ultimately, this is exactly what happened in the General American case. Engaged puts were not honored and at General American's request, state regulators took over the administrative supervision of the insurer and froze surrenders until sometime after the Met Life acquisition of General American.

Structural Contract Risk

FAs pose structural risk based on the fact that they are individually negotiated and unregistered (SEC) private placements. The market has not matured to the point where standard, boilerplate, legally tested, language is used for FAs. In addition, contracts may not be uniformly interpreted due to the industry's oversight by many local regulatory authorities.

Knowing Risk, Avoiding a Surprise

While FAs can be safe and rewarding investments for money market funds, they may not be appropriate for all money market funds. Moody's believes that it is important for investors to understand why their money market funds invest in FAs, and whether FAs fall within the investment strategy for the fund. Also important is whether the incremental exposure to an insurance company's risk is worth the boost in yield.

The relatively high yields paid by FAs may provide more satisfaction to money market funds and investors when risks are known and there are no surprises. Investors who hold FAs should therefore take it upon themselves to understand the risks of the FA contracts into which they enter. Each FA will incorporate a range of structural issues and product features that require discrimination and understanding. Investors and insurers alike must also anticipate relevant market and credit events that affect the FA market in order to maintain proper balance between their industries.

Chapter 10

Floating-Rate Securities

Frank J. Fabozzi, Ph.D., CFA
Adjunct Professor of Finance
School of Management
Yale University

Steven V. Mann, Ph.D.
Associate Professor of Finance
The Darla Moore School of Business
University of South Carolina

Cash managers invest in not only short-term fixed-rate securities but also floating-rate securities that exhibit little price volatility when interest rates change. In this chapter, we will discuss the general features of floating-rate securities (or simply "floaters"), their price volatility characteristics, and "spread" measures used by market participants. There are floaters in the agency debenture and corporate bond markets. There are also floating-rate products created in the mortgage-backed and asset-backed securities markets. These securities will be discussed in Chapters 11 and 12, along with short-term fixed-rate products created in these markets.

GENERAL FEATURES OF FLOATERS

A floater is a debt obligation whose coupon rate is reset at designated dates based on the value of some designated reference rate. The coupon formula for a pure floater (i.e., a floater with no embedded options) can be expressed as follows:

coupon rate = reference rate ± quoted margin

The quoted margin is the adjustment (in basis points) that the issuer agrees to make to the reference rate. For example, consider a floating-rate note issued by Enron Corp. that matured on March 30, 2000. This floater made quarterly cash flows and had a coupon formula equal to 3-month LIBOR plus 45 basis points.

Under the rubric of floating-rate securities, there are several different types of securities with the feature that the coupon rate varies over the instrument's life. A

Parts of this chapter are adapted from Frank J. Fabozzi and Steven V. Mann, *Floating-Rate Securities* (New Hope, PA: Frank J. Fabozzi Associates, 2000).

floater's coupon rate can be reset semiannually, quarterly, monthly or weekly. The term "adjustable-rate" or "variable-rate" typically refers to those securities with coupon rates reset not more than annually or based on a longer-term interest rate. We will refer to both floating-rate securities and adjustable-rate securities as floaters.

As noted, the reference rate is the interest rate or index that appears in a floater's coupon formula and it is used to determine the coupon payment on each reset date within the boundaries designated by embedded caps and/or floors. Common reference rates are LIBOR (with different maturities), Treasury bills yields, the prime rate, the federal funds rate, and domestic CD rates. There are other reference rates utilized in more specialized taxable fixed-income markets such as the mortgage-backed securities and asset-backed securities markets. For example, the most common reference rates for adjustable-rate mortgages (ARMs) or collateralized mortgage obligation (CMO) floaters include: (1) the 1-year Constant Maturity Treasury rate (i.e., 1-year CMT); (2) the Eleventh District Cost of Funds (COFI); (3) 6-month LIBOR; and (4) the National Monthly Median Cost of Funds Index.

Restrictions on the Coupon Rate

A floater often imposes limits on how much the coupon rate can float. Specifically, a floater may have a restriction on the maximum coupon rate that will be paid on any reset date. This is called a *cap*. Consider a hypothetical floater whose coupon formula is 3-month LIBOR plus 50 basis points with a cap of 7.5%. If 3-month LIBOR at a coupon reset date is 8%, then the coupon formula would suggest the new coupon rate is 8.5%. However, the cap restricts the maximum coupon rate to 7.5%. Needless to say, a cap is an unattractive feature from the investor's perspective.

In contrast, a floater may also specify a minimum coupon rate called a *floor*. For example, First Chicago (now 1st Chicago NBD Corp.) issued a floored floating rate note in July 1993 that matures in July 2003. This issue delivers quarterly coupon payments with a coupon formula of 3-month LIBOR plus 12.5 basis points with a floor of 4.25%. So if 3-month LIBOR ever fell below 4.125% the coupon rate would remain at 4.25%. A floor is an attractive feature from the investor's perspective.

When a floater possesses both a cap and a floor, this feature is referred to as a *collar*. Thus, a collared floater's coupon rate has a maximum and a minimum value. For example, the Economic Development Corporation issued a collared floater in February 1993 that makes semiannual coupon payments and matures in 2003. The coupon formula is 6-month LIBOR flat with a floor of 5% and a cap of 8%.[1]

Inverse Floaters

While a floater's coupon rate typically moves in the same direction as the reference rate, there are floaters whose coupon rate moves in the opposite direction to

---

[1] Here, the term flat means without a quoted margin or a quoted margin of zero.

the change in the reference rate. These securities are called *inverse floaters* or *reverse floaters*. The general coupon formula for an inverse floater is:

$$K - L \times (\text{Reference rate}).$$

From the formula, it is easy to see that as the reference rate goes up (down), the coupon rate goes down (up).

As an example, consider an inverse floater issued by one of the Federal Home Loan Banks in April 1999 due in April 2002. This issue delivers quarterly coupon payments according to the formula:

$$18\% - 2.5 \times (3\text{-month LIBOR})$$

In addition, this inverse floater has a floor of 3% and a cap of 15.5%. Note that for this floater the value for L (called the *coupon leverage*) in the coupon reset formula is 2.5. Assuming neither the cap rate nor the floor rate are binding, this means that for every one basis point change in 3-month LIBOR the coupon rate changes by 2.5 basis points in the opposite direction. When L is greater than 1, the security is referred to as a *leveraged inverse floater.*

Unfortunately, some cash managers and managers of short-duration portfolios have purchased inverse floaters based on the belief that these floating-rate products provide a hedge against a decline in interest rates. While the coupon rate does increase when the reference rate decreases, inverse floaters have the unfavorable property that their durations are typically very high. That is, they typically have high effective durations, a characteristic not understood by managers who still view "duration" in temporal terms (i.e., in terms of years). Certainly, these two features of an inverse floater — higher coupon rate when rates decline and substantial price appreciation due to a high effective duration — are appealing to a manager who wants to bet on a downward movement of rates. But clearly, this is not the approach that should be pursued by a manager who seeks to maintain a stable value for a portfolio when rates change.

Other Types of Floaters

There is a wide variety of floaters that have special features that may appeal to certain types of investors. For example, some issues provide for a change in the quoted margin (i.e., the spread added to or subtracted from the reference in the coupon reset formula) at certain intervals over a floater's life. These issues are called *stepped spread floaters* because the quoted margin can either step to a higher or lower level over time. Consider Standard Chartered Bank's floater due in December 2006. From its issuance in December 1996 until December 2001, the coupon formula is 3-month LIBOR plus 40 basis points. However, from December 2001 until maturity, the quoted margin "steps up" to 90 basis points.

A *range note* is a floater where the coupon payment depends upon the number of days that the specified reference rate stays within a preestablished collar. For instance, Sallie Mae issued a range note in August 1996 (due in August 2003) that makes coupon payments quarterly. For every day during the quarter that 3-month LIBOR is between 3% and 9%, the investor earns 3-month LIBOR plus 155 basis points. Interest will accrue at 0% for each day that 3-month LIBOR is outside this collar.

There are also floaters whose coupon formula contains more than one reference rate. A *dual-indexed floater* is one such example. The coupon rate formula is typically a fixed percentage plus the difference between two reference rates. For example, the Federal Home Loan Bank System issued a floater in July 1993 (due in July 1996) whose coupon rate was the difference between the 10-year Constant Maturity Treasury rate and 3-month LIBOR plus 160 basis points.

Although the reference rate for most floaters is an interest rate or an interest rate index, numerous kinds of reference rates appear in coupon formulas. This is especially true for structured notes. Potential reference rates include movements in foreign exchange rates, the price of a commodity (e.g., gold), movements in an equity index (e.g., the Standard & Poor's 500 Index), or an inflation index (e.g., CPI). Financial engineers are capable of structuring floaters with almost any reference rate. For example, Merrill Lynch issued in April 1983 Stock Market Reset Term Notes which matured in December 1999. These notes delivered semiannual coupon payments using a formula of 0.65 multiplied by the annual return of the Standard & Poor's MidCap 400 during the calendar year. These notes have a cap rate of 10% and a floor rate of 3%.

Of course, with these non-traditional (i.e., non-interest rate reference rates) floaters expose portfolios to different types of risks. Moreover, some of them are not simple to value — an undesireable feature for a cash portfolio.

Call and Prepayment Provisions

Just like fixed-rate issues, a floater may be *callable*. The call option gives the issuer the right to buy back the issue prior to the stated maturity date. The call option may have value to the issuer some time in the future for two reasons. First, market interest rates may fall so that the issuer can exercise the option to retire the floater and replace it with a fixed-rate issue. Second, the required margin decreases so that the issuer can call the issue and replace it with a floater with a lower quoted margin.[2] The issuer's call option is a disadvantage to the investor since the proceeds received must be reinvested either at a lower interest rate or a lower margin. Consequently, an issuer who wants to include a call feature when issuing a floater must compensate investors by offering a higher quoted margin.

For amortizing securities (e.g., mortgage-backed and some asset-backed securities) that are backed by loans that have a schedule of principal repayments, individual borrowers typically have the option to pay off all or part of their loan prior to the scheduled date. Any principal repayment in excess of the scheduled amount is

---

[2] The required margin is the spread (either positive or negative) the market requires as compensation for the risks embedded in the issue. If the required margin equals the quoted margin, a floater's price will be at par on coupon reset dates.

called a *prepayment*. The right of borrowers to prepay is called the *prepayment option*. Basically, the prepayment option is analogous to a call option. However, unlike a call option, there is not a call price that depends on when the borrower pays off the issue. Typically, the price at which a loan is prepaid is its par value.

Put Provisions

Floaters may also include a *put provision* which gives the security holder the option to sell the security back to the issuer at a specified price on designated dates. The specified price is called the *put price*. The put's structure can vary across issues. Some issues permit the holder to require the issuer to redeem the issue on any coupon payment date. Others allow the put to be exercised only when the coupon is adjusted.

The advantage of the put provision to the holder of the floater is that if after the issue date the margin required by the market for a floater to trade at par rises above the issue's quoted margin, absent the put option the price of the floater will decline. However, with the put option, the investor can force the issuer to redeem the floater at the put price and then reinvest the proceeds in a floater with the higher quoted margin.

PRICE VOLATILITY CHARACTERISTICS OF FLOATERS

The change in the price of a fixed-rate security when market rates change is due to the fact that the security's coupon rate differs from the prevailing market rate. So, an investor in a 10-year 7% coupon bond purchased at par, for example, will find that the price of this bond will decline below par value if the market requires a yield greater than 7%. By contrast, for a floater, the coupon is reset periodically, reducing a floater's price sensitivity to changes in rates. For this reason, floaters are said to more "defensive" securities. However, this does not mean that a floater's price will not change.

Factors that Affect the Price of a Floater

A floater's price will change depending on the following factors:

1. time remaining to the next coupon reset date
2. whether or not the market's required margin changes
3. whether or not the cap or floor is reached

Below we discuss the impact of each of these factors.

Time Remaining to the Next Coupon Reset Date

The longer the time to the next coupon reset date, the greater a floater's potential price fluctuation. Conversely, the less time to the next coupon reset date, the smaller the floater's potential price fluctuation.

To understand why, consider a floater with five years remaining to maturity whose coupon formula is the 1-year Treasury bill rate plus 50 basis points and the coupon is reset today when the 1-year Treasury bill rate is 5.5%. The coupon rate will then be set at 6% for the year. One month from now, the investor in this floater would effectively own an 11-month instrument with a 6% coupon. Suppose that at that time, the market wants a 6.2% yield on comparable issues with 11 months remaining to maturity. Then, our floater would be offering a below market rate (6% versus 6.2%). The floater's price must decline below par to compensate for the sub-market yield. Similarly, if the yield that the market requires on a comparable instrument with a maturity of 11 months is less than 6%, the price of a floater will trade above par. For a floater in which the cap is not reached and for which the market does not demand a margin different from the quoted margin, a floater that resets daily will trade at par value.

Whether or Not the Market's Required Margin Changes

At the initial offering of a floater, the issuer will set the quoted margin based on market conditions so that the security will trade near par. If after the initial offering the market requires a higher margin, the floater's price will decline to reflect the higher spread. We shall refer to the margin that is demanded by the market as the required margin. So, for example, consider a floater whose coupon formula is 1-month LIBOR plus 40 basis points. If market conditions change such that the required margin increases to 50 basis points, this floater would be offering a below market quoted margin. As a result, the floater's price will decline below par value. The price can trade above par value if the required margin is less than the quoted margin — less than 40 basis points in our example.

The required margin for a specific issue depends on: (1) the margin available in competitive funding markets, (2) the credit quality of the issue, (3) the presence of the embedded call or put options, and (4) the liquidity of the issue. In the case of floaters, an alternative funding source is a syndicated loan. Consequently, the required margin will be affected by margins available in the syndicated loan market.

The portion of the required margin attributable to credit quality is referred to as the *credit spread*. The risk that there will be an increase in the credit spread required by the market is called *credit spread risk*. The concern for credit spread risk applies not only to an individual issue, but to a sector and the economy as a whole. For example, the credit spread of an individual issuer may change not due to that issuer but to the sector or the economy as a whole.

A portion of the required margin will reflect the call risk associated with the floater. Because the call feature is a disadvantage to the investor, the greater the call risk, the higher the quoted margin at issuance. After issuance, depending on how rates and margins change in the market, the perceived call risk and the margin attributable to this risk will change accordingly. In contrast to call risk due to the presence of the call provision, a put provision is an advantage to the investor. If a floater is putable at par, all other factors constant, its price should trade at par near the put date.

Finally, a portion of the quoted margin at issuance will reflect the perceived liquidity of the issue. The risk that the required margin attributable to liquidity will increase due to market participants' perception of a deterioration in the issue's liquidity is called *liquidity risk*. Investors in non-traditional floater products are particularly concerned with liquidity risk.

Whether or Not the Cap or Floor Is Reached
For a floater with a cap, once the coupon rate as specified by the coupon formula rises above the cap, the floater then offers a below market coupon rate, and its price will decline below par. The floater will trade more and more like a fixed-rate security the further the capped rate is below the prevailing market rate. This risk that the value of the floater will decline because the cap is reached is referred to as cap risk.

On the other side of the coin, if the floater has a floor, once the floor is reached, all other factors constant, the floater will trade at par value or at a premium to par if the coupon rate is above the prevailing rate for comparable issues.

Duration of Floaters
We have just described how a floater's price will react to a change in the required margin, holding all other factors constant. Duration is the measure used by managers to quantify the sensitivity of the price of any security or a portfolio to changes in interest rates. Basically, the duration of a security is the approximate percentage change in a bond's price or a portfolio's value for a 100 basis point change in rates.

Two measures have been developed to estimate the sensitivity of a floater to each component of the coupon formula. *Index duration* is a measure of the price sensitivity of a floater to changes in the reference rate holding the quoted margin constant. *Spread duration* measures a floater's price sensitivity to a change in the "spread" or "quoted margin" assuming that the reference rate is unchanged.

SPREAD MEASURES

Participants in the floater market commonly refer to various "spread" measures that an issue is trading over its reference rate. These measures include spread for life, adjusted simple margin, adjusted total margin, discount margin, and option-adjusted spread. We conclude this chapter with an explanation of these measures along with their limitations. All of these spread measures are available on *Bloomberg's Yield Analysis* (YA) screen. We begin with a discussion of the concept of current yield and how to compare floaters with different reset dates.

Current Yield

The current yield of a floater is calculated by dividing the security's annual dollar cash flow (assuming that the reference rate does not change over the security's life) by the market price. The formula for the current yield is

$$\text{Current yield} = \frac{\text{Annual dollar cash flow}}{\text{Price}} \tag{1}$$

To illustrate the calculation, suppose that the coupon formula for a 6-year floater selling for \$99.3098 is 6-month LIBOR plus 80 basis points (i.e., the quoted margin). The coupon rate is reset every six months. Assume the current value for the reference rate is 10%. The calculation is shown below:

Annual dollar cash flow = \$100 × 0.1080 = \$10.80

$$\text{Current yield} = \frac{\$10.80}{\$99.3098} = 0.10875 = 10.875\%$$

Current yield possesses a number of drawbacks as a potential return measure. First, the measure assumes that the reference rate will not change over the security's life. Second, current yield considers only coupon interest and no other source of return that will affect an investor's yield. Simply put, the current yield assumes that the floater delivers a perpetual annuity. Third, current yield ignores the potential impact of any embedded options.

Comparing Floaters with Different Reset Dates

To compare the current yields of two floaters with different coupon reset dates, an adjustment known as the *weighted average rate* is utilized. The comparison requires two assumptions: (1) the coupon payments of the two floaters are determined using the same reference rate and (2) the frequency with which the coupon payments are reset is the same (e.g., semiannually, monthly, etc.). It is presumed that two floaters that share these attributes will produce the same current yield regardless of their respective terms to maturity.

The weighted average rate is simply the weighted average coupon rate over some anticipated holding period where the weights are the fraction of the holding period prior to the coupon reset date and the fraction of the holding period subsequent to the coupon reset date. (The holding period is assumed to contain only one coupon reset date. Accordingly, it is presumed an investor is considering the purchase of a floater as an alternative to a money market instrument.) On the reset date, it is assumed the new coupon rate is the current value of the reference rate adjusted for a spread. The formula for the weighted average rate is given by:

Weighted average rate

$$= \frac{(\text{Current coupon} \times w) + [\text{Assumed new coupon} \times (1 - w)]}{\text{Number of days in the holding period}} \tag{2}$$

where w is the number of days to the coupon reset date divided by the number of days in the anticipated holding period. The floater's current yield is then determined by dividing the weighted average rate by the market price.

To illustrate the calculation, suppose an investor is considering the purchase of one of two floaters for an anticipated holding period of 180 days. The purchase candidates are two issues with identical coupon formulas of 6-month LIBOR plus 90 basis points. Security A has a current coupon of 6.80%, matures in three years, and is trading at 99.50. Security B has a current coupon of 7%, matures in five years, and is trading at 99.125. These two securities also differ in coupon reset dates: Security A resets in 30 days while Security B resets in 90 days. Suppose the current value of the reference rate (6-month LIBOR) is 6.20%. Accordingly, the assumed new coupon rate for both Securities A and B is 7.10% since they share the same quoted margin.

The weighted average rate for Security A and the accompanying current yield using the weighted average rate is computed below:

$$\text{Weighted average rate} = \frac{(6.80\% \times 30) + (7.10\% \times 150)}{180} = 7.05\%$$

Annual dollar cash flow $= \$100 \times 0.0705 = \$7.05$

$$\text{Current yield using weighted average rate} = \frac{\$7.05}{\$99.50} = 0.07085 = 7.085\%$$

The weighted average rate for Security B and the accompanying current yield using the weighted average rate is computed below:

$$\text{Weighted average rate} = \frac{(7\% \times 90) + (7.10\% \times 90)}{180} = 7.05\%$$

Annual dollar cash flow $= \$100 \times 0.0705 = \$7.05$

$$\text{Current yield using weighted average rate} = \frac{\$7.05}{\$99.125} = 7.11\%$$

Although Security A carries a lower coupon rate, it resets sooner to the higher rate. As a result, the current yield of the two securities is closer than one would expect.

Margin Measures

There are several yield spread measures or margins that are routinely used to evaluate floaters. The four margins commonly used are spread for life, adjusted simple margin, adjusted total margin, and discount margin. We will illustrate the calculations of these margins with a floating-rate note issued by Enron Corp. (ticker symbol "ENE 03/00") that matured March 30, 2000. This issue contained no embedded options. The floater had a coupon formula equal to 3-month LIBOR plus 45 basis points and delivered cash flows quarterly. The Yield Analysis screen (YA) from Bloomberg is presented in Exhibit 1. We will illustrate the calculation of each of the four margin measures in turn.

Exhibit 1: Bloomberg's Yield Analysis Screen for Enron Floater

```
2                                              DG41 Corp   Y A
ENTER ALL VALUES AND HIT <GO>.
ENRON CORP             ENE Float 03/00   N O T   P R I C E D
                       F L O A T I N G   R A T E   N O T E S
```

INPUTS		DATE	FIX RATE	DATE	FIX RATE	DATE	FIX RATE
SETTLE DATE	4/20/99	3/30/99	5.45000				
MATURITY	3/30/00	6/30/99					
PREV PAY DATE	3/30/99						
NEXT PAY DATE	6/30/99						
REDEMPTION	100.0000						
CPN FREQUENCY	4						
REFIX FREQ	4						
BENCHMARK US00	-3 MNTH						
ASSUMED INDEX	5.0000						
QUOTED MARGIN	45.000						

```
REPO TO    6/30/99  4.9755   FACE AMOUNT(M)          1000  M/M EQUIV TO NEXT FIX
INDEX TO   6/30/99  4.9755   PRINCIPAL          999900.00  PRICE @ FIX =   99.991
     P R I C E S            ACCRUED INTEREST      3179.17  ON  6/30/99-   71 DAYS
PRICE              99.99000  TOTAL             1003079.17  CD(ACT/360) =    5.438
NEUTRAL PRICE      99.99089                                FIX PRICES? (Y/N)  N
ADJUSTED PRICE     99.90031              M A R G I N S
ADJUSTED SIMPLE MARGIN       55.458 BPS  (  5.555)  SPREAD FOR LIFE
ADJUSTED TOTAL MARGIN        55.957 BPS  (  5.560)     46.06 BPS
DISCOUNT MARGIN              46.231 BPS  (  5.462)  VOLATILITY = 0.00
```

```
Copyright 1999 BLOOMBERG L.P.  Frankfurt:69-920410  Hong Kong:2-977-6000  London:171-330-7500  New York:212-318-2000
Princeton:609-279-3000  Singapore:226-3000  Sydney:2-9777-8686  Tokyo:3-3201-8900  Sao Paulo:11-3048-4500
                                                          G279-532-3 15-Apr-99 17:34:08
```

Source: Bloomberg Financial Markets

Spread for Life

When a floater is selling at a premium/discount to par, a potential buyer of a floater will consider the premium or discount as an additional source of dollar return. Spread for life (also called *simple margin*) is a measure of potential return that accounts for the accretion (amortization) of the discount (premium) as well as the constant index spread over the security's remaining life. Spread for life is calculated using the following formula:

$$\text{Spread for life} = \left[\frac{100(100 - P)}{\text{Maturity}} + \text{Quoted margin} \right] \frac{100}{P} \tag{3}$$

where P is the market price (per \$100 of par value) and Maturity is in years using the appropriate day count convention. The quoted margin is measured in basis points.

To illustrate this calculation, at the time of the analysis the Enron floater had a current coupon of 5.45, matured in 345 days or 0.9583 of a year using an ACT/360. Although there is no current market quote available for this floater as indicated by the words "NOT PRICED" at the top center of the screen, we will use the Bloomberg default price of 99.99 for the current market price P. The simple margin is calculated as follows

$$\text{Spread for life} = \left[\frac{100(100 - 99.99)}{0.9583} + 45 \right] \frac{100}{99.99} = 46.0481 \text{ basis points}$$

At the bottom of the YA screen in Exhibit 1 is a box labeled "MARGINS." The Enron floater's spread for life is 46.06. The slight difference between our calculation and Bloomberg's is likely due to rounding error. Note also that spread for life considers only the accretion/amortization of the discount/premium over the floater's remaining term to maturity and considers neither the level of the coupon rate nor the time value of money.

Adjusted Simple Margin

The *adjusted simple margin* (also called *effective margin*) is an adjustment to spread for life. This adjustment accounts for a one-time cost of carry effect when a floater is purchased with borrowed funds. Suppose an investor has purchased $10 million of a particular floater. A leveraged investor has a number of alternative ways to finance the position, the most common being via a repurchase agreement. Regardless of the method selected, the investor must make a one-time adjustment to the floater's price to account for the cost of carry from the settlement date to next coupon reset date. Given a particular financing rate, a carry-adjusted forward price can be determined as of the next coupon reset date. Once the carry-adjusted price is determined, the floater's adjusted price is simply the carry-adjusted price discounted to the settlement date by the reference rate. As before, the reference rate is assumed to remain constant until maturity. Note the cost of carry adjustment is simply an adjustment to the purchase price of the floater. If the cost of carry is positive (negative), the purchase price will be adjusted downward (upward). A floater's adjusted price is calculated as below:

$$\text{Adjusted price} = P - \frac{[(\text{Coupon rate})100 - (P + AI)rf]w}{[1 + (w)(rr_{avg})]} \qquad (4)$$

where

Coupon rate	=	current coupon rate of the floater (in decimal)
P	=	market price (per $100 of par value)
AI	=	accrued interest (per $100 of par value)
rf	=	financing rate (e.g., the repo rate) (in decimal)

$$w = \frac{\text{Number of days between settlement and the next coupon payent}}{\text{Number of days in a year using the appropriate day-count}}$$

rr_{avg} = assumed (average) value for the reference rate until maturity (in decimal)

To illustrate this calculation, we revisit the Enron floater. The following information is taken from the YA screen in Exhibit 1. The market price is 99.99 is taken from the "PRICES" box on the left-hand side of the screen. For the coupon rate, we use 0.0545 (in decimal) which is located under "FIX RATE." The accrued interest is 0.3179 (per $100 of par value). Under "INPUTS", we find the repo rate (0.049755) to the next coupon reset date. There are 71 days between the settlement date (4/20/99) and the next coupon reset date (6/30/99) and the day count is ACT/360. Given this information, w = 71/360 or 0.1972. Lastly, the assumed value of the reference rate until maturity (rr_{avg}) is simply the current value of the reference rate which is 0.05 (in decimal) and is labeled "ASSUMED INDEX" under the "INPUTS" section.

$$\text{Adjusted price} = 99.99 - \frac{[(0.0545)100 - (99.99 + 0.3179)0.049755]0.1972}{[1 + (0.1972)(0.05)]}$$

$$= 99.90033$$

The adjusted price as computed by Bloomberg is 99.90031 and is found under "PRICES."

Once the adjusted price is determined, the adjusted simple margin is computed using the formula below.

$$\text{Adjusted simple margin} = \left[\frac{100(100 - P_A)}{\text{Maturity}} + \text{Quoted margin}\right]\frac{100}{P_A} \qquad (5)$$

where P_A is the adjusted price, Maturity is measured in years using the appropriate day count convention, and Quoted margin is measured in basis points.

To compute the adjusted simple margin for the Enron floater, we gather the following information from Exhibit 1. We use the adjusted price of 99.90031 for P_A. There are 345 days between the settlement date (4/20/99) and the maturity date (3/30/00). Since the day count convention is ACT/360, the maturity is 345/360 or 0.9583. The quoted margin of 45 basis points is obtained from the "INPUTS" box. Plugging this information into equation (5), we obtain the adjusted simple margin.

$$\text{Adjusted simple margin} = \left[\frac{100(100 - 99.90031)}{0.9583} + 45\right]\frac{100}{99.90031} \qquad (6)$$

$$= 55.458 \text{ basis points}$$

The adjusted simple margin from Bloomberg is 55.458 which is also located in the "MARGINS" box at the bottom of Exhibit 1.

Adjusted Total Margin

The *adjusted total margin* (also called *total adjusted margin*) adds one additional refinement to the adjusted simple margin. Specifically, the adjusted total margin is the adjusted simple margin plus the interest earned by investing the difference between the floater's par value and the adjusted price. The current value of the reference rate (i.e., the assumed index) is assumed to be the investment rate. The adjusted total margin is calculated using the following expression:

Adjusted total margin

$$= \left[\frac{100(100 - P_A)}{\text{Maturity}} + \text{Quoted margin} + 100(100 - P_A)rr_{avg}\right]\frac{100}{P_A} \qquad (7)$$

The notation used is the same as given above.

For the Enron floater we used in previous illustrations, the adjusted total margin is:

Adjusted total margin

$$= \left[\frac{100(100 - 99.90031)}{0.9583} + 45 + 100(100 - 99.90031)0.05 \right] \frac{100}{99.90031}$$

$$= 55.957 \text{ basis points}$$

In Exhibit 1, Bloomberg's adjusted total margin is 55.957 which is obtained from the "MARGINS" box.

Discount Margin

One common method of measuring potential return that employs discounted cash flows is *discount margin*. This measure indicates the average spread or margin over the reference rate the investor can expect to earn over the security's life given a particular assumption of the path the reference rate will take to maturity. The assumption that the future levels of the reference rate are equal to today's level is the usual assumption. The procedure for calculating the discount margin is as follows:

> *Step 1*. Determine the cash flows assuming that the reference rate does not change over the security's life.
> *Step 2*. Select a margin.
> *Step 3*. Discount the cash flows found in Step 1 by the current value of the reference rate plus the margin selected in Step 2.
> *Step 4*. Compare the present value of the cash flows as calculated in Step 3 to the price. If the present value is equal to the security's price, the discount margin is the margin assumed in Step 2. If the present value is not equal to the security's price, go back to Step 2 and select a different margin.

For a security selling at par, the discount margin is simply the quoted margin.

For example, suppose that a 6-year floater selling for $99.3098 pays the reference rate plus a quoted margin of 80 basis points. The coupon resets every six months. Assume that the current value of the reference rate is 10%.

Exhibit 2 presents the calculation of the discount margin for this security. Each period in the security's life is enumerated in Column (1), while Column (2) shows the current value of the reference rate. Column (3) sets forth the security's cash flows. For the first 11 periods, the cash flow is equal to the reference rate (10%) plus the quoted margin of 80 basis points multiplied by 100 and then divided by 2. In last 6-month period, the cash flow is $105.40 — the final coupon payment of $5.40 plus the maturity value of $100. Different assumed margins appear at the top of the last five columns. The rows below the assumed margin indicate the present value of each period's cash flow for that particular value of assumed margin. Finally, the last row gives the total present value of the cash flows for each assumed margin.

Exhibit 2: Calculation of the Discount Margin for a Floater

Floater: Maturity   = 6 years
            Coupon rate   = Reference rate + 80 basis points
                                 Resets every 6 months
            Maturity value   = $100

(1)	(2)	(3)	(4)	(5)	(6)	(7)	(8)
			Assumed Margin				
Period	Rate (%)	Flow ($)*	80	84	88	96	100
1	10	5.40	$5.1233	$5.1224	$5.1214	$5.1195	$5.1185
2	10	5.40	4.8609	4.8590	4.8572	4.8535	4.8516
3	10	5.40	4.6118	4.6092	4.6066	4.6013	4.5987
4	10	5.40	4.3755	4.3722	4.3689	4.3623	4.3590
5	10	5.40	4.1514	4.1474	4.1435	4.1356	4.1317
6	10	5.40	3.9387	3.9342	3.9297	3.9208	3.9163
7	10	5.40	3.7369	3.7319	3.7270	3.7171	3.7122
8	10	5.40	3.5454	3.5401	3.5347	3.5240	3.5186
9	10	5.40	3.3638	3.3580	3.3523	3.3409	3.3352
10	10	5.40	3.1914	3.1854	3.1794	3.1673	3.1613
11	10	5.40	3.0279	3.0216	3.0153	3.0028	2.9965
12	10	105.40	56.0729	55.9454	55.8182	55.5647	55.4385
		Present value =	$100.00	$99.8269	$99.6541	$99.3098	$99.1381

* For periods 1-11: Cash flow = 100(Reference rate + 80 basis points) (0.5)
For period 12: Cash flow = 100(Reference rate + 80 basis points) (0.5) + 100

For the five assumed margins, the present value of the cash flows is equal to the floater's price ($99.3098) when the assumed margin is 96 basis points. Accordingly, the discount margin on a semiannual basis is 48 basis points and correspondingly 96 basis points on an annual basis. (Notice that the discount margin is 80 basis points (i.e., the quoted margin) when the floater is selling at par.)

Now that we have a sense about how to calculate discount margin, let's return to our Enron floater in Exhibit 1. The floater was trading at 99.99 with a coupon rate of 5.45% as of the last coupon reset date, 3/30/99. Accrued interest on this floater from the last coupon date (3/30/99) to the settlement date (4/20/00) was 0.3179 (per $100 of par value) which appears in the box in the middle of the screen. Given this information, we know the floater's full price (i.e., flat price plus accrued interest) is 100.307917 (per $100 of par value). In the box labeled "MARGINS" at the bottom of the screen, we see that the discount margin is 46.231 basis points. Accordingly, if we discount the floater's four remaining quarterly cash flows using an annual discount of 5.46321% (i.e., the reference rate plus the discount margin), we should recover the floater's full price of 100.307917 (per $100 of par value).

At the time of the analysis, the Enron floater had four remaining quarterly cash flows of $1.3625 [(0.0545 × 100)/4] delivered on 6/30/99, 9/30/99, 12/30/99, and 3/30/99. In addition, on the day the floater matures (3/30/00) the investor will receive the floater's terminal cash flow of $100 (per $100 of par value).

Since the floater was being valued between coupon payment dates, we determined the present value of cash flows received over fractional coupon periods using an ACT/360 day count convention. The present value calculation is as follows:

$$100.3156$$
$$= \frac{\$1.3625}{1.0546321^{71/360}} + \frac{\$1.3625}{1.0546321^{163/360}} + \frac{\$1.3625}{1.0546321^{254/360}} + \frac{\$101.3625}{1.0546321^{345/360}}$$

This calculation is within rounding error of Bloomberg's full price of 100.3079 (per $100 of par value).

There are several drawbacks of the discount margin as a measure of potential return from holding a floater. First and most obvious, the measure assumes the reference rate will not change over the security's life. Second, the price of a floater for a given discount margin is sensitive to the path that the reference rate takes in the future except in the special case when the discount margin equals the quoted margin.

Option-Adjusted Spread

The spread measures discussed thus far fail to recognize any embedded options that may be present in a floater. A spread measure that takes into account embedded options is the *option-adjusted spread*. A discussion of how this spread measure is computed is beyond the scope of this chapter.[3] Basically, it is a byproduct of a model that is used for valuing a security with an embedded option. The spread is referred to as "option adjusted" because the valuation model adjusts the cash flows based on how changes in the reference rates might be expected to change the cash flows of the security, taking into account any embedded options.

Despite its widespread use, the OAS has a number of limitations. Specifically, the OAS is model-dependent. Changing the assumptions of the valuation model may produce substantial differences in the computed OAS.

---

[3] See Chapter 4 in Frank J. Fabozzi and Steven V. Mann, *Floating-Rate Securities* (New Hope, PA: Frank J. Fabozzi Associates, 2000).

Chapter 11

Short-Term Fixed-Rate and Floating-Rate Mortgage-Backed Securities

Frank J. Fabozzi, Ph.D., CFA
Adjunct Professor of Finance
School of Management
Yale University

An asset-backed security (ABS) is a security supported by a pool of loans or receivables. That is, the cash flow to pay the holders of the security comes from the cash flow of the underlying loans or receivables. A mortgage-backed security (MBS) refers to an ABS created by pooling mortgage loans on real estate property. While technically the MBS market is part of the ABS market, in the United States the two markets are viewed as being separate. There are many short-term fixed-rate products and floating-rate products in this market that have characteristics sought by cash managers. In this chapter we discuss mortgage-backed securities and in the next we focus on asset-backed securities.

MORTGAGE LOANS

While any type of mortgage loans — residential or commercial — can be used as collateral for an MBS, most are backed by residential mortgages. We begin our coverage of MBS products with a description of the raw product — the mortgage loan.

Mortgage Designs

There are many types of mortgage designs. By a mortgage design we mean the specification of the interest rate (fixed or floating), the term of the mortgage, and the manner in which the principal is repaid. We summarize the major mortgage designs below.

Fixed-Rate, Level-Payment, Fully Amortized Mortgage

The basic idea behind the design of the fixed-rate, level payment, fully amortized mortgage is that the borrower pays interest and repays principal in equal installments over an agreed-upon period of time, called the maturity or term of the mort-

143

gage. The frequency of payment is typically monthly. Each monthly mortgage payment for this mortgage design is due on the first of each month and consists of:

1. interest of $\frac{1}{12}$th of the annual interest rate times the amount of the outstanding mortgage balance at the beginning of the previous month, and
2. a repayment of a portion of the outstanding mortgage balance (principal).

The difference between the monthly mortgage payment and the portion of the payment that represents interest equals the amount that is applied to reduce the outstanding mortgage balance. The portion of the monthly mortgage payment applied to interest declines each month and the portion applied to reducing the mortgage balance increases each month. The reason for this is that as the mortgage balance is reduced with each monthly mortgage payment, the interest on the mortgage balance declines. Since the monthly mortgage payment is fixed, an increasingly larger portion of the monthly payment is applied to reduce the outstanding principal in each subsequent month. The monthly mortgage payment is designed so that after the last scheduled monthly payment of the loan is made, the amount of the outstanding mortgage balance is zero (i.e., the mortgage is fully repaid or amortized).

The cash flow from this mortgage loan, as well as all mortgage designs, is not simply the interest payment and the scheduled principal repayments. There are two additional factors — servicing fees and prepayments.

Every mortgage loan must be serviced. The servicing fee is a portion of the mortgage rate. If the mortgage rate is 8.125% and the servicing fee is 50 basis points, then the investor receives interest of 7.625%. The interest rate that the investor receives is said to be the net interest or net coupon. The servicing fee is commonly called the *servicing spread*. The dollar amount of the servicing fee declines over time as the mortgage amortizes. This is true for not only the mortgage design that we have just described, but for all mortgage designs.

The second modification to the cash flow is that the borrower typically has the right to pay off any portion of the mortgage balance prior to the scheduled due date typically without a penalty. Payments made in excess of the scheduled principal repayments are called *prepayments*. When less than the entire amount of the outstanding mortgage balance is prepaid in a month, this type of prepayment is called a *curtailment* because it shortens or curtails the life of the loan. The effect of prepayments is that the amount and timing of the cash flows from a mortgage loan are not known with certainty. This risk is referred to as *prepayment risk*. This is true for all mortgage loans, not just fixed-rate, level-payment, fully amortized mortgages.

Balloon Mortgages

In a balloon mortgage, the borrower is given long-term financing by the lender but at specified future dates the mortgage rate is renegotiated. Thus, the lender is providing long-term funds for what is effectively a short-term borrowing, how short depending on the frequency of the renegotiation period. Effectively it is a short-term balloon loan in which the lender agrees to provide financing for the remainder of the term of the mortgage if certain conditions are met. The balloon payment is the original amount borrowed less the amount amortized. Thus, in a balloon mortgage, the actual maturity is shorter than the stated maturity.

Adjustable-Rate Mortgages

As the name implies, an adjustable-rate mortgage (ARM) has an adjustable or floating coupon instead of a fixed one. The coupon adjusts periodically — monthly, semiannually, or annually. Some ARMs even have coupons that adjust every three years or five years. The coupon formula for an ARM is specified in terms of a reference rate plus a quoted margin.

At origination, the mortgage usually has an initial rate for an initial period (teaser period) which is slightly below the rate specified by the coupon formula. This is called a "teaser rate" and makes it easier for first time home buyers to qualify for the loan. At the end of the teaser period, the loan rate is reset based on the coupon formula. Once the loan comes out of its teaser period and resets based on the coupon formula, it is said to be fully indexed.

To protect the homeowner from interest rate shock, there are caps imposed on the coupon adjustment level. There are periodic caps and lifetime caps. The *periodic cap* limits the amount of coupon reset upward from one reset date to another. The *lifetime cap* is the maximum absolute level for the coupon rate that the loan can reset to for the life of the mortgage.

Two categories of reference rates have been used in ARMs: (1) market determined rates and (2) calculated cost of funds for thrifts. The most common market determined rates used are the 1-year, 3-year or 5-year CMT and 3-month or 6-month London interbank offered rate (LIBOR). The most popular cost of funds for thrift index used is the Eleventh Federal Home Loan Bank Board District Cost of Funds Index (COFI).

MORTGAGE PASSTHROUGH SECURITIES

A mortgage passthrough is an MBS where the cash flows from the underlying pool of mortgage loans is distributed to the security holders on a pro rata basis. That is, if there are X certificates issued against a pool of mortgage loans, then a certificate holder is entitled to $1/X$ of the cash flow from the pool of mortgage loans. The cash flow for the certificate holder depends on the cash flow of the underlying mortgages: monthly mortgage payments representing interest, the scheduled repayment of principal, and any prepayments.

Payments are made to security holders each month. Neither the amount nor the timing, however, of the cash flows from the pool of mortgages are identical to that of the cash flows passed through to investors. The monthly cash flows for a passthrough are less than the monthly cash flows of the underlying mortgages by an amount equal to the servicing fee and other fees. The other fees are those charged by the issuer or guarantor of the passthrough for guaranteeing the issue. The coupon rate on a passthrough, called the "passthrough coupon rate," is less than the mortgage rate on the underlying pool of mortgage loans by an amount equal to the servicing fee and guarantee fee.

Not all of the mortgages that are included in a pool of mortgages that are securitized have the same mortgage rate and the same maturity. Consequently, when describing a passthrough security, a *weighted average coupon rate* and a *weighted average maturity* are determined. A weighted average coupon rate, or WAC, is found by weighting the mortgage rate of each mortgage loan in the pool by the amount of the mortgage balance outstanding. A weighted average maturity, or WAM, is found by weighting the remaining number of months to maturity for each mortgage loan in the pool by the amount of the mortgage balance outstanding.

Agency Mortgage Passthrough Securities

There are three government agencies that issue passthrough securities: Government National Mortgage Association, Federal National Mortgage Association, and Federal Home Loan Mortgage Corporation. The first is a federally related government agency. The last two are government sponsored enterprises. There are also MBS issued by nonagencies. We will postpone discussion of nonagency MBS until later in this chapter.

The Government National Mortgage Association (nicknamed "Ginnie Mae") passthroughs are guaranteed by the full faith and credit of the U.S. government. For this reason, Ginnie Mae passthroughs are viewed as risk-free in terms of default risk, just like Treasury securities. The security guaranteed by Ginnie Mae is called a *mortgage-backed security* (MBS). All Ginnie Mae MBS are guaranteed with respect to the timely payment of interest and principal, meaning the interest and principal will be paid when due, even if any of the borrowers fail to make their monthly mortgage payments.

Only mortgage loans insured or guaranteed by either the Federal Housing Administration, the Veterans Administration, or the Rural Housing Service can be included in a mortgage pool guaranteed by Ginnie Mae. The maximum loan size is set by Congress, based on the maximum amount that the FHA, VA, or RHS may guarantee. The maximum for a given loan varies with the region of the country and type of residential property.

The passthroughs issued by the Federal National Mortgage Association (nicknamed "Fannie Mae") are called *mortgage-backed securities* (MBSs). Although a guarantee of Fannie Mae is not a guarantee by the U.S. government, most market participants view Fannie Mae MBSs as similar, although not identical, in credit worthiness to Ginnie Mae passthroughs. All Fannie Mae MBSs carry its guarantee of timely payment of both interest and principal.

The Federal Home Loan Mortgage Corporation (nicknamed "Freddie Mac") is a government sponsored enterprise that issues a passthrough security that is called a *participation certificate* (PC). As with Fannie Mae MBS, a guarantee of Freddie Mac is not a guarantee by the U.S. government, but most market participants view Freddie Mac PCs as similar, although not identical, in credit worthiness to Ginnie Mae passthroughs. Freddie Mac has issued PCs with different types of guarantee. The old PCs issued by Freddie Mac guarantee the timely payment of interest; the scheduled principal is passed through as it is collected, with Freddie Mac only guaranteeing that the scheduled payment will be made no later than one year after it is due. Today, Freddie Mac issues PCs under its "Gold Program" in which both the timely payment of interest and principal are guaranteed.

Price Quotes and Trading Procedures

Passthroughs are quoted in the same manner as U.S. Treasury coupon securities. A quote of 94-05 means 94 and 5⁄32nds of par value, or 94.15625% of par value. The price that the buyer pays the seller is the agreed upon sale price plus accrued interest. Given the par value, the dollar price (excluding accrued interest) is affected by the amount of the mortgage pool balance outstanding. The pool factor indicates the percentage of the initial mortgage balance still outstanding. So, a pool factor of 90 means that 90% of the original mortgage pool balance is outstanding. The pool factor is reported by the agency each month.

The dollar price paid for just the principal is found as follows given the agreed upon price, par value, and the month's pool factor provided by the agency:

Price = Par value × Pool factor

For example, if the parties agree to a price of 92 for $1 million par value for a passthrough with a pool factor of 85, then the dollar price paid by the buyer in addition to accrued interest is:

$0.92 \times \$1,000,000 \times 0.85 = \$782,000$

Many trades occur while a pool is still unspecified, and therefore no pool information is known at the time of the trade. This kind of trade is known as a "TBA" (to be announced) trade. In a TBA trade for a fixed-rate passthrough, the two parties agree on the agency type, the agency program, the coupon rate, the face value, the price, and the settlement date. The actual pools underlying the agency passthrough are not specified in a TBA trade. However, this information is provided by the seller to the buyer before delivery. In contrast to a TBA trade, there are specified pool trades wherein the actual pool numbers to be delivered are specified.

Prepayment Conventions and Cash Flows

To value a security it is necessary to project its cash flows. The difficulty for an MBS is that the cash flows are unknown because of prepayments. The only way to project cash flows is to make some assumption about the prepayment rate over the life of the underlying mortgage pool. The prepayment rate is sometimes referred to as the *prepayment speed*, or simply *speed*. Two conventions have been used as a benchmark for prepayment rates — conditional prepayment rate and Public Securities Association prepayment benchmark.

Conditional Prepayment Rate

One convention for describing the pattern of prepayments and the cash flows of a passthrough assumes that some fraction of the remaining principal in the pool is prepaid each month for the remaining term of the mortgage. The prepayment rate assumed for a pool, called the *conditional prepayment rate* (CPR), is based on the characteristics of the pool (including its historical prepayment experience) and the current and expected future economic environment.

The CPR is an annual prepayment rate. To estimate monthly prepayments, the CPR must be converted into a monthly prepayment rate, commonly referred to as the *single-monthly mortality rate* (SMM). The following formula is used to determine the SMM for a given CPR:

$$SMM = 1 - (1 - CPR)^{1/12}$$

Suppose that the CPR used to estimate prepayments is 6%. The corresponding SMM is:

$$SMM = 1 - (1 - 0.06)^{1/12}$$
$$= 1 - (0.94)^{0.08333} = 0.005143$$

An SMM of $w\%$ means that approximately $w\%$ of the remaining mortgage balance at the beginning of the month, less the scheduled principal payment, will prepay that month. That is,

Prepayment for month t = SMM
  × (Beginning mortgage balance for month t
  − Scheduled principal payment for month t)

For example, suppose that an investor owns a passthrough in which the remaining mortgage balance at the beginning of some month is $290 million. Assuming that the SMM is 0.5143% and the scheduled principal payment is $3 million, the estimated prepayment for the month is:

$$0.005143 \times (\$290,000,000 - \$3,000,000) = \$1,476,041$$

PSA Prepayment Benchmark

The Public Securities Association (PSA) prepayment benchmark is expressed as a monthly series of CPRs. The PSA benchmark assumes that prepayment rates are low for newly originated mortgages and then will speed up as the mortgages become seasoned.

The PSA prepayment benchmark assumes the following prepayment rates for 30-year mortgages: (1) a CPR of 0.2% for the first month, increased by 0.2% per year per month for the next 30 months when it reaches 6% per year, and (2) a 6% CPR for the remaining years. This benchmark is referred to as "100% PSA" or simply "100 PSA." Slower or faster speeds are then referred to as some percentage of 100 PSA. For example, 50 PSA means one-half the CPR of the PSA benchmark prepayment rate; 150 PSA means 1.5 times the CPR of the PSA benchmark prepayment rate; 300 PSA means three times the CPR of the benchmark prepayment rate. A prepayment rate of 0 PSA means that no prepayments are assumed.

It is important to understand that the PSA benchmark is commonly referred to as a prepayment model, suggesting that it can be used to estimate prepayments. Characterization of this benchmark as a prepayment model is incorrect. It is simply a market convention describing what the PSA believes the pattern will be for prepayments.

It is worthwhile to see a monthly cash flow for a hypothetical passthrough given a PSA assumption since we can use the information in our discussion of collateralized mortgage obligations in the next section. Exhibit 1 shows the cash flow for selected months assuming 165 PSA for a passthrough security in which the underlying loans are assumed to be fixed-rate, level-payment, fully amortized mortgages with a WAC of 8.125%. It is assumed that the passthrough rate is 7.5% with a WAM of 357 months. The cash flow in Exhibit 1 is broken down into three components: (1) interest (based on the passthrough rate), (2) the regularly scheduled principal repayment, and (3) prepayments based on 165 PSA.

Since the WAM is 357 months, the underlying mortgage pool is seasoned an average of three months. Therefore, the CPR for month 27 is 1.65 times 6%.

Average Life Measure

Because an MBS is an amortizing security, market participants do not talk in terms of an issue's maturity. Instead, the average life of an MBS is computed. The average life is the average time to receipt of principal payments (scheduled principal payments and projected prepayments). Specifically, the average life is found by first calculating:

$$\frac{\begin{array}{l} 1 \times (\text{Projected principal received in month 1}) \\ 2 \times (\text{Projected principal received in month 2}) \\ 3 \times (\text{Projected principal received in month 3}) \\ \cdots \\ + \quad T \times (\text{Projected principal received in month } T) \end{array}}{\text{Weighted monthly average of principal received}}$$

where T is the last month that principal is expected to be received.

Exhibit 1: Monthly Cash Flow for a $400 Million Passthrough with a 7.5% Passthrough Rate, a WAC of 8.125%, and a WAM of 357 Months Assuming 165 PSA

(1)	(2)	(3)	(4)	(5)	(6)	(7)	(8)	(9)
Month	Outstanding Balance	SMM	Mortgage Payment	Net Interest	Scheduled Principal	Prepayment	Total Principal	Cash Flow
1	$400,000,000	0.00111	$2,975,868	$2,500,000	$267,535	$442,389	$709,923	$3,209,923
2	399,290,077	0.00139	2,972,575	2,495,563	269,048	552,847	821,896	3,317,459
3	398,468,181	0.00167	2,968,456	2,490,426	270,495	663,065	933,560	3,423,986
4	397,534,621	0.00195	2,963,513	2,484,591	271,873	772,949	1,044,822	3,529,413
5	396,489,799	0.00223	2,957,747	2,478,061	273,181	882,405	1,155,586	3,633,647
6	395,334,213	0.00251	2,951,160	2,470,839	274,418	991,341	1,265,759	3,736,598
7	394,068,454	0.00279	2,943,755	2,462,928	275,583	1,099,664	1,375,246	3,838,174
8	392,693,208	0.00308	2,935,534	2,454,333	276,674	1,207,280	1,483,954	3,938,287
9	391,209,254	0.00336	2,926,503	2,445,058	277,690	1,314,099	1,591,789	4,036,847
10	389,617,464	0.00365	2,916,666	2,435,109	278,631	1,420,029	1,698,659	4,133,769
11	387,918,805	0.00393	2,906,028	2,424,493	279,494	1,524,979	1,804,473	4,228,965
24	356,711,789	0.00775	2,698,575	2,229,449	283,338	2,761,139	3,044,477	5,273,926
25	353,667,312	0.00805	2,677,670	2,210,421	283,047	2,843,593	3,126,640	5,337,061
26	350,540,672	0.00835	2,656,123	2,190,879	282,671	2,923,885	3,206,556	5,397,435
27	347,334,116	0.00865	2,633,950	2,170,838	282,209	3,001,955	3,284,164	5,455,002
28	344,049,952	0.00865	2,611,167	2,150,312	281,662	2,973,553	3,255,215	5,405,527
29	340,794,737	0.00865	2,588,581	2,129,967	281,116	2,945,400	3,226,516	5,356,483
30	337,568,221	0.00865	2,566,190	2,109,801	280,572	2,917,496	3,198,067	5,307,869
100	170,142,350	0.00865	1,396,958	1,063,390	244,953	1,469,591	1,714,544	2,777,933
101	168,427,806	0.00865	1,384,875	1,052,674	244,478	1,454,765	1,699,243	2,751,916
102	166,728,563	0.00865	1,372,896	1,042,054	244,004	1,440,071	1,684,075	2,726,128
103	165,044,489	0.00865	1,361,020	1,031,528	243,531	1,425,508	1,669,039	2,700,567
200	56,746,664	0.00865	585,990	354,667	201,767	489,106	690,874	1,045,540
201	56,055,790	0.00865	580,921	350,349	201,377	483,134	684,510	1,034,859
202	55,371,280	0.00865	575,896	346,070	200,986	477,216	678,202	1,024,273
203	54,693,077	0.00865	570,915	341,832	200,597	471,353	671,950	1,013,782
300	11,758,141	0.00865	245,808	73,488	166,196	100,269	266,465	339,953
301	11,491,677	0.00865	243,682	71,823	165,874	97,967	263,841	335,664
302	11,227,836	0.00865	241,574	70,174	165,552	95,687	261,240	331,414
303	10,966,596	0.00865	239,485	68,541	165,232	93,430	258,662	327,203
353	760,027	0.00865	155,107	4,750	149,961	5,277	155,238	159,988
354	604,789	0.00865	153,765	3,780	149,670	3,937	153,607	157,387
355	451,182	0.00865	152,435	2,820	149,380	2,611	151,991	154,811
356	299,191	0.00865	151,117	1,870	149,091	1,298	150,389	152,259
357	148,802	0.00865	149,809	930	148,802	0	148,802	149,732

Note: Since the WAM is 357 months, the underlying mortgage pool is seasoned an average of three months. Therefore, the CPR for month 27 is $1.65 \times 6\%$.

Then the average life is found as follows:

$$\text{Average life} = \frac{\text{Weighted monthly average of principal received}}{12(\text{Total principal to be received})}$$

The average life of a passthrough depends on the prepayment assumption. To see this, the average life is shown below for different PSA prepayment speeds for the passthrough we used to illustrate the cash flows for 165 PSA in Exhibit 1:

PSA speed	50	100	165	200	300	400	500	600	700
Average life	15.11	11.66	8.76	7.68	5.63	4.44	3.68	3.16	2.78

Closer Look at Prepayment Risk:
Contraction Risk and Extension Risk

Just like the owner of any security that contains an embedded option, investors in passthrough securities do not know what their cash flows will be because of prepayments — the borrower's option to alter the mortgage's cash flows. As we noted earlier, this risk is called prepayment risk. To understand the significance of prepayment risk, suppose an investor buys an 8.5% coupon Ginnie Mae at a time when mortgage rates are 8.5%. Let's consider what will happen to prepayments if mortgage rates decline to, say, 6.5%. There will be two adverse consequences. First, a basic property of fixed-income securities is that the price of an option-free bond increases at an increasing rate as interest rates decline. However, for a passthrough security with an embedded prepayment option, the rise in price will not be as large as that of an option-free bond because a drop in interest rates will give the borrower an incentive to prepay the loan and refinance at a lower rate. In other words, the borrower is altering the mortgage's flows (i.e., exercising the prepayment option) when this action enhances his/her economic value. Thus, the upside price potential of a passthrough security is truncated because of prepayments in a manner similar to that of a callable bond. The second adverse consequence is that the cash flows must be reinvested at a lower rate. These two adverse consequences when mortgage rates decline are referred to as *contraction risk*. In essence, contraction risk is all the consequences resulting from borrowers prepaying at a faster rate than anticipated.

Now let's look at what happens if mortgage rates rise to 10.5%. The price of the passthrough, like the price of any bond, will decline. But again it will decline more because the higher rates will tend to slow down the rate of prepayment, in effect increasing the amount invested at the coupon rate, which is lower than the market rate. Prepayments will slow down because homeowners will not refinance or partially prepay their mortgages when mortgage rates are higher than the contract rate of 8.5%. Of course, this is just the time when investors want prepayments to speed up so that they can reinvest the prepayments at the higher market interest rate. This adverse consequence of rising mortgage rates is called *extension risk* and results from borrowers prepaying at a slower rate than anticipated.

Therefore, prepayment risk encompasses contraction risk and extension risk. Prepayment risk makes passthrough securities unattractive for certain individuals and financial institutions to hold for purposes of accomplishing their investment objectives. Some individuals and institutional investors such as cash managers and managers of short-duration portfolios are concerned with extension risk and others with contraction risk when they purchase a passthrough security. Is it possible to alter the cash flows of a mortgage passthrough security so as to reduce the contraction risk or extension risk for institutional investors? This can be done as we will see in the next section.

COLLATERALIZED MORTGAGE OBLIGATIONS

Cash managers may find adjustable-rate mortgages and fixed-rate passthrough securities with a short WAC attractive investments. Now we will see how mortgage passthroughs securities backed by fixed-rate mortgage loans with a long WAC can be used to create a structure called a *collateralized mortgage obligation* (CMO). Two types of bond classes that can be created within the structure is a floating-rate bond class and a fixed-rate bond class with a short average life.

We will discuss CMOs issued by the three agencies that issue mortgage passthrough securities and CMOs issued by private entities. CMOs are also referred to as "paythroughs" or "multi-class passthroughs." Because they are created so as to comply with a provision in the tax law called the Real Estate Mortgage Investment Conduit, or REMIC, they are also referred to as "REMICs." Throughout this chapter we refer to these structures as simply CMOs. We will see similar paythrough or multi-class passthrough structures when we cover other asset-backed security structures in the next chapter.

Basic Principles of a CMO

By investing in a mortgage passthrough security an investor is exposed to prepayment risk. Furthermore, as explained earlier, prepayment risk can be divided into extension risk and contraction risk. Some investors are concerned with extension risk and others with contraction risk when they invest in a passthrough. An investor may be willing to accept one form of prepayment risk but seek to avoid the other. For example, a cash manager seeks a short-term security and is concerned with extension risk. A portfolio manager who seeks a long-term security, and wants to avoid reinvesting unexpected principal prepayments due to refinancing of mortgages should interest rates drop, is concerned with contraction risk.

By redirecting how the cash flows of passthrough securities are paid to different bond classes that are created, securities can be created that have different exposure to prepayment risk. When the cash flows of mortgage-related products are redistributed to different bond classes, the resulting securities are called CMOs. Simply put, CMOs set forth rules for dividing up cash flows among bond classes.

The basic principle is that redirecting cash flows (interest and principal) to different bond classes, called *tranches*, mitigates different forms of prepayment risk. It is never possible to eliminate prepayment risk. If one tranche in a CMO structure has less prepayment risk than the mortgage passthrough securities that are collateral for the structure, then another tranche in the same structure has greater prepayment risk than the collateral.

Agency Collateralized Mortgage Obligations

Issuers of CMOs are the same three entities that issue agency passthrough securities: Freddie Mac, Fannie Mae, and Ginnie Mae. However, Freddie Mac and Fannie Mae have used Ginnie Mae passthroughs as collateral for their own CMOs. CMOs issued by any of these entities are referred to as *agency CMOs*.

When an agency CMO is created it is structured so that even under the worst circumstances regarding prepayments, the interest and principal payments from the collateral will be sufficient to meet the interest obligation of each tranche and pay off the par value of each tranche. Defaults are ignored because the agency that has issued the passthroughs used as collateral is expected to make up any deficiency. Thus, the credit risk of agency CMOs is minimal. However, the guarantee of a government sponsored enterprise does not carry the full faith and credit of the U.S. government. Fannie Mae and Freddie Mac CMOs created from Ginnie Mae passthroughs effectively carry the full faith and credit of the U.S. government.

Types of Bond Classes

There have been a good number of products created in the CMO market that would be acceptable investments for cash managers. But there are also a good number that cash managers should avoid given the typical interest rate exposure a cash manager seeks.

Sequential-Pay Tranches

The first CMO was structured so that each tranche would be retired sequentially. Such structures are referred to as *sequential-pay CMOs*. To illustrate a sequential-pay CMO, we will use a hypothetical deal that we will refer to as Deal 1. The collateral for Deal 1 is a hypothetical passthrough with a total par value of $400 million and the following characteristics: (1) the passthrough coupon rate is 7.5%, (2) the WAC is 8.125%, and (3) the WAM is 357 months. This is the same passthrough that we used in Exhibit 1 to describe the cash flows of a passthrough based on an assumed 165 PSA prepayment speed.

From this $400 million of collateral, four tranches are created. Their characteristics are summarized in Exhibit 2. The total par value of the four tranches is equal to the par value of the collateral (i.e., the passthrough security). In this simple structure, the coupon rate is the same for each tranche and also the same as the collateral's coupon rate. There is no reason why this must be so, and, in fact, typically the coupon rate varies by tranche. Specifically, if the yield curve

154 Short-Term Fixed-Rate and Floating-Rate Mortgage-Backed Securities

is upward-sloping, the coupon rates of the tranches will usually increase with average life.

Now remember that a CMO is created by redistributing the cash flow — interest and principal — to the different tranches based on a set of payment rules. The payment rules at the bottom of Exhibit 2 set forth how the monthly cash flow from the passthrough (i.e., collateral) is to be distributed among the four tranches. There are separate rules for the payment of the coupon interest and the payment of principal, the principal being the total of the regularly scheduled principal payment and any prepayments.

In Deal 1, each tranche receives periodic coupon interest payments based on the amount of the outstanding balance. The disbursement of the principal, however, is made in a special way. A tranche is not entitled to receive principal until the entire principal of the tranche before it has been paid off. More specifically, tranche A receives all the principal payments until the entire principal amount owed to that tranche, $194,500,000, is paid off; then tranche B begins to receive principal and continues to do so until it is paid the entire $36,000,000. Tranche C then receives principal, and when it is paid off, tranche D starts receiving principal payments.

While the payment rules for the disbursement of the principal payments are known, the precise amount of the principal in each period is not. This will depend on the cash flow, and therefore principal payments, of the collateral, which depends on the actual prepayment rate of the collateral. An assumed PSA speed allows the monthly cash flow to be projected. Exhibit 1 shows the monthly cash flow (interest, regularly scheduled principal repayment, and prepayments) assuming 165 PSA. Assuming that the collateral does prepay at 165 PSA, the cash flows available to all four tranches of Deal 1 will be precisely the cash flows shown in Exhibit 1.

Exhibit 2: Deal 1: A Hypothetical Four-Tranche Sequential-Pay Structure

Tranche	Par Amount	Coupon Rate (%)
A	$194,500,000	7.5
B	36,000,000	7.5
C	96,500,000	7.5
D	73,000,000	7.5
Total	$400,000,000	

Payment rules:

1. For payment of periodic coupon interest: Disburse periodic coupon interest to each tranche on the basis of the amount of principal outstanding at the beginning of the period.

2. For disbursement of principal payments: Disburse principal payments to tranche A until it is completely paid off. After tranche A is completely paid off, disburse principal payments to tranche B until it is completely paid off. After tranche B is completely paid off, disburse principal payments to tranche C until it is completely paid off. After tranche C is completely paid off, disburse principal payments to tranche D until it is completely paid off.

Exhibit 3: Monthly Cash Flow for Selected Months for Deal 1 Assuming 165 PSA

Month	Tranche A			Tranche B		
	Balance	Principal	Interest	Balance	Principal	Interest
1	194,500,000	709,923	1,215,625	36,000,000	0	225,000
2	193,790,077	821,896	1,211,188	36,000,000	0	225,000
3	192,968,181	933,560	1,206,051	36,000,000	0	225,000
4	192,034,621	1,044,822	1,200,216	36,000,000	0	225,000
5	190,989,799	1,155,586	1,193,686	36,000,000	0	225,000
6	189,834,213	1,265,759	1,186,464	36,000,000	0	225,000
7	188,568,454	1,375,246	1,178,553	36,000,000	0	225,000
8	187,193,208	1,483,954	1,169,958	36,000,000	0	225,000
9	185,709,254	1,591,789	1,160,683	36,000,000	0	225,000
10	184,117,464	1,698,659	1,150,734	36,000,000	0	225,000
11	182,418,805	1,804,473	1,140,118	36,000,000	0	225,000
12	180,614,332	1,909,139	1,128,840	36,000,000	0	225,000
75	12,893,479	2,143,974	80,584	36,000,000	0	225,000
76	10,749,504	2,124,935	67,184	36,000,000	0	225,000
77	8,624,569	2,106,062	53,904	36,000,000	0	225,000
78	6,518,507	2,087,353	40,741	36,000,000	0	225,000
79	4,431,154	2,068,807	27,695	36,000,000	0	225,000
80	2,362,347	2,050,422	14,765	36,000,000	0	225,000
81	311,926	311,926	1,950	36,000,000	1,720,271	225,000
82	0	0	0	34,279,729	2,014,130	214,248
83	0	0	0	32,265,599	1,996,221	201,660
84	0	0	0	30,269,378	1,978,468	189,184
85	0	0	0	28,290,911	1,960,869	176,818
95	0	0	0	9,449,331	1,793,089	59,058
96	0	0	0	7,656,242	1,777,104	47,852
97	0	0	0	5,879,138	1,761,258	36,745
98	0	0	0	4,117,880	1,745,550	25,737
99	0	0	0	2,372,329	1,729,979	14,827
100	0	0	0	642,350	642,350	4,015
101	0	0	0	0	0	0
102	0	0	0	0	0	0
103	0	0	0	0	0	0
104	0	0	0	0	0	0
105	0	0	0	0	0	0

To demonstrate how the payment rules for Deal 1 work, Exhibit 3 shows the cash flow for selected months assuming the collateral prepays at 165 PSA. For each tranche, the exhibit shows: (1) the balance at the end of the month, (2) the principal paid down (regularly scheduled principal repayment plus prepayments), and (3) interest. In month 1, the cash flow for the collateral consists of a principal payment of $709,923 and interest of $2.5 million (0.075 times $400 million divided by 12). The interest payment is distributed to the four tranches based on the amount of the par value outstanding. So, for example, tranche A receives $1,215,625 (0.075 times $194,500,000 divided by 12) of the $2.5 million. The principal, however, is all distributed to tranche A. Therefore, the cash flow for tranche A in month 1 is $1,925,548.

The principal balance at the end of month 1 for tranche A is $193,790,076 (the original principal balance of $194,500,000 less the principal payment of $709,923). No principal payment is distributed to the three other tranches because there is still a principal balance outstanding for tranche A. This will be true for months 2 through 80.

Exhibit 3 (Concluded)

Month	Tranche C			Tranche D		
	Balance	Principal	Interest	Balance	Principal	Interest
1	96,500,000	0	603,125	73,000,000	0	456,250
2	96,500,000	0	603,125	73,000,000	0	456,250
3	96,500,000	0	603,125	73,000,000	0	456,250
4	96,500,000	0	603,125	73,000,000	0	456,250
5	96,500,000	0	603,125	73,000,000	0	456,250
6	96,500,000	0	603,125	73,000,000	0	456,250
7	96,500,000	0	603,125	73,000,000	0	456,250
8	96,500,000	0	603,125	73,000,000	0	456,250
9	96,500,000	0	603,125	73,000,000	0	456,250
10	96,500,000	0	603,125	73,000,000	0	456,250
11	96,500,000	0	603,125	73,000,000	0	456,250
12	96,500,000	0	603,125	73,000,000	0	456,250
95	96,500,000	0	603,125	73,000,000	0	456,250
96	96,500,000	0	603,125	73,000,000	0	456,250
97	96,500,000	0	603,125	73,000,000	0	456,250
98	96,500,000	0	603,125	73,000,000	0	456,250
99	96,500,000	0	603,125	73,000,000	0	456,250
100	96,500,000	1,072,194	603,125	73,000,000	0	456,250
101	95,427,806	1,699,243	596,424	73,000,000	0	456,250
102	93,728,563	1,684,075	585,804	73,000,000	0	456,250
103	92,044,489	1,669,039	575,278	73,000,000	0	456,250
104	90,375,450	1,654,134	564,847	73,000,000	0	456,250
105	88,721,315	1,639,359	554,508	73,000,000	0	456,250
175	3,260,287	869,602	20,377	73,000,000	0	456,250
176	2,390,685	861,673	14,942	73,000,000	0	456,250
177	1,529,013	853,813	9,556	73,000,000	0	456,250
178	675,199	675,199	4,220	73,000,000	170,824	456,250
179	0	0	0	72,829,176	838,300	455,182
180	0	0	0	71,990,876	830,646	449,943
181	0	0	0	71,160,230	823,058	444,751
182	0	0	0	70,337,173	815,536	439,607
183	0	0	0	69,521,637	808,081	434,510
184	0	0	0	68,713,556	800,690	429,460
185	0	0	0	67,912,866	793,365	424,455
350	0	0	0	1,235,674	160,220	7,723
351	0	0	0	1,075,454	158,544	6,722
352	0	0	0	916,910	156,883	5,731
353	0	0	0	760,027	155,238	4,750
354	0	0	0	604,789	153,607	3,780
355	0	0	0	451,182	151,991	2,820
356	0	0	0	299,191	150,389	1,870
357	0	0	0	148,802	148,802	930

Exhibit 4: Average Life for the Collateral and the Four Tranches of Deal 1

Prepayment speed (PSA)	Average life for				
	Collateral	Tranche A	Tranche B	Tranche C	Tranche D
50	15.11	7.48	15.98	21.02	27.24
100	11.66	4.90	10.86	15.78	24.58
165	8.76	3.48	7.49	11.19	20.27
200	7.68	3.05	6.42	9.60	18.11
300	5.63	2.32	4.64	6.81	13.36
400	4.44	1.94	3.70	5.31	10.34
500	3.68	1.69	3.12	4.38	8.35
600	3.16	1.51	2.74	3.75	6.96
700	2.78	1.38	2.47	3.30	5.95

After month 81, the principal balance will be zero for tranche A. For the collateral the cash flow in month 81 is $3,318,521, consisting of a principal payment of $2,032,196 and interest of $1,286,325. At the beginning of month 81 (end of month 80), the principal balance for tranche A is $311,926. Therefore, $311,926 of the $2,032,196 of the principal payment from the collateral will be disbursed to tranche A. After this payment is made, no additional principal payments are made to this tranche as the principal balance is zero. The remaining principal payment from the collateral, $1,720,271, is disbursed to tranche B. According to the assumed prepayment speed of 165 PSA, tranche B then begins receiving principal payments in month 81.

Exhibit 3 shows that tranche B is fully paid off by month 100, when tranche C begins to receive principal payments. Tranche C is not fully paid off until month 178, at which time tranche D begins receiving the remaining principal payments. The maturity (i.e., the time until the principal is fully paid off) for these four tranches assuming 165 PSA is 81 months for tranche A, 100 months for tranche B, 178 months for tranche C, and 357 months for tranche D.

The *principal pay down window* for a tranche is the time period between the beginning and the ending of the principal payments to that tranche. So, for example, for tranche A, the principal pay down window would be month 1 to month 81 assuming 165 PSA. For tranche B it is from month 81 to month 100. In confirmation of trades involving CMOs, the principal pay down window is specified in terms of the initial month that principal is expected to be received based on an assumed PSA speed to the final month that principal is expected to be received.

Let's look at what has been accomplished by creating the CMO. First, earlier we saw that the average life of the passthrough is 8.76 years, assuming a prepayment speed of 165 PSA. Exhibit 4 reports the average life of the collateral and the four tranches assuming different prepayment speeds. Notice that the four tranches have average lives that are both shorter and longer than the collateral, thereby attracting investors who have a preference for an average life different from that of the collateral.

Exhibit 5: Deal 2: A Hypothetical Four-Tranche Sequential-Pay Structure with an Accrual Bond Class

Tranche	Par Amount	Coupon rate (%)
A	$194,500,000	7.5
B	36,000,000	7.5
C	96,500,000	7.5
Z (Accrual)	73,000,000	7.5
Total	$400,000,000	

Payment rules:

1. *For payment of periodic coupon interest:* Disburse periodic coupon interest to tranches A, B, and C on the basis of the amount of principal outstanding at the beginning of the period. For tranche Z, accrue the interest based on the principal plus accrued interest in the previous period. The interest for tranche Z is to be paid to the earlier tranches as a principal paydown.

2. *For disbursement of principal payments:* Disburse principal payments to tranche A until it is completely paid off. After tranche A is completely paid off, disburse principal payments to tranche B until it is completely paid off. After tranche B is completely paid off, disburse principal payments to tranche C until it is completely paid off. After tranche C is completely paid off, disburse principal payments to tranche Z until the original principal balance plus accrued interest is completely paid off.

There is still a major problem: there is considerable variability of the average life for the tranches. We'll see how this can be tackled later on. However, there is some protection provided for each tranche against prepayment risk. This is because prioritizing the distribution of principal (i.e., establishing the payment rules for principal) effectively protects the shorter-term tranche A in this structure against extension risk. This protection must come from somewhere — it comes from the three other tranches. Similarly, tranches C and D provide protection against extension risk for tranche B. At the same time, tranches C and D benefit because they are provided protection against contraction risk, the protection coming from tranches A and B.

Accrual Tranches

In Deal 1, the payment rules for interest provide for all tranches to be paid interest each month. In many sequential-pay CMO structures, at least one tranche does not receive current interest. Instead, the interest for that tranche would accrue and be added to the principal balance. Such a bond class is commonly referred to as an *accrual tranche* or a *Z bond* (because the bond is similar to a zero-coupon bond). The interest that would have been paid to the accrual tranche is then used to speed up pay down of the principal balance of earlier tranches.

To see this, consider Deal 2, a hypothetical CMO structure with the same collateral as Deal 1 and with four tranches, each with a coupon rate of 7.5%. The difference is in the last tranche, Z, which is an accrual tranche. The structure for Deal 2 is shown in Exhibit 5.

It can be shown that the expected final maturity for tranches A, B, and C will shorten as a result of the inclusion of tranche Z. The final payout for tranche A is 64 months rather than 81 months; for tranche B it is 77 months rather than

100 months; and for tranche C it is 112 months rather than 178 months. The average lives for tranches A, B, and C are shorter in Deal 2 compared to Deal 1 because of the inclusion of the accrual tranche. For example, at 165 PSA, the average lives are as follows:

Structure	Tranche A	Tranche B	Tranche C
Deal 1	3.48	7.49	11.19
Deal 2	2.90	5.86	7.87

The reason for the shortening of the non-accrual tranches is that the interest that would be paid to the accrual tranche is being allocated to the other tranches. Tranche Z in Deal 2 will have a longer average life than tranche D in Deal 1. These shorter term average life tranches are more attractive to cash managers than the deal without an accrual tranche.

Floating-Rate Tranches

Now let's see how a floating-rate tranche can be created from a fixed-rate tranche. This is done by creating a floater and an inverse floater. We will illustrate the creation of a floater and an inverse floater tranche using the hypothetical CMO structure Deal 2, which is a four tranche sequential-pay structure with an accrual tranche. We can select any of the tranches from which to create a floater tranche and an inverse floater tranche. In fact, we can create these two securities for more than one of the four tranches or for only a portion of one tranche.

In this case, we created a floater and an inverse floater from tranche C. The par value for this tranche is $96.5 million, and we create two tranches that have a combined par value of $96.5 million. We refer to this CMO structure with a floater and an inverse floater as Deal 3. It has five tranches, designated A, B, FL, IFL, and Z, where FL is the floating-rate tranche and IFL is the inverse floating-rate tranche. Exhibit 6 describes Deal 3. Any reference rate can be used to create a floater and the corresponding inverse floater. The reference rate selected for setting the coupon rate for FL and IFL in Deal 3 is 1-month LIBOR. The principal paydown for the floater and inverse floater is proportionate to the amount of the principal paydown of tranche C.

The amount of the par value of the floater tranche will be some portion of the $96.5 million. There are an infinite number of ways to cut up the $96.5 million between the floater and inverse floater, and final partitioning will be driven by the demands of investors. In Deal 3, we made the floater from $72,375,000 or 75% of the $96.5 million. Therefore, for every $100 of principal received in a month, the floater receives $75 and the inverse floater receives $25. The coupon rate on the floater is set at 1-month LIBOR plus 50 basis points. So, for example, if LIBOR is 3.75% at the coupon reset date, the coupon rate on the floater is 3.75% + 0.5%, or 4.25%. There is a cap on the coupon rate for the floater (discussed later).

Exhibit 6: Deal 3: A Hypothetical Five-Tranche Sequential-Pay Structure with Floater, Inverse Floater, and Accrual Tranches

Tranche	Par amount	Coupon rate
A	$194,500,000	7.50%
B	36,000,000	7.50%
FL	72,375,000	1-mo. LIBOR + 0.50
IFL	24,125,000	28.50 − 3 × (1-mo. LIBOR)
Z (Accrual)	73,000,000	7.50%
Total	$400,000,000	

Payment rules:

1. *For payment of periodic coupon interest:* Disburse periodic coupon interest to tranches A, B, FL, and IFL on the basis of the amount of principal outstanding at the beginning of the period. For tranche Z, accrue the interest based on the principal plus accrued interest in the previous period. The interest for tranche Z is to be paid to the earlier tranches as a principal paydown. The maximum coupon rate for FL is 10%; the minimum coupon rate for IFL is 0%.

2. *For disbursement of principal payments:* Disburse principal payments to tranche A until it is completely paid off. After tranche A is completely paid off, disburse principal payments to tranche B until it is completely paid off. After tranche B is completely paid off, disburse principal payments to tranches FL and IFL until they are completely paid off. The principal payments between tranches FL and IFL should be made in the following way: 75% to tranche FL and 25% to tranche IFL. After tranches FL and IFL are completely paid off, disburse principal payments to tranche Z until the original principal balance plus accrued interest is completely paid off.

Unlike the floaters discussed in Chapter 10 whose principal is unchanged over the life of the instrument, the floater's principal balance declines over time as principal repayments are made. The principal payments to the floater are determined by the principal payments from the tranche from which the floater is created. In Deal 3, this is tranche C.

Since the floater's par value is $72,375,000 of the $96.5 million, the balance is the inverse floater. Assuming that 1-month LIBOR is the reference rate, the coupon reset formula for an inverse floater takes the following form:

$$K - L \times (\text{1-month LIBOR})$$

In Deal 3, K is set at 28.50% and L at 3. Thus, if 1-month LIBOR is 3.75%, the coupon rate for the month is:

$$28.50\% - 3 \times (3.75\%) = 17.25\%$$

K is the cap or maximum coupon rate for the inverse floater. In Deal 3, the cap for the inverse floater is 28.50%.

The L or multiple in the coupon reset formula for the inverse floater is called the "coupon leverage." The higher the coupon leverage, the more the inverse floater's coupon rate changes for a given change in 1-month LIBOR. For example, a coupon leverage of 3 means that a 1-basis point change in 1-month LIBOR will change the coupon rate on the inverse floater by 3 basis points.

Exhibit 7: Deal 4: Structure with One PAC Bond and One Support Bond

Tranche	Par amount	Coupon rate (%)
P (PAC)	$243,800,000	7.5
S (Support)	156,200,000	7.5
Total	$400,000,000	

Payment rules:
1. *For payment of periodic coupon interest:* Disburse periodic coupon interest to each tranche on the basis of the amount of principal outstanding at the beginning of the period.
2. *For disbursement of principal payments:* Disburse principal payments to tranche P based on its schedule of principal repayments. Tranche P has priority with respect to current and future principal payments to satisfy the schedule. Any excess principal payments in a month over the amount necessary to satisfy the schedule for tranche P are paid to tranche S. When tranche S is completely paid off, all principal payments are to be made to tranche P regardless of the schedule.

Because 1-month LIBOR is always positive, the coupon rate paid to the floating-rate tranche cannot be negative. If there are no restrictions placed on the coupon rate for the inverse floater, however, it is possible for the coupon rate for that tranche to be negative. To prevent this, a floor, or minimum, is placed on the coupon rate. In many structures, the floor is set at zero. Once a floor is set for the inverse floater, a cap is imposed on the floater. In Deal 3, a floor of zero is set for the inverse floater. The floor results in a cap for the floater of 10%.

As noted in Chapter 10, inverse floaters have substantial price volatility, a point that was unfortunately not recognized by some cash or short-duration managers who purchased them in anticipation of a decline in interest rates.

Planned Amortization Class Tranches

A *planned amortization class* (PAC) bond is one in which a schedule of principal payments is set forth in the prospectus. The PAC bondholders have priority over all other bond classes in the structure with respect to the receipt of the scheduled principal payments. While there is no assurance that the principal payments will be actually realized so as to satisfy the schedule, a PAC bond is structured so that if prepayment speeds are within a certain range of prepayment speeds, the collateral will generate sufficient principal to meet the schedule of principal payments.[1]

The greater certainty of the cash flow for the PAC bonds comes at the expense of the non-PAC classes, called the *support* or *companion tranches*. It is these tranches that absorb the prepayment risk. Because PAC bonds have protection against both extension risk and contraction risk, they are said to provide "two-sided" prepayment protection.

Exhibit 7 shows a CMO structure, Deal 4, created from the $400 million 7.5% coupon passthrough with a WAC of 8.125% and a WAM of 357 months. There are just two tranches in this structure: a 7.5% coupon PAC bond created

---

[1] For an explanation of how a PAC schedule is created, see Chapter 6 in Frank J. Fabozzi and Chuck Ramsey, *Collateralized Mortgage Obligations: Structures and Analysis* (New Hope, PA: Frank J. Fabozzi Associates, 1999).

assuming 90 to 300 PSA with a par value of $243.8 million, and a support bond with a par value of $156.2 million. The two speeds used to create a PAC bond are called the *initial PAC collars* (or *initial PAC bands*). For Deal 4, 90 PSA is the lower collar and 300 PSA the upper collar.

Exhibit 8 reports the average life for the PAC bond and the support bond in Deal 4 assuming various actual prepayment speeds. Notice that between 90 PSA and 300 PSA, the average life for the PAC bond is stable at 7.26 years. However, at slower or faster PSA speeds the schedule is broken and the average life changes, lengthening when the prepayment speed is less than 90 PSA and shortening when it is greater than 300 PSA. Even so, there is much greater variability for the average life of the support bond.

Most CMO PAC structures have more than one class of PAC bonds. Exhibit 9 shows six PAC bonds created from the single PAC bond in Deal 4. We will refer to this CMO structure as Deal 5. Information about this CMO structure is provided in Exhibit 9. The total par value of the six PAC bonds is equal to $243.8 million, which is the amount of the single PAC bond in Deal 4,

Exhibit 10 shows the average life for the six PAC bonds and the support bond in Deal 5 at various prepayment speeds. From a PAC bond in Deal 4 with an average life of 7.26, we have created six PAC bonds with an average life as short as 2.58 years (P-A) and as long as 16.92 years (P-F) if prepayments stay within 90 PSA and 300 PSA.

As expected, the average lives are stable if the prepayment speed is between 90 PSA and 300 PSA. Notice that even outside this range the average life is stable for several of the shorter PAC bonds. For example, PAC P-A is stable even if prepayment speeds are as high as 400 PSA. For the PAC P-B, the average life does not vary when prepayments are between 90 PSA and 350 PSA. Why is it that the shorter the PAC, the more protection it has against faster prepayments?

Exhibit 8: Average Life for PAC Bond and Support Bond in Deal 4 Assuming Various Prepayment Speeds

Prepayment rate (PSA)	PAC Bond (P)	Support Bond (S)
0	15.97	27.26
50	9.44	24.00
90	7.26	18.56
100	7.26	18.56
150	7.26	12.57
165	7.26	11.16
200	7.26	8.38
250	7.26	5.37
300	7.26	3.13
350	6.56	2.51
400	5.92	2.17
450	5.38	1.94
500	4.93	1.77
700	3.70	1.37

Exhibit 9: Deal 5: Structure with Six PAC Bonds and One Support Bond

Tranche	Par amount	Coupon rate (%)
P-A	$85,000,000	7.5
P-B	8,000,000	7.5
P-C	35,000,000	7.5
P-D	45,000,000	7.5
P-E	40,000,000	7.5
P-F	30,800,000	7.5
S	156,200,000	7.5
Total	$400,000,000	

Payment rules:

1. *For payment of periodic coupon interest:* Disburse periodic coupon interest to each tranche on the basis of the amount of principal outstanding at the beginning of the period.

2. *For disbursement of principal payments:* Disburse principal payments to tranches P-A to P-F based on their respective schedules of principal repayments. Tranche P-A has priority with respect to current and future principal payments to satisfy the schedule. Any excess principal payments in a month over the amount necessary to satisfy the schedule for tranche P-A are paid to tranche S. Once tranche P-A is completely paid off, tranche P-B has priority, then tranche P-C, etc. When tranche S is completely paid off, all principal payments are to be made to the remaining PAC tranches in order of priority regardless of the schedule.

Exhibit 10: Average Life for PAC Bond and Support Bond in Deal 5 Assuming Various Prepayment Speeds

Prepayment rate (PSA)	PAC Bonds					
	P-A	P-B	P-C	P-D	P-E	P-F
0	8.46	14.61	16.49	19.41	21.91	23.76
50	3.58	6.82	8.36	11.30	14.50	18.20
90	2.58	4.72	5.78	7.89	10.83	16.92
100	2.58	4.72	5.78	7.89	10.83	16.92
150	2.58	4.72	5.78	7.89	10.83	16.92
165	2.58	4.72	5.78	7.89	10.83	16.92
200	2.58	4.72	5.78	7.89	10.83	16.92
250	2.58	4.72	5.78	7.89	10.83	16.92
300	2.58	4.72	5.78	7.89	10.83	16.92
350	2.58	4.72	5.94	6.95	9.24	14.91
400	2.57	4.37	4.91	6.17	8.33	13.21
450	2.50	3.97	4.44	5.56	7.45	11.81
500	2.40	3.65	4.07	5.06	6.74	10.65
700	2.06	2.82	3.10	3.75	4.88	7.51

To understand why this is so, remember that there are $156.2 million in support bonds that are protecting the $85 million of PAC P-A. Thus, even if prepayments are faster than the initial upper collar, there may be sufficient support bonds to assure the satisfaction of the schedule. In fact, as can been from Exhibit 10, even if prepayments are 400 PSA over the life of the collateral, the average life is unchanged.

Now consider PAC P-B. The support bonds are providing protection for both the $85 million of PAC P-A and $93 million of PAC P-B. As can be seen from Exhibit 10, prepayments could be 350 PSA and the average life is still unchanged. From Exhibit 10 it can be seen that the degree of protection against extension risk increases the shorter the PAC. Thus, while the initial collar may be 90 to 300 PSA, the effective collar is wider for the shorter PAC tranches.

PAC Floaters Given a series of PAC bonds, any of the tranches can be carved up to make a floater and an inverse floater. The advantage of the PAC floater compared to a sequential-pay floater is that there is two-sided prepayment protection and therefore the uncertainty of the average life is less. The trade-off is that this greater prepayment protection is not free. All other factors constant, the margin over the same reference rate offered on a PAC floater will be less than that on a sequential-pay floater and/or the cap will be the lower.

Effective Collars and Actual Prepayments As we have emphasized, the creation of an MBS cannot make prepayment risk disappear. This is true for both a passthrough and a CMO. Thus, the reduction in prepayment risk (both extension risk and contraction risk) that a PAC bond offers must come from somewhere.

The prepayment protection comes from the support bonds. It is the support bonds that have principal payments deferred if the collateral prepayments are slow; support bonds do not receive any principal until the PAC bonds receive the scheduled principal repayment. This reduces the risk that the PAC bonds will extend. Similarly, it is the support bonds that absorb any principal payments in excess of the scheduled principal payments that are made. This reduces the contraction risk of the PAC bonds. Thus, the key to the prepayment protection offered by a PAC bond is the amount of support bonds outstanding. If the support bonds are paid off quickly because of faster-than-expected prepayments, then there is no longer any protection for the PAC bonds. In fact, in Deal 5, if the support bond is paid off, the structure is effectively reduced to a sequential-pay CMO. In such cases, the schedule is unlikely to be maintained, and the structure is referred to as a *busted PAC*.

The support bonds can be thought of as bodyguards for the PAC bondholders. When the bullets fly — i.e., prepayments occur — it is the bodyguards that get killed first. The bodyguards are there to absorb the bullets. Once all the bodyguards are killed off (i.e., the support bonds paid off with faster-than-expected prepayments), the PAC bonds must fend for themselves: they are exposed to all the bullets.

With the bodyguard metaphor for the support bonds in mind, let's consider two questions asked by buyers of PAC bonds:

1. Will the schedule of principal repayments be satisfied if prepayments are faster than the initial upper collar?
2. Will the schedule of principal repayments be satisfied as long as prepayments stay within the initial collar?

Let's address the first question. The initial upper collar for Deal 4 is 300 PSA. Suppose that actual prepayments are 500 PSA for seven consecutive months. Will this disrupt the schedule of principal repayments? The answer is: it depends!

There are two pieces of information we will need to answer this question. First, when does the 500 PSA occur? Second, what has been the actual prepayment experience up to the time that prepayments are 500 PSA? For example, suppose six years from now is when the prepayments reach 500 PSA, and also suppose that for the past six years the actual prepayment speed has been 90 PSA every month. What this means is that there are more bodyguards (i.e., support bonds) around than was expected when the PAC was structured at the initial collar. In establishing the schedule of principal repayments, it is assumed that the bodyguards would be killed off at 300 PSA. But the actual prepayment experience results in them being killed off at only 90 PSA. Thus, six years from now when the 500 PSA is assumed to occur, there are more bodyguards than expected. Thus, a 500 PSA for seven consecutive months may have no effect on the ability of the schedule of principal repayments to be met.

In contrast, suppose that the actual prepayment experience for the first six years is 300 PSA (the upper collar of the initial PAC collar). In this case, there are no extra bodyguards around. As a result, any prepayment speeds faster than 300 PSA, such as 500 PSA in our example, jeopardize satisfaction of the principal repayment schedule and increase contraction risk. What this means is that the prepayment protection is reduced.

It should be clear from these observations that the initial collars are not particularly useful in assessing the prepayment protection for a seasoned PAC bond. This is most important to understand, as it is common for CMO buyers to compare prepayment protection of PACs in different CMO structures, and conclude that the greater protection is offered by the one with the wider initial collars. This approach is inadequate because it is actual prepayment experience that determines the degree of prepayment protection going forward, as well as the expected future prepayment behavior of the collateral.

The way to determine this protection is to calculate the *effective collar* for a PAC bond. An effective collar for a PAC is the lower and the upper PSA that can occur in the future and still allow maintenance of the schedule of principal repayments.

The effective collar changes every month. An extended period over which actual prepayments are below the upper range of the initial PAC collar will result in an increase in the upper range of the effective collar. This is because there will be more bodyguards around than anticipated. An extended period of prepayments slower than the lower range of the initial PAC collar will raise the lower range of the effective collar. This is because it will take faster prepayments to make up the shortfall of the scheduled principal payments not made plus the scheduled future principal payments.

It is important to understand that the PAC schedule may not be satisfied even if the actual prepayments never fall outside of the initial collar. This may seem surprising since our previous analysis indicated that the average life would not change if prepayments are at either extreme of the initial collar. However, recall that all of our previous analysis has been based on a single PSA speed for the life of the structure. If we vary the PSA speed over time rather than keep it constant over the life of the CMO, we can see what happens to the effective collar if the prepayments are at the initial upper collar for a certain number of months. For example, if one computed the average life two years from now for the PAC bond in Deal 4 assuming that prepayments are 300 PSA for the first 24 months, one would find that the average life is stable at six years if the prepayments for the following months are between 115 PSA and 300 PSA. That is, the effective PAC collar is no longer the initial collar. Instead, the lower collar has shifted upward. This means that the protection from year 2 on is for 115 PSA to 300 PSA, a narrower band than initially, even though the earlier prepayments did not exceed the initial upper collar.

Support Bonds

The support bonds are the bonds that provide prepayment protection for the PAC tranches. Consequently, support tranches expose investors to the greatest level of prepayment risk. Because of this, investors must be particularly careful in assessing the cash flow characteristics of support bonds to reduce the likelihood of adverse portfolio consequences due to prepayments.

The support bond typically is divided into different tranches. All the tranches we have discussed earlier are available, including sequential-pay support tranches and floater and inverse floater support tranches. The support bond can even be partitioned so as to create support tranches with a schedule of principal payments. That is, support tranches that are PAC bonds can be created. In a structure with a PAC bond and a support bond with a PAC schedule of principal payments, the former is called a *PAC I bond* or *Level I PAC bond* and the latter a *PAC II bond* or *Level II PAC bond* or *scheduled bond*. While PAC II bonds have greater prepayment protection than the support tranches without a schedule of principal repayments, the prepayment protection is less than that provided PAC I bonds.

There is more that can be done with the PAC II bond. A series of PAC IIs can be created just as we did with the PACs in Deal 5. PAC IIs can also be used to create any other type of bond class, such as a PAC II floater and inverse floater, for example. The support bond without a principal repayment schedule can be used to create any type of bond class. In fact, a portion of the non-PAC II support bond can be given a schedule of principal repayments. This bond class would be called a *PAC III bond* or a *Level III PAC bond*. While it provides protection against prepayments for the PAC I and PAC II bonds and is therefore subject to considerable prepayment risk, such a bond class has greater protection than the support bond class without a schedule of principal repayments.

NONAGENCY CMOS

There are short-term fixed-rate bonds and floaters created in CMO deals in which the issuer is a private entity rather than Ginnie Mae, Fannie Mae, or Freddie Mac. These securities are called *nonagency mortgage-backed securities* (referred to as *nonagency securities* hereafter). Other mortgage-backed products that are separately classified in the industry as asset-backed securities are home equity loan-backed securities and manufactured housing-backed securities. These products are discussed in the next chapter. Since all of these mortgage-related securities expose an investor to credit risk, these securities are sometimes referred to as *credit-sensitive mortgage-backed securities*.

For agency CMOs, the concern is with the redistribution or "tranching" of prepayment risk. For nonagency CMOs, the bonds issued are not guaranteed by a federally related agency or a government sponsored enterprise. Consequently, there is concern with credit risk. As a result, nonagency CMOs expose the investor to both prepayment risk and credit risk. The same types of tranches are created in nonagency CMO structures as described earlier for agency CMO structures. What is unique is the mechanisms for enhancing the credit of a nonagency CMO so that an issuer can obtain any credit rating desired for a tranche in a deal. The same credit enhancement mechanisms are used for ABS structures discussed in the next chapter.

Agency CMOs are created from pools of passthrough securities. In the nonagency market, a CMO can be created from either a pool of passthroughs or unsecuritized mortgage loans. It is uncommon for nonconforming mortgage loans to be securitized as passthroughs and then the passthroughs carved up to create a CMO. Instead, in the nonagency market a CMO is carved out of mortgage loans that have not been securitized as passthroughs. Since a mortgage loan is commonly referred to as a whole loan, nonagency CMOs are also referred to as *whole-loan CMOs*.

The underlying loans for agency securities are those that conform to the underwriting standards of the agency issuing or guaranteeing the issue. That is, only conforming loans are included in pools that are collateral for an agency mortgage-backed security. The three main underwriting standards deal with (1) the maximum loan-to-value ratio, (2) the maximum payment-to-income ratio, and (3) the maximum loan amount. A nonconforming mortgage loan is one that does not conform to the underwriting standards established by any of the agencies.

Credit Enhancement Mechanisms
Typically a double A or triple A rating is sought for the most senior tranche in a nonagency CMO. The amount of credit enhancement necessary depends on rating agency requirements. There are two general types of credit enhancement mechanisms: external and internal. We describe each type below

External Credit Enhancements
External credit enhancements come in the form of third-party guarantees that provide for first protection against losses up to

a specified level, for example, 10%. The most common forms of external credit enhancement are (1) a corporate guarantee, (2) a letter of credit, (3) pool insurance, and (4) bond insurance.

Pool insurance policies cover losses resulting from defaults and foreclosures. Policies are typically written for a dollar amount of coverage that continues in force throughout the life of the pool. However, some policies are written so that the dollar amount of coverage declines as the pool seasons as long as two conditions are met: (1) the credit performance is better than expected and (2) the rating agencies that rated the issue approve. Since only defaults and foreclosures are covered, additional insurance must be obtained to cover losses resulting from bankruptcy (i.e., court mandated modification of mortgage debt — "cramdown"), fraud arising in the origination process, and special hazards (i.e., losses resulting from events not covered by a standard homeowner's insurance policy).

Bond insurance provides the same function as in municipal bond structures. The major insurers are AMBAC, MBIA, FSA, and FGIC.

A nonagency CMO with external credit support is subject to the credit risk of the third-party guarantor. Should the third-party guarantor be downgraded, the issue itself could be subject to downgrade even if the structure is performing as expected. This is based on the "weak link" test followed by rating agencies. According to this test, when evaluating a proposed structure, the credit quality of the issue is only as good as the weakest link in credit enhancement regardless of the quality of the underlying loans. This is the chief disadvantage of third-party guarantees, sometimes referred to as "event risk." Therefore, it is imperative that investors monitor the third-party guarantor as well as the collateral.

External credit enhancements do not materially alter the cash flow characteristics of a CMO structure except in the form of prepayments. In case of a default resulting in net losses within the guarantee level, investors will receive the principal amount as if a prepayment has occurred. If the net losses exceed the guarantee level, investors will realize a shortfall in the cash flows.

Internal Credit Enhancements Internal credit enhancements come in more complicated forms than external credit enhancements and may alter the cash flow characteristics of the loans even in the absence of default. The most common forms of internal credit enhancements are reserve funds and senior/subordinated structures.

Reserve funds come in two forms, cash reserve funds and excess servicing spread. Cash reserve funds are straight deposits of cash generated from issuance proceeds. In this case, part of the underwriting profits from the deal are deposited into a fund which typically invests in money market instruments. *Cash reserve funds* are typically used in conjunction with letters of credit or other kinds of external credit enhancements.

Excess servicing spread accounts involve the allocation of excess spread or cash into a separate reserve account after paying out the net coupon, servicing fee, and all other expenses on a monthly basis. For example, suppose that the gross WAC is 7.75%, the servicing and other fees are 0.25%, and the net WAC is 7.25%. This means that there is excess servicing of 0.25%. The amount in the reserve account will gradually increase and can be used to pay for possible future losses. This form of credit enhancement relies on the assumption that defaults occur infrequently in the very early life of the loans but gradually increase in the following two to five years.

The most widely used internal credit enhancement structure is the *senior/ subordinated structure*. Today a typical structure will have a senior tranche and several junior tranches. The junior tranches represent the subordinated tranches of the structure. The issuer will seek a triple A or double A rating for the senior tranche. The junior tranches will have lower ratings — investment grade and non-investment grade. Typically, the most junior tranche — called the *first loss piece* — will not be rated.

Exhibit 11 shows a hypothetical $200 million structure with a senior tranche representing 92.25% of the deal and five junior tranches representing 7.75% of the deal. Note that all that has been done in this structure is "credit tranching." The senior or any of the junior tranches can then be carved up to create other CMO tranches such as sequential pays.

The first loss piece in this hypothetical deal is tranche X5. The subordination level in this hypothetical structure is 7.75%. The junior classes will absorb all losses up to $15.5 million and the senior tranche will start to experience losses thereafter. So, if there is a $10 million loss, no loss will be realized by the senior tranche. If, instead, there is a $20 million loss, the senior tranche will experience a loss of $4.5 million ($20 million minus $15.5 million) or a 2.4% loss ($4.5/$184.5).

In the case where the loss is $10 million, the first loss piece (tranche X5), tranche X4, and tranche X3 absorb $9.5 million. These tranches will realize a loss experience of 100%. Tranche X2 will realize a loss of $0.5 million, thereby having a loss experience of 25% ($0.5/$2.0). Tranche X1 will not realize any loss. If the loss is $20 million, all junior bonds will have a loss experience of 100%.

Exhibit 11: Hypothetical $200 Million Senior/Subordinated Structure

Bond	Rating	Amount ($ in millions)	Percent of deal(%)
Senior	AAA	$184.50	92.25
Junior			
X1	AA	4.00	2.00
X2	A	2.00	1.00
X3	BBB	3.00	1.50
X4	BB	4.00	2.00
X5*	Not rated	2.50	1.25

* First loss piece.

The junior tranches obviously would require a yield premium to take on the greater credit risk exposure relative to the senior tranche. This setup is a form of self-insurance wherein investors in the senior tranche are giving up yield spread to the investors in the junior tranches. This form of credit enhancement still does not affect the cash flow characteristics of the senior tranche except in the form of prepayments. To the extent that losses are within the subordination level, investors in the senior tranche will receive principal as if a prepayment has occurred.

The basic concern is that while the subordinate tranche provides a certain level of credit protection for the senior tranche at the closing of the deal, the level of protection changes over time due to prepayments and certain liquidation proceeds. The objective is to distribute these payments of principal such that the credit protection for the senior tranche does not deteriorate over time.

To accomplish this, almost all existing senior/subordinated structures incorporate a *shifting interest structure*. A shifting interest structure redirects prepayments disproportionally from the subordinated classes to the senior class according to a specified schedule. An example of such a schedule would be as follows:

Months	Percentage of prepayments directed to senior class
1-60	100%
61-72	70%
73-84	60%
85-96	40%
97-108	20%
109+	pro rata

The rationale for the shifting interest structure is to have enough insurance outstanding to cover future losses. Because of the shifting interest structure, the subordination amount may actually grow in time especially in a low default and fast prepayment environment. Using the same example of our previous $200 million deal with 7.75% initial subordination and assuming a cumulative paydown (prepayments at 165 PSA and regularly scheduled repayments) of $40 million by year 3, the subordination will actually increase to 10.7% [$15.5/($184.50 − $40)] without any net losses. Even if the subordinated classes have experienced some losses, say, $1 million, the subordination will still increase to 9.3% [($15.5 − $1)/($184.50 − $40)].

While the shifting interest structure is beneficial to the senior tranche from a credit standpoint, it does alter the cash flow characteristics of the senior tranche even in the absence of defaults.

Chapter 12

Short-Term Fixed-Rate and Floating-Rate Asset-Backed Securities

Frank J. Fabozzi, Ph.D., CFA
Adjunct Professor of Finance
School of Management
Yale University

While residential mortgage loans are by far the most commonly securitized asset type, securities backed by other assets (consumer and business loans and receivables) have also been securitized. In this chapter we discuss the various asset-backed securities products.

Just as with collateralized mortgage obligations (CMOs), structures with multiple tranches can be created from a pool of loans or receivables to create short-term average life tranches. Floating-rate asset-backed securities are typically created where the underlying pool of loans or receivables pay a floating rate. The most common are securities backed by credit card receivables, home equity line of credit receivables, closed-end home equity loans with an adjustable rate, student loans, Small Business Administration loans, and trade receivables. As demonstrated in the previous chapter, fixed-rate loans also can be used to create a structure that has one or more floating-rate tranches. For example, there are closed-end home equity loans with a fixed rate that can be pooled to create a structure with one or more floating-rate tranches.

CREDIT RISK

Asset-backed securities expose investors to credit risk. The three nationally recognized statistical rating organizations rate asset-backed securities. In analyzing credit risk, all three rating companies focus on similar areas of analysis: (1) credit quality of the collateral, (2) the quality of the seller/servicer, (3) cash flow stress and payment structure, and (4) legal structure.

The credit enhancements — internal and external — that were described in the previous chapter for nonagency CMOs are also used for all ABS products. The amount of enhancement necessary to obtain a specific rating for each tranche in an ABS deal is determined by a rating agency after analysis of the collateral and the structure.

BASIS RISK AND FLOATING-RATE ABS

A floating-rate ABS is often exposed to *basis risk*. This risk is defined as any mismatch between adjustments to the coupon rate paid to bondholders and the interest rate paid on the floating-rate collateral. Two common sources of basis risk are index risk and reset risk.

Index risk is a type of yield curve risk that arises because the ABS floater's coupon rate and the interest rate of the underlying collateral are usually determined at different ends of the yield curve. Specifically, the floater's coupon rate is typically spread off the short-term sector of the yield curve (e.g., U.S. Treasury) while the collateral's interest rate is spread off a longer maturity sector of the same yield curve or in some cases a different yield curve (e.g., LIBOR). This mismatch is a source of risk. For example, for home equity loan-backed securities in which the collateral is adjustable-rate loans, the reference rate for the loans may be 6-month LIBOR while the reference rate for the bonds is usually 1-month LIBOR. Both the collateral and the bonds are indexed off LIBOR, but different sectors of the Eurodollar yield curve. The reference rate for some home equity loans is a constant maturity Treasury. Thus, the collateral is based on a spread off the 1-month sector of the Eurodollar yield curve while the bonds are spread off a longer maturity sector of the Treasury yield curve. As another example, for credit card-backed ABS the interest rate paid is usually a spread over the prime rate (a spread over the Treasury yield curve) while the coupon rate for the bonds is usually a spread over 1-month LIBOR (a spread over the Eurodollar yield curve).

Reset risk is the risk associated with the mismatch between the frequency of the resetting of the interest rate on the floating-rate collateral and the frequency of reset of the coupon rate on the bonds. This risk is common for ABS. For home equity loan-backed securities, for example, the underlying collateral for the adjustable-rate loans is either reset semiannually or annually. However, the coupon rate on the bonds is reset every month. For credit card-backed securities, the coupon rate for the bonds is set monthly, while the finance charges on the outstanding credit card balances are computed daily at a fixed spread over the prime rate.

Basis risk has an impact on the cap of an ABS floater. For a non-ABS floater, the coupon rate has a fixed cap (typically, for the life of the floater). In contrast, the cap for an ABS floater depends on the performance of the underlying collateral. For ABS floaters, basis risk affects the excess spread available to pay the coupon rate for the bondholders. In the case of home equity loan-backed ABS and student loan ABS, the cap on the bondholder's coupon is called the *available funds cap*. Typically, the large spread on the collateral loans compared to the spread offered on the bonds provides protection for ABS investors against basis risk.

Where there is an available funds cap, typically there is a provision for carrying any interest shortfall resulting from the cap forward to future months.

So, for example, suppose that in one month the full coupon rate would be 6.5% but the available fund cap restricts the coupon rate for that month to 6.2%. The 30 basis point difference between the full coupon rate and the rate due to the available funds cap is capitalized and paid in a subsequent month (or months) when the funds are available to pay the bondholder. As a result, the presence of an available funds cap does not have the same impact on cash flow as a typical cap which does not have a catch-up provision.

CASH FLOW OF ASSET-BACKED SECURITIES

The collateral for an ABS can be classified as either amortizing or non-amortizing assets. Amortizing assets are loans in which the borrower's periodic payment consists of scheduled principal and interest payments over the life of the loan. The schedule for the repayment of the principal is called the amortization schedule. The standard residential mortgage loan falls into this category. Auto loans and certain types of home equity loans (specifically, closed-end home equity loans discussed later in this chapter) are amortizing assets. Any excess payment over the scheduled principal payment is called a prepayment. Prepayments can be made to pay off the entire balance or a partial prepayment, called a curtailment.

In contrast to amortizing assets, non-amortizing assets do not have a schedule for the periodic payments that the borrower must make. Instead, a non-amortizing asset is one in which the borrower must make a minimum periodic payment. If that payment is less than the interest on the outstanding loan balance, the shortfall is added to the outstanding loan balance. If the periodic payment is greater than the interest on the outstanding loan balance, then the difference is applied to the reduction of the outstanding loan balance. There is no schedule of principal payments (i.e., no amortization schedule) for a non-amortizing asset. Consequently, the concept of a prepayment does not apply. Credit card receivables and certain types of home equity loans described later in this chapter are examples of non-amortizing assets.

For an amortizing asset, projection of the cash flows requires projecting prepayments. One factor that may affect prepayments is the prevailing level of interest rates relative to the interest rate on the loan. In projecting prepayments it is critical to estimate the extent to which borrowers are expected to take advantage of a possible decline in interest rates below the loan rate by refinancing the loan.

Modeling defaults for the collateral is critical in estimating the cash flow of an ABS. Proceeds that are recovered in the event of a default of a loan prior to the scheduled principal repayment date of an amortizing asset represent a prepayment. Projecting prepayments for amortizing assets requires an assumption of the default rate and the recovery rate. For a non-amortizing asset, while the concept of a prepayment does not exist, a projection of defaults is still necessary to project how much will be recovered and when.

MAJOR ABS SECTORS

Below we review the major sectors of the asset-backed securities market

Auto Loan-Backed Securities

Auto loan-backed securities are issued by (1) the financial subsidiaries of auto manufacturers (domestic and foreign), (2) commercial banks, and (3) independent finance companies and small financial institutions specializing in auto loans.

Cash Flow and Prepayments

The cash flow for auto loan-backed securities consists of regularly scheduled monthly loan payments (interest and scheduled principal repayments) and any prepayments. For securities backed by auto loans, prepayments result from (1) sales and tradeins requiring full payoff of the loan, (2) repossession and subsequent resale of the automobile, (3) loss or destruction of the vehicle, (4) payoff of the loan with cash to save on the interest cost, and (5) refinancing of the loan at a lower interest cost.

Prepayments due to repossessions and subsequent resale are sensitive to the economic cycle. In recessionary economic periods, prepayments due to this factor increase. While refinancings may be a major reason for prepayments of mortgage loans, they are of minor importance for automobile loans. Moreover, the interest rates for the automobile loans underlying several issues are substantially below market rates if they are offered by manufacturers as part of a sales promotion.

Prepayments for auto loan-backed securities are measured in terms of the *absolute prepayment speed* (ABS). The ABS is the monthly prepayment expressed as a percentage of the original collateral amount. Recall that the SMM (monthly CPR) expresses prepayments based on the prior month's balance. There is a mathematical relationship between the SMM and the ABS measures.[1]

Payment Structure

There are auto loan-backed deals that are passthrough structures and paythrough structures. A typical passthrough structure for an auto loan-backed deal is as follows:[2]

Tranche	Amount ($)	Average Life (Years)	Coupon Rate
A	$187,050,000	1.87	Fixed
B	18,499,000	1.87	Fixed
IO	6,000,000	1.46	Fixed

---

[1] Letting M denote the number of months after loan origination, the SMM rate can be calculated from the ABS rate using the following formula:

$$SMM = \frac{ABS}{1 - ABS \times (M - 1)}$$

where the ABS and SMM rates are expressed in decimal form.

[2] Thomas Zimmerman and Leo Burrell, "Auto Loan-Backed Securities," Chapter 4 in Anand K. Bhattacharya and Frank J. Fabozzi (eds.) *Asset-Backed Securities* (New Hope, PA: Frank J. Fabozzi Associates, 1996).

In this typical passthrough structure there is a senior tranche (A) and a subordinated tranche (B). There is also an interest-only class. While more deals are structured as passthroughs, this structure is typically used for smaller deals.

Larger deals usually have a paythrough structure. A typical auto loan-backed paythrough structure is as follows:[3]

Tranche	Amount ($)	Average Life (Years)	Coupon Rate
A1	$250,000,000	0.2	Fixed
A2	545,000,000	0.8	Floating
A3	400,000,000	1.9	Fixed
A4	248,760,000	3.0	Fixed
B	56,240	3.3	Fixed

In this typical paythrough structure, the senior pieces are tranched to create a range of average lives.

Credit Card Receivable ABS

Credit cards are originated by banks (e.g., Visa and MasterCard), retailers (e.g., JCPenney and Sears), and travel and entertainment companies (e.g., American Express). Deals are structured as a master trust. With a master trust the issuer can sell several series from the same trust. Each series issued by the master trust shares the cash flow and therefore the credit risk of one pool of credit card receivables of the issuer.

For a pool of credit card receivables, the cash flow consists of finance charges collected, fees, interchange, and principal. Finance charges collected represent the periodic interest the credit card borrower is charged based on the unpaid balance after the grace period. Fees include late payment fees and any annual membership fees. For Visa and Mastercharge, a payment is made to originators. This payment is called interchange and is made to the originator for providing funding and accepting risk during the grace period. The principal is the amount of the borrowed funds repaid. Interest to security holders is paid periodically (e.g, monthly, quarterly, or semiannually). The interest rate may be fixed or floating.

A credit card receivable-backed security is a non-amortizing security. For a specified period of time, referred to as the *lockout period* or *revolving period*, the principal payments made by credit card borrowers comprising the pool are retained by the trustee and reinvested in additional receivables. The lockout period can vary from 18 months to 10 years. So, during the lockout period, the cash flow that is paid out is based on finance charges collected and fees. After the lockout period, the principal is no longer reinvested but paid to investors. This period is referred to as the *principal-amortization period*.

There are provisions in credit card receivable-backed securities that require early amortization of the principal if certain events occur. Such provisions, which are referred to as *early amortization* or *rapid amortization provi-*

---

[3] Zimmerman and Burrell, "Auto Loan-Backed Securities," p. 92.

sions, are included to safeguard the credit quality of the issue. The only way that the cash flows can be altered is by the triggering of the early amortization provision. When early amortization occurs, the credit card tranches are retired sequentially (i.e., first the AAA bond, then the AA rated bond, and so on).

There are several concepts that must be understood in order to assess the performance of the portfolio of receivables and the ability of the issuer to meet its interest obligation and repay principal as scheduled.

We begin with the concept of *gross portfolio yield*. This yield includes finance charges collected and fees. Some issuers include interchange in the computation of portfolio yield. *Charge-offs* represent the accounts charged off as uncollectible. *Net portfolio yield* is equal to gross portfolio yield minus charge-offs. *Delinquencies* are the percentage of receivable that are past due a specified number of months.

The *monthly payment rate* (MPR) expresses the monthly payment (which includes finance charges, fees, and any principal repayment) of a credit card receivable portfolio as a percentage of debt outstanding in the previous month. For example, suppose a $500 million credit card receivable portfolio in January realized $50 million of payments in February. The MPR would then be 10% ($50 million divided by $500 million).

MPR is an important indicator for two reasons. With a low level of MPR, extension risk with respect to the principal payments may increase. Also a low MPR, indicating low cash flows to satisfy principal payments, may trigger early amortization of the principal.

Closed-End Home Equity Loan-Backed Securities

A home equity loan (HEL) is a loan backed by residential property. At one time, the loan was typically a second lien on property that has already been pledged to secure a first lien. In some cases, the lien may be a third lien. In recent years, the character of a home equity loan has changed. Today, a home equity loan is often a first lien on property where the borrower has an impaired credit history so that the loan cannot qualify as a conforming loan for Ginnie Mae, Fannie Mae, or Freddie Mac. Typically, the borrower uses a home equity loan to consolidate consumer debt using the current home as collateral rather than to obtain funds to purchase a new home. Borrowers are segmented into four general credit quality groups, A, B, C, and D. There is no standard industrywide criteria for classifying a borrower.

Home equity loans can be either open end or closed end. An open-end home equity loan is discussed in the next section. A closed-end HEL is structured the same way as a fully amortizing residential mortgage loan. That is, it has a fixed maturity and the payments are structured to fully amortize the loan by the maturity date. There are both fixed-rate and variable-rate closed-end HELs. Typically, variable-rate loans have a reference rate of 6-month LIBOR and have periodic caps and lifetime caps, just as the adjustable-rate mortgages discussed in the previous chapter. The cash flow of a pool of closed-end HELs is comprised of interest, regularly scheduled principal repayments, and prepayments, just as with mortgage-backed securities. Thus, it is necessary to have a prepayment model and a default model to forecast cash flows. The prepayment speed is measured in terms of a conditional prepayment rate (CPR).

Cash Flow

The monthly cash flow for a security backed by closed-end HELs is the same as for mortgage-backed securities. That is, the cash flow consists of (1) net interest, (2) regularly scheduled principal payments, and (3) prepayments. The uncertainty about the cash flow arises from prepayments.

Borrower characteristics must be kept in mind when trying to assess prepayments for a particular deal. In the prospectus of an offering, a base case prepayment assumption is made — the initial speed and the amount of time until the collateral is expected to season. Thus, the prepayment benchmark is issue specific and is called the *prospectus prepayment curve* or PPC.

Payment Structure

There are passthrough and paythrough home equity loan-backed structures. Typically, home equity loan-backed securities are securitized by both closed-end fixed-rate and adjustable-rate (or variable-rate) HELs. The securities backed by the latter are called *HEL floaters*. The reference rate of the underlying loans is typically 6-month LIBOR. The cash flow of these loans is affected by periodic and lifetime caps on the loan rate.

To increase the attractiveness of home equity loan-backed securities to short-term investors, the securities typically have been created in which the reference rate is 1-month LIBOR. Because of (1) the mismatch between the reference rate on the underlying loans and that of the HEL floater and (2) the periodic and lifetime caps of the underlying loans, there is an available funds cap on the coupon rate for the HEL floater.

Tranches have been structured in HEL deals so as to give some senior tranches greater prepayment protection than other senior tranches. The two types of structures that do this are the *planned amortization class* (PAC) *tranche* and *non-accelerating senior* (NAS) *tranche.* In our discussion of CMOs issued by the agencies in the previous chapter we explained how a planned amortization class tranche can be created. These tranches are also created in HEL structures

A NAS tranche receives principal payments according to a schedule. The schedule is not a dollar amount. Rather, it is a principal schedule that shows for a given month the share of pro rata principal that must be distributed to the NAS tranche. A typical principal schedule for a NAS tranche is as follows:

Months	Share of pro rata principal
1 through 36	0%
37 through 60	45%
61 through 72	80%
73 through 84	100%
After month 84	300%

The average life for the NAS tranche is stable for a large range of pre-payments because for the first three years all prepayments are made to the other senior tranches. This reduces the risk of the NAS tranche contracting (i.e., short-ening) due to fast prepayments. After month 84, 300% of its pro rata share is paid to the NAS tranche thereby reducing its extension risk.

Open-End Home Equity Loan-Backed Securities

With an open-end home equity loan (HELOC) the homeowner is given a credit line and can write checks or use a credit card for up to the amount of the credit line. The amount of the credit line depends on the amount of the equity the bor-rower has in the property.

The revolving period for a HELOC is the period during which the bor-rower can take down all or part of the line of credit. The revolving period can run from 10 to 15 years. At the end of the revolving period, the HELOC can specify either a balloon payment or an amortization schedule (of up to 10 years). Almost all HELOCs are floating-rate loans, with the interest rate paid by about 75% of HELOC borrowers resets monthly to the prime rate as reported in *The Wall Street Journal* plus a spread.

The securities created in HELOC deals are floating-rate tranches. While the underlying loans are priced based on a spread over the prime rate, the securi-ties created are based on a spread over 1-month LIBOR.

Because HELOCs are for revolving lines, the deal structures are quite different for HELOCs and closed-end HELs. As with other ABS involving revolv-ing credit lines such as credit card deals, there is a revolving period, an amortiza-tion period, and a rapid amortization period.

Manufactured Housing-Backed Securities

Manufactured housing-backed securities are backed by loans for manufactured homes. In contrast to site-built homes, manufactured homes are built at a factory and then transported to a manufactured home community or private land. The loan may be either a mortgage loan (for both the land and the home) or a con-sumer retail installment loan.

Manufactured housing-backed securities are issued by Ginnie Mae and private entities. The former securities are guaranteed by the full faith and credit of the U.S. government. Loans not backed by the FHA or VA are called conventional loans. Manufactured housing-backed securities that are backed by such loans are called conventional manufactured housing-backed securities.

The typical loan for a manufactured home is 15 to 20 years. The loan repayment is structured to fully amortize the amount borrowed. Therefore, as with residential mortgage loans and HELs, the cash flow consists of net interest, regularly scheduled principal, and prepayments. However, prepayments are more stable for manufactured housing-backed securities because they are not sensitive to refinancing.

There are several reasons for this. First, the loan balances are typically small so that there is no significant dollar savings from refinancing. Second, the rate of depreciation of mobile homes may be such that in the earlier years depreciation is greater than the amount of the loan paid off. This makes it difficult to refinance the loan. Finally, typically borrowers are of lower credit quality and therefore find it difficult to obtain funds to refinance. As with residential mortgage loans and HELs, prepayments on manufactured housing-backed securities are measured in terms of CPR.

The payment structure is the same as with nonagency mortgage-backed securities and home equity loan-backed securities.

Student Loan-Backed Securities

Student loans are made to cover college costs (undergraduate, graduate, and professional programs such as medical school and law school) and tuition for a wide range of vocational and trade schools. Securities backed by student loans, popularly referred to as SLABS (student loan asset-backed securities), have similar structural features as the other ABS products we discussed above.

The student loans that have been most commonly securitized are those that are made under the Federal Family Education Loan Program (FFELP). Under this program, the government makes loans to students via private lenders. The decision by private lenders to extend a loan to a student is not based on the applicant's ability to repay the loan. If a default of a loan occurs and the loan has been properly serviced, then the government will guarantee up to 98% of the principal plus accrued interest. The federal government has a direct lending program — the Federal Direct Student Loan Program (FDSLP) — in which the Department of Education (DOE) makes loans directly to students; however, these loans are retained by the DOE and not securitized. Loans that are *not* part of a government guarantee program are called *alternative loans*. These loans are basically consumer loans and the lender's decision to extend an alternative loan will be based on the ability of the applicant to repay the loan. Alternative loans have been securitized.

As Congress did with the creation of Fannie Mae and Freddie Mac to provide liquidity in the mortgage market by allowing these entities to buy mortgage loans in the secondary market, it created the Student Loan Marketing Association ("Sallie Mae") as a government-sponsored enterprise to purchase student loans in the secondary market and to securitize pools of student loans. Its first issuance was in 1995. Sallie Mae is now the major issuer of SLABS and its issues are viewed as the benchmark issues. Other entities that issue SLABS are traditional corporate entities (e.g., the Money Store and PNC Bank) and non-profit organizations (Michigan Higher Education Loan Authority and the California Educational Facilities Authority). The SLABS of the latter are typically issued as tax-exempt securities and therefore trade in the municipal market.

Let's first look at the cash flow for the student loans themselves. There are different types of student loans under the FFELP, including subsidized and unsubsidized Stafford loans, Parental Loans for Undergraduate Students (PLUS), and Supplemental Loans to Students (SLS). These loans involve three periods with respect to the borrower's payments — deferment period, grace period, and loan repayment period. Typically, student loans work as follows. While in school, no payments are made by the student on the loan. This is the deferment period. Upon leaving school, the student is extended a grace period of usually six months when no payments on the loan need to be made. After this period, payments are made on the loan by the borrower.

Prior to July 1, 1998, the reference rate for student loans originated under the FFELP program was the 3-month Treasury bill rate plus a margin of either 250 basis points (during the deferment and grace periods) or 310 basis points (during the repayment period). Since July 1, 1998, the Higher Education Act changed the reference rate to the 10-year Treasury note. The interest rate is the 10-year Treasury note plus 100 basis points. The spread over the reference rate varies with the cycle period for the loan.

As with other ABS, the reference rate need not be the same as that of the underlying loans. For investors in non-Sallie Mae issues, there is exposure to collateral performance due to basis risk discussed earlier in this chapter. Typically, non-Sallie Mae issues have been LIBOR-based floaters. For Sallie Mae issues, there is an indirect government guarantee. Sallie Mae has typically issued SLABS indexed to the 3-month Treasury bill rate. However, late in the second quarter of 1999, Sallie Mae issued bonds in which the buyer of the 2-year tranche had the choice of receiving either LIBOR plus 8 basis points or the 3-month Treasury bill rate plus 87 basis points. There are available funds caps in ABS deals because of the different reference rates.

Prepayments typically occur due to defaults or loan consolidation. Even if there is no loss of principal faced by the investor when defaults occur, the investor is still exposed to contraction risk. This is the risk that the investor must reinvest the proceeds at a lower spread and in the case of a bond purchased at a premium, the premium will be lost. Studies have shown student loan prepayments are insensitive to the level of interest rates. Consolidations of loans occur when the students who have loans over several years combine them into a single loan. The proceeds from the consolidation are distributed to the original lender and, in turn, distributed to the bondholders.

SBA Loan-Backed Securities

The Small Business Administration (SBA) is an agency of the federal government empowered to guarantee loans made by approved SBA lenders to qualified borrowers. The loans are backed by the full faith and credit of the U.S. government. Most SBA loans are variable-rate loans where the reference rate is the prime rate. The rate on the loan is either reset monthly on the first of the month or quarterly on the first of January, April, July, and October. SBA regulations specify the maximum coupon allowable in the secondary market. As of this writing, the maximum coupon rate is equal to the prime rate plus 1.625%. SBA loans typically do not have caps. Newly originated loans have maturities between 5 and 25 years.

The Small Business Secondary Market Improvement Act passed in 1984 permitted the pooling of SBA loans. When pooled, the underlying loans must have similar terms and features. The maturities typically used for pooling loans are 7, 10, 15, 20, and 25 years. Loans without caps are not pooled with loans that have caps.

Most variable-rate SBA loans make monthly payments consisting of interest and principal repayment. The amount of the monthly payment for an individual loan is determined as follows. Given the coupon formula of the prime rate plus the loan's quoted margin, the interest rate is determined. Given the interest rate, a level payment amortization schedule is determined. It is this level payment that is paid for the months until the coupon rate is reset. When variable-rate SBA loans are pooled, the amortization schedule is based on the net pool rate and the rate is recomputed either every month or every quarter.

Prepayments for SBA-backed securities are measured in terms of CPR. Voluntary prepayments can be made by the borrower without any penalty. There are several factors contributing to the prepayment speed of a pool of SBA loans. A factor affecting prepayments is the maturity date of the loan. It has been found that the fastest speeds on SBA loans and pools occur for shorter maturities. The purpose of the loan also affects prepayments. There are loans for working capital purposes and loans to finance real estate construction or acquisition. It has been observed that SBA pools with maturities of 10 years or less made for working capital purposes tend to prepay at the fastest speed. In contrast, loans backed by real estate that have long maturities tend to prepay at a slow speed. All other factors constant, pools that have capped loans tend to prepay more slowly than pools of uncapped loans.

Collateralized Bond Obligations

A *collateralized bond obligation* (CBO) is an ABS backed by a diversified pool of one or more of the following types of debt obligations:

1. non-investment grade (i.e., high yield) corporate bonds
2. emerging market bonds
3. bank loans to corporate entities

When an asset-backed security has only bank loans, it is referred to as a *collateralized loan obligation* (CLO).

There is an asset manager responsible for managing the portfolio. There are restrictions imposed by the rating agencies as to what the asset manager may do and certain tests that must be satisfied for the tranches in the CBO to maintain their original credit rating.

The typical structure of a CBO is as follows. There is (1) a senior tranche, (2) different layers of subordinated or junior debt tranches, and (3) an equity tranche. The senior tranche is between 70% and 80% of the deal and receives a floating-rate payment — a tranche that may be of interest to cash managers. The junior tranches, in contrast, receive a fixed coupon rate. So, the collateral from the diversified pool of debt obligations is going to pay the tranche holders, the majority of whom (i.e., the senior tranche investors) are being paid a floating rate. While the bank loans are typically floating rate, the other debt obligations in which the asset manager invests are typically fixed rate. Now this presents a problem — paying the majority of the tranche investors a floating rate when the majority of the debt obligations pay a fixed rate.

Because of the mismatch between the nature of the cash flows of the debt obligations in which the asset manager invests and the floating-rate liability due to the senior tranche, the asset manager uses an interest rate swap. A rating agency will require the use of swaps to eliminate this mismatch.

The junior tranches receive a fixed rate. The rate is a spread over a comparable maturity Treasury security. The amount of the spread varies with market conditions and the credit rating of a junior tranche. The equity tranche receives any remaining interest that is received from the collateral but not paid to the debt tranches (i.e., the senior and junior tranches).

There are three phases in the life of a CBO. The first phase is the startup phase or ramp phase. In this phase, which is one or two months, the asset manager assembles the portfolio with the proceeds received from the sale of the CBO tranches. Once the portfolio is assembled, the manager monitors the portfolio and is responsible for reinvesting any principal repayments due to any calls or proceeds received from any defaulted issues. This phase is called the reinvestment phase. This phase varies from three years to five years. Finally, principal payments to the senior and junior tranches must be made over the balance of the CBO's life. This phase is called the pay down phase.

The CBO structure described above is the most common type that is issued today. The CBO is structured to generate cash flow for the senior and junior tranches without the active trading of bonds. Older CBO deals were typically structured so that the cash flow for the structure was based on the active trading of bonds. The cash flow needed to pay principal and interest to the senior and junior tranches had to be generated from capital gains as well as coupon interest. With the difficulties encountered in the high-yield bond sector in the late 1980s and early 1990s, CBOs structured in this way lost their appeal.

Because the cash flows from the structure are designed to accomplish the objective for each tranche, restrictions are imposed on the asset managers. The asset manager is not free to buy and sell bonds. The conditions for disposing of issues held are specified. Also, in assembling the portfolio during the startup phase, the asset manager must meet certain requirements set forth by the rating agency or agencies that rate the deal. These requirements have to do with constructing a diversified portfolio and minimum ratings for the issues acquired. The asset manager during the reinvestment and pay down phases must monitor the collateral to ensure that certain tests or covenants are being met.

Index